Sunset Travel Guide to
SOUTHERN CALIFORNIA

By the Editors of Sunset Books
and Sunset Magazine

Lane Publishing Co., Menlo Park, California

Hours, admission fees, prices, telephone numbers, and highway designations in this book are accurate as of November, 1974.

Maps have been provided in each chapter for the special purpose of highlighting significant regions, routes, or attractions in the area. More detailed road maps of Southern California are available from automobile clubs, oil companies, and chambers of commerce or visitors bureaus in major cities.

Acknowledgments

Special thanks go to Christiana Hills and other members of the Southern California Visitors Council. To other city and county chambers of commerce throughout the area goes our sincere appreciation: Bill Burris, San Diego Convention and Visitors Bureau; Frank Coony, San Bernardino Economic Development Department; Thomas Hanlon, Richard Lee, and Gerald Stewart, Palm Springs Convention and Visitors Bureau; Roz Meyers, Beverly Hills Chamber of Commerce; Marilyn Randle, Santa Barbara Chamber of Commerce; and Allen Trecartin, Ventura Visitors and Convention Bureau. Other individuals who offered aid include Jim Bishop, Marina del Rey; Marcie Buckley, Historian of Hotel Del Coronado; Mr. and Mrs. Roy Clayton of Newport Beach and Palm Springs; Jim Garber, Disneyland; Milt Jones, *Palm Springs Life*; Shirley McFadzean, Kern County Museum; Janet Rogers, Sea World; Mr. and Mrs. Glen Settle of Tropico; and Frederick W. Sleight, Director, Palm Springs Desert Museum.

Supervising Editor: Robert G. Bander
Research and Text: Barbara Braasch

Special Consultant: Walter Houk,
Southwest Editor, *Sunset* Magazine

Design: JoAnn Masaoka

Cartography: Jeannette Todd, Jack Doonan

Illustrations: Susan Colton

Front cover: Horseback riders at Palm Springs.
Photo: Palm Springs Convention and Visitors Bureau.

Back cover: Left photo: Jack McDowell.
Top right photo: Ken Niles. Bottom right photo: Glenn Christiansen.

Executive Editor, Sunset Books: David E. Clark

Second Printing May 1975

Contents

Special Features

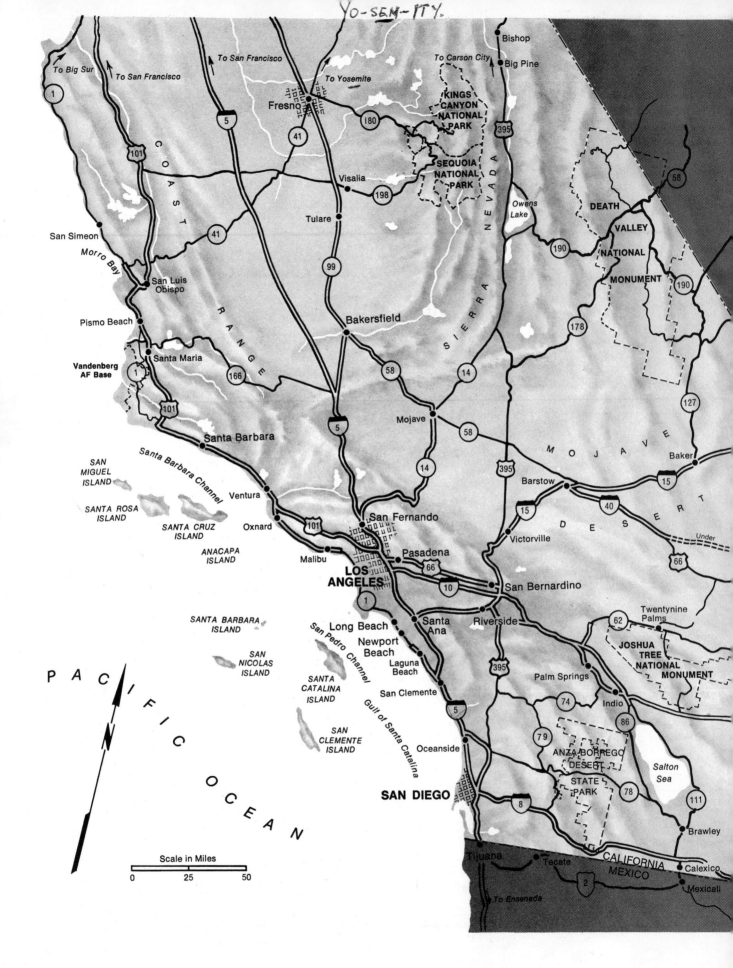

YO-SEM-ITY.

To Big Sur
To San Francisco
To San Francisco
To Yosemite
To Carson City
Bishop
Big Pine

1
101
5
41
Fresno
180
KINGS CANYON NATIONAL PARK
395

COAST
Visalia
198
SEQUOIA NATIONAL PARK
DEATH

41
Tulare
Owens Lake
VALLEY

San Simeon
190
NATIONAL

Morro Bay
San Luis Obispo
RANGE
99
Bakersfield
SIERRA
178
MONUMENT
190

Pismo Beach
166
58
14
NEVADA
127

Vandenberg AF Base
1
Santa Maria
5
Mojave
58
M O J A V E

101
Santa Barbara
14
395
Baker
15

SAN MIGUEL ISLAND
Santa Barbara Channel
Ventura
Barstow
15
40
D E S E R T

SANTA ROSA ISLAND
SANTA CRUZ ISLAND
Oxnard
101
San Fernando
Victorville
Under
66

ANACAPA ISLAND
Malibu
Pasadena
66
LOS ANGELES
10
San Bernardino
Twentynine Palms
62

SANTA BARBARA ISLAND
1
Long Beach
Santa Ana
Riverside
JOSHUA TREE NATIONAL MONUMENT

SAN NICOLAS ISLAND
Newport Beach
395
Palm Springs
Indio
86

San Pedro Channel
Laguna Beach
74

SANTA CATALINA ISLAND
San Clemente
79
ANZA BORREGO DESERT STATE PARK
Salton Sea

P A C I F I C
SAN CLEMENTE ISLAND
Gulf of Santa Catalina
Oceanside
5
78
111

SAN DIEGO
8
Brawley

O C E A N
Tijuana
Tecate
CALIFORNIA MEXICO
Calexico

Scale in Miles
2
To Ensenada
Mexicali

0   25   50

Introduction to Southern California

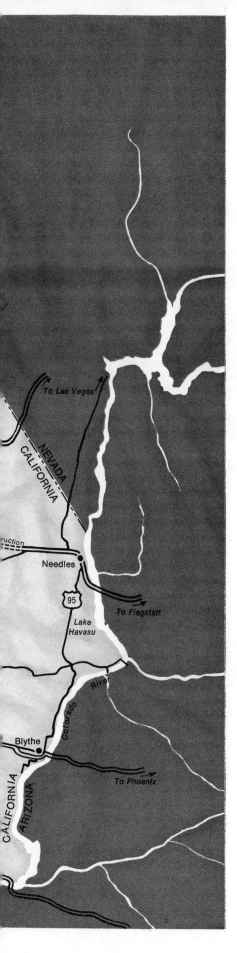

Why visit Southern California? One reason might be that no other single area offers the environmental diversity, natural and manmade attractions, or social and cultural achievements that are a part of this region. You could choose to vacation here for a year without running out of exciting things to see and do.

Nearly a century ago a massive advertising campaign by the Southern Pacific and Santa Fe railroads attracted thousands of settlers with visions of swimming in the blue Pacific, picking oranges from acres of fruit-filled groves, and playing in the snow of nearby mountains—all in one day. It's still possible.

Variety in the Southland does not stop there. Large cities (each different in character) add overlays to the landscape between ocean and mountain, and desert meets the mountains at their north and east faces. In Death Valley, Badwater is 282 feet below sea level, the lowest point in the western hemisphere. Across the valley in the Sierra Nevada, Mt. Whitney (14,495 feet) is the highest point in the United States (excluding Alaska).

Climate. Southern California's biggest asset is her dry, subtropical climate—the only one in the United States. Very little rain, low humidity, little variation in temperature, and lots of sun make it possible to enjoy casual outdoor living the year around. Sunbathing around a lovely pool is in the best Southern California tradition.

Mellowed by the fine weather, Southern Californians have adopted a new lifestyle, becoming trend-setters in food, fashion, architecture, and gardening. In this capital of casual living, it's possible to enter a fine restaurant without a tie, and a dinner invitation usually means an outdoor barbecue in a garden patio.

When to visit. Anytime of the year is good somewhere in Southern California. Summertime is more crowded, quite hot in the desert, and it's apt to be "smog season" around Los Angeles and

California's Southland *is a vast and vital region, encompassing deserts, mountains, beaches, cities.*

the surrounding area. This is the time to enjoy the miles of white sandy beaches, dotted with dramatic surfing areas, marinas, harbors, and noted coastal towns — Santa Barbara, Malibu, Santa Monica, Newport, Laguna Beach, La Jolla, and San Diego. Desert parks and resorts are the goal of winter sun-seekers, while skiers head for the mountains.

Spring and fall provide the region's mildest weather. Most of the fairs and festivals are held at this time. (For a calendar of monthly events, write the Southern California Visitors Council, 705 W. Seventh Street, Los Angeles 90017.) Wildflowers carpet desert and higher elevations, beginning in mid-February and lasting through June.

What to see. Amusement parks and other types of entertainment centers are a part of the Southern California experience. Such magic words as "Disneyland" and "Hollywood" and "Rose Bowl" and "Sunset Boulevard" had their origins here. But don't overlook the natural attractions. Wilderness areas remain as they have for centuries—mountain peaks reach high above the roads and energies of man, lovely waterfall canyons hide from the eyes of all but the most probing, and the desert stretches sand and silence for miles.

The Spaniards left their mark in California. Many towns grew up around the missions founded by indomitable Father Serra. A walk through San Diego's Old Town, Pueblo de Los Angeles, or Santa Barbara streets provides an insight into the history and romance of the Spanish era.

Southern California has something for everyone: from Marineland to missions; from the Hollywood Bowl concerts under the stars to the stars of Hollywood; from Sea World to sequoias.

A "Must See" box at the beginning of each chapter in the book lists some of the interesting attractions of that region. Many are famous; others not so well known. Intended only as suggestions, these are explained more fully in the text.

Where is Southern California? Although actual boundaries do not exist, the area known as Southern California is nevertheless a real place—one defined as much by personality as by geography.

Our travel guide to Southern California covers a generous scope, stretching north to the town of Fresno in the San Joaquin Valley and extending south across the Mexican border. In the east we stretch the boundary a bit above Death Valley, taking in both Inyo and Mono counties, major recreation targets for southland residents. Along the coast we inch north above San Luis Obispo (halfway between Los Angeles and San Francisco) to Morro Bay and San Simeon. The area north of this broad east-west dividing line is described in the Sunset book *Travel Guide to Northern California.*

Beginning with the sprawling Los Angeles region, this book includes the ocean world and coastal

Smiles come easily...

The beauty *along Olvera Street doesn't all lie in the Mexican architecture.*

resort towns, valleys fronting upon major mountain ranges, peaceful rolling hills with quiet villages and mission memories, desert resorts and wilderness, the winding Colorado River that divides Southern California and Arizona, and the grand southern section of the Sierra Nevada.

In addition to the general area map of Southern California, other maps scattered throughout the chapters focus on local points of interest. Detailed street maps of downtown Los Angeles, San Diego, and Santa Barbara can aid in planning walking tours. Freeways in the L.A. area are clearly marked to help motorists find their way around.

Information for both tourists and residents. Although the book is aimed primarily at the visitor and new resident, we included information on possible discoveries for "back yard" vacations for those who have lived in Southern California for some time.

But if you are new to Southern California, no matter how you enter it—at its busy harbor, on its teeming freeways, or through its sprawling international airport—you'll sense immediately that this is a young and forward-looking region, a land with a well-grounded sense of the future. Not too many Southern Californians look back.

...in the land of sunshine

In Southern California, *radiance is where you find it—even inside a delicatessen case.*

A nautical *Marina del Rey setting encourages lovers to smile private smiles.*

Street mimes *at plaza of Los Angeles County Museum on Wilshire Boulevard delight onlookers with their antics.*

Los Angeles

Big, busy, bustling Los Angeles is a city in motion. The best overall view of the heterogeneous communities making up the metropolis of Los Angeles is from a plane, particularly at night. Nowhere else does the criss-crossing light pattern of the main street grid seem so extensive.

Sprawling inland from the Pacific Ocean over some 460 square miles, L.A. occupies as much ground as the entire state of Rhode Island. The West's largest city is the focal point for one of the greatest population migrations in all recorded history. Three million people call Los Angeles their home, and natives are a minority outnumbered by immigrant residents and visitors.

Why did they come? The Mediterranean climate was—and still is—the key. People found the year-round sun exhilarating; it stimulated the crops they planted. Citrus groves thrived; oil was discovered. Because they could operate all year, the cinema and aviation industries flourished, generating technological offspring—television and aerospace—that eventually outdistanced them.

One of the paradoxes of forward-looking Los Angeles is the insistent presence of its rich past. A large part of the city's heritage is architectural, expressed in such forms as the indigenous Mexican adobe and the later California bungalow.

First major United States city to build *out* instead of *up*, the City of the Angels plunged rapidly into such pace-setting trends as urban decentralization, mass rapid transit systems, and the final result of reliance on the internal (some say "infernal") combustion engine: air pollution.

There's always pleasure to be found in Los Angeles. All you have to do is pin it down. You can sample the city in many ways: take in the basic natural gifts of sunshine, beach, and mountains or seek out the elaborate amusements of a city where entertainment is big business.

The developing Santa Monicas *will shape L.A.'s future. Mid-distance: Century City; beyond, downtown.*

ENJOYING THE CITY

It takes a sense of humor to savor unpredictable, offbeat Los Angeles. If you think museums and theaters are the measure of a city, you'll find some fine ones. But where else would you discover great art in a cemetery or look-alike replicas of once-trapped Ice Age creatures emerging from tar pits? Movie premieres may be things of the past, but if you follow the revolving lights in the sky, you can catch the opening of a new supermarket.

Getting there

Los Angeles has one of the largest and busiest airports in the country—Los Angeles International. Four other major airports in surrounding areas provide supplemental passenger service: Hollywood/Burbank, Long Beach, Ontario, and Orange County. You can make connections from one to the other by motor coach.

The city is also served by the nation's two big transcontinental bus companies (Continental Trailways and Greyhound) and by Amtrak rail service.

Settling in

First-timers and even those who haven't been to L.A. for a while may need some help in finding their way around this large, ever-changing city. A few words of orientation and advice on touring and accommodations from those who know the area will add greatly to the enjoyment of your visit. The Southern California Visitors Council, at 705 W. Seventh Street in downtown Los Angeles (90017), is the source for such information, as well as for free maps and booklets; the phone number is (213) 628-3101. They even have a brochure on "where the movie stars live," one of the most-asked questions. Their offices are open from 9 A.M. to 5 P.M. daily except Sunday. You can write for information in advance of your visit.

Gasoline station maps are getting more difficult to obtain; there will probably be a slight charge if you do find one. Motorists would be well advised to come prepared. Car rental agencies provide condensed maps showing main streets and freeways. Members of automobile clubs can request street maps of L.A. and surrounding areas.

Moving around

Once in Los Angeles, you can take guided bus tours of most major attractions. But if you plan any ambitious sightseeing, you will need a car.

Freeways are the lifelines of the city. Opinions vary as to whether they were designed by people of vision or madmen, but, at best, they get motorists long distances in astonishingly short periods of time. The often intertwining maze of routes may seem complicated at first, but a review of the freeway map on page 21 will help to simplify your driving. Try to avoid freeways during times of peak congestion—7 to 9 A.M. and 4 to 6 P.M.—when residents are traveling to and from work.

TOURING OLD LOS ANGELES

Los Angeles started as a Spanish village, then became Mexican, and finally Yankee. Today, the once somnolent Pueblo, aging but undergoing rebirth and restoration, is the nucleus of bustling districts. Close by you can savor the sights and sounds, foods, and goods of Mexico and early California, the Orient, and the Mediterranean, all at the Civic Center edge of downtown L.A.

Pueblo de Los Angeles and vicinity

In 1781, 11 families recruited by the provincial governor, Felipe de Neve, concluded a seven-month colonizing expedition from Sonora, Mexico, to the banks of the Los Angeles River. They marked off the lots that gave birth to the Spanish village with the tongue-tangling name *El Pueblo de Nuestra Señora la Reina de Los Angeles* (the town of Our Lady the Queen of the Angels). Although presently bogged down by lack of funds, restoration of L.A.'s birthplace as a 42-acre State Historical Landmark is underway.

Walking is the surest way to see the Pueblo well. Parking lots are nearby. Guided tours through the park are available free of charge Tuesdays through Saturdays, hourly from 10 A.M. to 2 P.M. For information, check at the Visitors Council, 100 Calle de la Plaza.

The Plaza, once the center of activity for the whole town, is now closed to traffic and remains the heart of the Pueblo. On summer Sunday afternoons, the circular, lacy *kiosko* (19th century, iron-grilled bandstand) is the scene of open-air concerts of Mexican and Spanish music. Colorful fiestas are held throughout the year. Stroll around the square to view the varied topiary.

Southwest of the Plaza on Main Street are three venerable structures: Masonic Hall (the first building restored, dating from 1858); the Merced Theater, the city's first theater; and the Pico House (on the Plaza), grandest hotel of its day when opened over a hundred years ago. Facades of the last two have been restored; both will eventually operate in their original roles.

These three buildings are all part of a block that includes the fire station and the Pico-Garnier Block, which is being restored as a pedestrian-access complex of shops. The future will be lively

Pool table *pacifies husband while wife shops in mod boutique.*

Whimsically *decorated roof of Los Angeles minibus enlivens Civic Center, site of upthrusting City Hall.*

Sign of the times *on Santa Monica freeway alerts drivers to congested areas ahead.*

"MUST SEES"

CIVIC CENTER (downtown Los Angeles) —panoramic city view from 27th-floor observation deck of City Hall; gardens, shops, and restaurants in the new L. A. Mall around City Hall East

PUEBLO DE LOS ANGELES (north of the Civic Center)—birthplace of L.A.; 19th century park restoration. Olvera Street, West's first mall with Mexican flavor

CHINATOWN-LITTLE TOKYO (north and east of the Civic Center)—smells, sights, and sounds of two cultures

MUSIC CENTER (Grand Avenue at First Street)—L.A.'s cultural "in" place; Chandler Pavilion, Mark Taper Forum, Ahmanson Theater

STUDIO TOURS—behind-scenes peek at television and movie studios; largest tours at Universal Studios and NBC

LOS ANGELES COUNTY MUSEUM OF ART (Hancock Park, Wilshire Boulevard) —one of the great art museums in the U.S.

LA BREA TAR PITS (Hancock Park)—site of prehistoric animals' entrapment in bubbling black pits

GRIFFITH PARK (off Hollywood Freeway) —L.A.'s superpark: see zoo, Travel Town, Fern Dell, Griffith Observatory, Greek Theater

CENTURY CITY (Santa Monica Boulevard just west of Beverly Hills)—city of tomorrow on former 20th Century Fox lot

BEVERLY HILLS (Wilshire Boulevard)— hotels, restaurants, galleries, fine homes, exciting shopping district with New York and European stores

EXPOSITION PARK (off Harbor Freeway) —California Museum of Science and Industry, Natural History Museum of L.A. County, University of Southern California

U.C.L.A. (Sunset Blvd.)—cultural center of western L.A.; four theaters, lively program of performing and exhibiting arts; Westwood

Groceries below, *mariachi musicians above in lively El Mercado, 3425 E. First Street.*

Colorful Mexican *clothing in El Pueblo stalls attracts Olvera Street shoppers.*

here, for only two buildings will be museums; the others will be actual commercial enterprises in historical surroundings.

Old Plaza Fire House, on the Plaza at Los Angeles Street, is the restored station of Engine Company No. 1, the oldest Los Angeles fire station. After serving as a fire house from 1884 to 1897, the two-story brick building became in turn a warehouse, a hotel, and a saloon. Inside is one of the first fire engines used in the city; the horse-drawn equipment was originally built in 1892 for the Chicago Columbia Exposition. Upstairs are the firemen's living quarters. The building is open from noon to 5 P.M. Friday, Saturday, and Sunday, and a guide is available to answer questions.

Plaza Church was first established as a chapel for the settlers in 1784. The diminutive church was originally only 18 by 24 feet. It was finally rebuilt in 1822 with proceeds from the sale of seven barrels of brandy from Mission San Gabriel. In 1860 heavy rains nearly ruined the adobe walls, so the front was taken down and rebuilt with brick. In recent years other changes have been made, including the rebuilding of the bell tower to fit in with the church's original architecture. The door has the classic river-of-life design.

Patterned after the Spanish tradition, the church's interior has an elaborate gold leaf altar, one of the finest in California, and colorful frescoed ceilings. In the grapevine-shaded courtyard is an adobe fountain with a wooden cross in its center. Under the arches are pictures and signs depicting Old Los Angeles.

Also on the Plaza, at the northeast corner of Main Street and Sunset Boulevard, is a bilingual bank operating in a one-time gambling house. Look in on its collection of antique firearms, including pistols used by Mexican insurrectionary Pancho Villa.

Fort Moore Pioneer Memorial is easy to sight. From the plaza, look west past the Plaza Church (over the parking lot that one day may be restored to the old cemetery it once was) to the great waterfall (turned off at present due to energy crisis) of the Pioneer Memorial. From this vantage point it becomes clear why the hill would make a good fort location—a cannon could command the entire Pueblo on the flat land below. Honoring the men and women who pioneered settlement in California, the fort also commemorates the raising of the first United States flag in Los Angeles during the Mexican War in 1847. The 400-foot-long memorial wall, one of the largest bas-reliefs in the United States, features a waterfall-fountain 47 feet high and 80 feet wide.

Olvera Street, a block-long, brick-paved pedestrian lane, is the greatest single magnet in the Pueblo and possibly the West's first pedestrian shopping mall. In its 45 years of existence, Olvera Street has developed its own distinct character, both Mexican and Californian, in shops, restaurants, color, and life. Visitors come, enjoy the experience, and return; the street is a continuous pageant. And its cheerful people are the best part of the show.

Shop for candles, leather goods, silver jewelry, pottery, and Mexican candies. Or dine on good Mexican food with music in the background. The more Mexican way is to eat in one of the little food *puestos* along the street, where you can see your enchiladas and tacos cook over charcoal *braseros.*

Watch the artisans at work. You may see a piñata being formed around a clay *olla* (you can have one made to order); wrought iron being fashioned; three players performing on one marimba; and candles, leather goods, blown glass, and pottery being made. Stalls and shops open at 10 A.M.

Olvera Street actually hits its colorful peak in the evening when lanterns light the shops and Mexican music from the cafes spills into the streets.

Avila Adobe, at 14 Olvera Street, was once a major attraction but is now temporarily closed because of earthquake damage. Oldest dwelling in Los Angeles (perhaps dating back to 1818), the house with its high ceilings, many windows, multiple rooms, and patio-facing corridor was considered a mansion in its day. During the American occupation of the Pueblo in 1847, it served as headquarters for General Kearny and Commodore Robert Stockton. Lieutenant Colonel John Charles Fremont, who accepted Mexico's capitulation ending the war in California, was also billeted here for a while.

The interesting church on the east side of the entrance to Olvera Street is La Plaza Iglesia Metodista (Methodist Church). Built in 1929, its architecture is in the Mexican tradition. Services are conducted in Spanish.

East of El Pueblo, at 737 Lamar Street, is another historic site, the San Antonio Winery. It stands in the heart of what were once Old Town's vast vineyards, now completely urbanized. A visit to the last producing winery in L.A. includes a tour of bottling, aging, and tasting rooms. It is open daily from 9 A.M. Self-guided winery tours take about 20 minutes.

Union Passenger Terminal, one of the last great rail depots built in the United States, celebrated its 35th birthday in 1974. White-stuccoed towers, arches, passageways, soaring interior spaciousness, and a red-tiled roof make the attractive Union Passenger Terminal at 800 N. Alameda Street (east of the Plaza) one of the city's landmarks. Its patios provide the first view of the city for incoming passengers. Stroll the concourses and go up a level above the street to view the railroad tracks.

You can begin a walking tour of cosmopolitan Los Angeles from this stately terminal. It is a good place to park (for a modest fee); from here you can walk to Little Tokyo, City Hall, the Plaza, and New Chinatown. Taken in that order, the round-trip walking tour is about 3 miles long.

New Chinatown really isn't so new. It opened in 1939 to replace the Chinatown ripped out for the Union Station. Located off N. Broadway near College Street, this two-block-long pedestrian mall has small, shop-lined lanes with names like Gin Ling, Sun Mun, and Lei Ling.

Although devoted to much the same kinds of enterprise as Olvera Street, New Chinatown has not aged as well. The emphasis here seems to lean more toward tourism, but in a few shops you can find some excellent Oriental wares. Two food markets have a wide variety of foods, teas, and utensils; there are good Chinese restaurants. One confectionary is a deservedly popular shop.

Liveliest at night, the main mall is bright with lights and often bustling with crowds of after-dinner shoppers and sightseers. The most colorful season here is during Chinese New Year week in late winter. But special occasions throughout the year are likely to bring forth firecracker explosions and parades.

The most authentic Chinese section of the city is on N. Spring Street, southeast of New Chinatown. Here you'll see Chinese markets, restaurants, a Chinese cinema, and a fascinating juxtaposition of Chinese and Spanish-language signs.

Elysian Park

Close to downtown, the 550 acres of Elysian Park seem nevertheless remote. The park is little known and seldom crowded because of its hill and canyon seclusion and its complicated pattern of access roads. Curving around Dodger Stadium, the park is entered from North Broadway or Sunset Boulevard. (Except for two small parks, one downtown and one near it, the acreage contained in Elysian Park represents all that's left of the 17,172-acre Spanish land grant from which the city of Los Angeles grew.)

In the park you can walk forest paths, explore a little known arboretum, picnic under tropical trees, and take in some striking views. On a clear day the park's ridges and promontories afford a rare look over the metropolis, dispelling the illusion that the city is far away.

You can drive through the park in a half hour, but it reveals its delights chiefly to the walker or the cyclist. One of the least strenuous walks takes you through the largest level area in the park. The route is from Scott Avenue up the gentle canyon to the head of Chavez Ravine, where Elysian Drive joins Stadium Way. Selected by horticulturists in 1893 for its frostfree climate (so tropical trees

Government and culture *mix at Civic Center. Night-lighted Water and Power building looms rear, next to Music Center's Chandler Pavilion (left middle ground), Taper Forum (right).*

could survive) and its excellent soil, the Chavez Ravine section of the park was Southern California's first botanical garden. In 1973 it was revived with a program of annual tree plantings by citizens' donations.

Dodger Stadium is adjacent to Elysian Park. Home of L.A.'s first major league baseball team, the stadium has a seating capacity of 56,000, and you park your car on the same level as your stadium seat. Contrary to popular belief, Dodger Stadium was not built in Chavez Ravine but in an adjoining canyon, known before landfill as Sulfur Canyon.

CIVIC CENTER AND VICINITY

The scene of much redevelopment in recent years, Los Angeles' Civic Center is separated from the Old Pueblo area to the north by the Hollywood-Santa Ana Freeway. First Street is the southern extremity, while Figueroa and San Pedro streets are the western and eastern boundaries, respectively.

"The Stack," a much-photographed, four-level freeway interchange, is a few blocks northeast. First of its kind in the world when it opened in the 1950s, it is now outmoded by newer, wider interchanges.

City Hall

For years the City Hall was the tallest building in Southern California, rising 32 stories above the then low-roofed city, kept this way by a ruling against other high-rise buildings. Set on one side of the new City Mall, probable site of the Indian village of Yang-na which antedated the Pueblo, the City Hall tower provides a panorama of the city on a clear day. From the observation deck on the 27th floor, you'll see Union Station to the north and, 15 miles distant, Mt. Wilson.

To the northwest is Hollywood along the Santa Monica Mountains and, closer in, historic Fort Moore Hill. The beach cities along the Pacific Ocean are 16 miles to the west. To the south you'll see Los Angeles Harbor and possibly Catalina Island. The imposing peak to the northeast is Mt. San Antonio. To the east and southeast are the city's industrial sections.

The Los Angeles Mall, or City Mall, opened in the fall of 1974. A handsomely landscaped complex of shops and restaurants, it is two blocks long around City Hall East (Aliso to First Street between Main and Los Angeles streets). Containing submerged gardens and subterranean parking, the mall is served by the downtown minibus.

The Civic Center Complex of Los Angeles is the largest concentration of public buildings outside Washington, D.C. Dominating the group at the head of the west mall is the dramatic Water and Power Building. When illuminated, it can be seen for miles at night. Between it and the City Hall is the County Mall, a setting of promenades, fountains, and pools.

The Music Center—L.A.'s cultural heart

The cultural "in" place of Los Angeles, the Music Center at First Street and Grand Avenue is a $34.5 million complex specially designed to accommodate theatrical and musical presentations.

The Dorothy Chandler Pavilion, an elegant marble and black glass music hall, is the home of the Los Angeles Philharmonic Orchestra. Completed in 1964, it was the first of the three-theater complex, linked on the surface by a landscaped mall and underground by a parking cavern. Acoustics are close to perfection anywhere in the 3,250-seat hall.

The pavilion provides a glittering setting for opera, symphony, musical comedy, and dance performances. You'll find its current attraction listed in local newspapers.

Mark Taper Forum, intimate and innovative, is usually committed to experimental drama by the resident Center Theater Group, lured away from its long-time U.C.L.A. home. Occasionally the 750-seat building is used for lectures, chamber music, and less-than-grand opera.

The building is linked to its larger companion, the Ahmanson Theatre, by a lofty colonnade that echoes the design of the Chandler Pavilion across the court.

Ahmanson Theater, a spacious 2,000-seat auditorium, completes the triple complex of the Music Center. Dedicated to attracting first-class plays and musicals, it is operated most of the year by the Center Theater Group and the rest of the time by the Los Angeles Civic Light Opera.

Although rehearsals are usually in progress in the Forum and the Ahmanson, free daytime tours are conducted through the six-level pavilion on weekdays (except Wednesdays) from May through October and Monday through Thursday from November through April. (Of course, the best way to visit the Music Center is by attending a performance.) Underground parking costs are moderate for a half-hour.

Little Tokyo, a Japanese neighborhood bounded by Central Avenue, Los Angeles, First, and Second streets, is mostly shops and restaurants, but its redevelopment program is bringing new office buildings onto the scene. Walk down the north side of First Street as far as Central and then back on the south side. You pass restaurants, tea houses, sushi bars, confectioners' shops, markets specializing in Oriental cookery ingredients, and some tourist shops. Good buys are imported ceramics, fabrics, tailor-made kimonos, garden accessories, and Japanese carpenter's tools.

During Nisei Week in early August, colorful pageantry stresses cultural achievements and traditions of ancient Japan. On the final Sunday night, the *Ondo* parade sing-songs through the streets.

DOWNTOWN LOS ANGELES

L.A. is experiencing a long overdue downtown renaissance. It is finally beginning to grow upward. Height restrictions placed on tall buildings (previously set at 150 feet) because of earthquake scares were removed in 1957. Today's skyline is dominated by towering office buildings with rooftop dining and "in city" apartments where once elegant 19th century Bunker Hill residences stood. Underneath the two towers of the Atlantic Richfield Plaza is one of America's largest subterranean shopping centers, lined with stores and restaurants. Fashion shows, concerts, and art exhibits are regularly featured. Occidental Center (Twelfth, Hill, and Olive streets) is one of the most interesting business complexes in the West. Guided tours take you through the big auditorium, Japanese garden and courtyard, and up to the observation deck on the 32nd floor. Recently added to the outskirts of the downtown center area is the much-needed and heavily used Convention Center—a sprawling, commodious building with easy access and acres of parking.

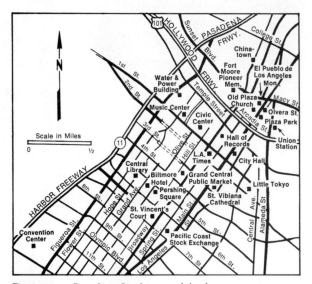

Downtown Los Angeles *is surprisingly compact, offers a variety of cultures close to Civic Center.*

It's easy to get around in the working heart of the city. Downtown traffic is not bad, except during weekday rush hours. And the minibus fleet operated by the Southern California Rapid Transit District shows a fair sampling of the downtown sector on a tour: the retail district, from Fourth to Eighth streets; the big new generation high-rises on Figueroa from Seventh to Fifth; the historic Bradbury Building and the Grand Central Market near Third and Broadway; the Music Center and the monumental Civic Center on First from Flower to Los Angeles Street. You can also visit the Plaza and Olvera Street, Chinatown, and Little Tokyo. Buses run at 5-minute intervals on a continuous loop route from 9 A.M. to 4 P.M. daily except Sunday and holidays. Bus stop signs indicate the route and your location; you can get a pocket-sized map on board. It's quite a tour for 10 cents a ride; but you'll need exact change.

Walking is still the best way to see some of the landmarks. Leave your car in one of the city's many parking lots.

Near the heart of working Los Angeles, you can view some things unique to the city's center: the buildings that record its development since the boom of the 1880s, a great market, the financial district, and downtown shopping.

To get there, turn off the Harbor Freeway at Sixth Street and drive to Pershing Square. You can park there or in nearby lots for a few dollars a day (less on Sunday). Sunday morning is a good time for suburban youngsters to experience the deep canyons of downtown without weekend crowds. Saturday is good for both walking and shopping. Weekdays are the liveliest.

Pershing Square, called Central Park before 1918, is L.A.'s only downtown park, located in the center of the business district. The statue of brooding Beethoven is a reminder that this park used to be the cultural center of downtown Los Angeles. His statue faces the former Philharmonic Auditorium across Fifth Street, which reverted to church use after the new Music Center opened.

The Biltmore Hotel, across Olive Street from the square, belongs to another era. Untouched by the

"Double Ascension," *massive metal-work at Richfield Plaza.*

Bradbury Building's *soaring, skylit central court is astonishing design.*

modernization that has been applied to its rooms, the lobby is ornate in the grand manner, as impressive today as it was in 1923 when the hotel was built. Turn left in the upper lobby toward the carriage entrance past an art gallery and shops; then turn right into another broad corridor to exit on Grand Avenue.

The Main Library, across from the Biltmore on Grand Avenue and reaching over to Flower Street, is part of the largest public library system in the nation. Built in 1926, the fortresslike structure was designed by architect Bertram Goodhue, who achieved fame as the architect of the 1915 San Diego Exposition (now metamorphosed into Balboa Park) that touched off a wave of mission-style building in Southern California.

The formal entrance is on Fifth and Flower streets. Oldtimers will remember that the State Normal School, predecessor of U.C.L.A., stood here for more than 50 years before Fifth Street was cut through to the west.

If you have time, see the pleasant gardens, impressive rotunda on the second floor, and mural-decorated History Room. The library is open 10 A.M. to 9 P.M. daily except Sunday and holidays.

Grand Central Market, a block and a half north from Pershing Square (Hill Street between Third and Fourth), is a food bazaar that could exist only in a metropolis. The giant Grand Central Public Market, a block deep, is open from 9 A.M. to 6 P.M. daily except Sunday and holidays.

Perhaps the main reason for shopping here is to find things you may not find anywhere else in town. One stall displays 13 kinds of beans, peas, and lentils; another offers 20 different varieties of tea. You can look over rare spices and chiles, rice in all grain sizes, different blends of olive oil, and all the ingredients for Mexican cookery. The store has so many Spanish-speaking customers that many stalls have bilingual signs and sales people.

The Bradbury Building, across from the Grand Central Market at 304 Broadway, is an ordinary-looking building on the outside. Once inside, you'll see why this 85-year-old structure is a city cultural-historic monument. (On Sunday and holidays you can only get a glimpse of its interior grandeur through locked glass doors.) Its surprising, five-story skylit interior, with cast-iron tracery on the open elevator cages and balcony rails, is a distinguished example of 19th century, Parisian-style architecture. One of the prototype hydraulic elevators is still in use.

Built by colorful Colonel Louis Bradbury of Bunker Hill, the building was once a fashionable address for law firms of a bygone era. Now it houses a gallery and offices for architects and other design professionals.

The Alexandria Hotel has managed to elude the urban renewal that is sweeping L.A. This turn-of-the-century hostelry, two blocks east of Pershing Square, once glittered with statesmen and celebrities of stage and screen. A victim of hard times, it has now recovered. Out from under the paint has emerged gleaming brass on stair rails and the stained glass ceiling of the lofty Palm Court (darkened for the blackouts of World War II).

Thick carpet, stained glass from razed Bunker Hill houses, antiques, and old photographs evoke nostalgia. Victorian rooms and suites are named after stars who once frequented the hotel: Valentino, Gloria Swanson, Francis X. Bushman.

The Pacific Coast Stock Exchange, at 618 S. Spring Street, has a visitors' gallery on the second floor where you can get a first-hand picture of what's happening on the trading floor. The gallery is open from 7 A.M. to 2:30 P.M. Monday through Friday (coinciding with hours of the New York Exchange).

Spring Street is all financial dignity, with a few appropriate shops: stationers, leather goods, and florists. Broadway, once the main retail street from Fourth to Eighth, is still bustling, crowded, often nerve-jangling in its profusion of signs and people on Sundays, when Spanish is heard as often as English. On Broadway, just north of Seventh Street, you can lunch at a Los Angeles institution: Clifton's Cafeteria. Its interior decor consists of rocks, tree trunks, and a waterfall. It's a good place to take small children; they like the atmosphere and can see what they're getting in advance. (There's another Clifton's on Olive Street.)

Seventh Street, west from Broadway, is the second major downtown retail street. Intended as a great artery to the west, its development was slowed because of the need to grade the hill on which the Los Angeles Hilton was built, and Wilshire overtook it as the main line. Between Broadway and Hill, look in on pleasant St. Vincent's Court, site of Los Angeles' first college. Now it is a shady retreat with bookstall, outdoor espresso bar, and sidewalk florist. The block between Hope and Flower streets contains the big new Broadway Plaza complex of stores, restaurants, hotel, offices, and parking.

SOUTH OF THE CITY

South and west of downtown Los Angeles are several of the area's largest sports centers, two big museums, one of the best known universities in the country, the international airport, and other scattered attractions. All can be reached from several freeways—the Santa Monica (Interstate 10), the San Diego (Interstate 405), the Harbor (State 11), and the Long Beach (State 7).

Exposition Park

A meeting place for nature, ideas and experiments, history, and activity, 114-acre Exposition Park is bordered by Exposition Boulevard, Figueroa Street, and Menlo and Santa Barbara avenues. A ramp from the Harbor Freeway takes you to Exposition Boulevard; the main entrance to the park is through the Memorial Gateway just west of the junction of Hoover and Figueroa streets.

In the center of Exposition Park, 16,000 fragrant rose bushes fill the Sunken Garden, a principal feature of the park's landscaping. The roses bloom from late spring through fall; all are identified.

The California Museum of Science and Industry, south of the Sunken Garden on State Drive, offers the opportunity for a do-it-yourself short course in basic science. It's a noisy museum: balls drop, a jet engine fires, a heart thumps. Some machines perform with soap bubbles and rubber balls. Others can be manipulated by a child to reveal the laws of orbiting bodies, to turn a car wheel or axle, or to play tic-tac-toe with an electronic brain that never loses. Throughout the museum you'll find gadgets that are not only fascinating but instructive. One of the most popular shows is the giant egg, where each day 150 chicks are hatched.

Contributed by industries and professions in Southern California, displays represent medicine and the computer, aircraft, gas, electricity, telephone, railroad, and automobile industries.

Its hours are 10 A.M. to 5 P.M.; the museum is closed only on Thanksgiving and Christmas. Admission is free. The main parking lot is behind the Hall of Health annex.

The Museum of Natural History is on the west side of the Sunken Garden. The most outstanding Southern California exhibit consists of the assembled skeletons of the Ice Age fossils exhumed from the Rancho La Brea tar pits (now called Hancock Park). Another exhibit features realistic, life-size dioramas of African elephants in natural settings. And to another world belongs the museum's most popular display: the Egyptian mummy.

Other halls in the museum (soon to be enlarged) depict Southern California life in the Indian, Spanish, Mexican, and American periods. Also on display are Polynesian, African, and pre-Columbian American artifacts.

In the Phantasmagoria show you can put a nickel in the nickelodeon for some sprightly background music while you browse among such diverse memorabilia as William S. Hart's fan mail, Tom Mix's Stetson hat, W. C. Field's billiard cue, and Mary Pickford's curls. You'll also see such early motion picture inventions as E. H. Amet's Magniscope, one of the first four motion picture projectors, and an 1895 Lumiere camera-projector.

Other windows show film animation, costumes, props, and early theaters. You can watch silent movies at 2-hour intervals beginning at 10:30 A.M. or a button-activated slide show history of color in motion pictures. Open from 10 A.M. to 5 P.M., the museum is closed Mondays and on Thanksgiving and Christmas. It also has an excellent ethnic arts gift shop, where you can find artifacts from the world over. Admission is free.

Memorial Coliseum, on the opposite side of the park from the museums, has an awesome seating capacity of nearly 95,000. The gateway to the park commemorates the Olympic Games that were held in this coliseum. The stadium, built in 1928 and remodeled for the 10th Olympiad in 1932, covers 17 acres. University of Southern California and University of California at Los Angeles play their home football games here, as do the Los Angeles Rams of the National Football League. Track meets, rodeos, and pageants are also staged here.

Behind the Coliseum, the Swim Stadium, with its Olympic-sized swimming pool (also built for the Olympics), is open to the public.

Sports centers tend to proliferate in this area. The modern indoor Sports Arena, in Exposition Park at the corner of Figueroa and Santa Barbara streets, has a maximum seating capacity of 16,300. Collegiate and professional basketball, track meets, boxing matches, tennis tournaments, and special sports events and shows are held here.

Another outstanding sports center, The Forum, is located in Inglewood, at the corner of Manchester Boulevard and Prairie Avenue. Professional basketball, hockey, ice shows, track meets, tennis, and boxing are the main attractions. The Forum seats 18,600.

University of Southern California covers several blocks along Exposition Boulevard opposite Exposition Park. Founded in 1876 by the Southern Conference of the Methodist Episcopal Church, it is the largest private university in California. Its architecture is a fine integration of the old and new; notice especially Doheny Library and the campanile. U.S.C. is noted for its Department of Cinema, the oldest (1929), largest, and one of the most respected in the country. Its faculty roster often includes prominent names from nearby Hollywood's motion picture industry.

Watts Towers

In Watts, most easily reached via the Harbor Freeway (State 11), three unusual towers, soaring 104 feet above the ground, stand as a strangely beautiful symbol of a man's ambition "to do something big." The man was Sabatino (or Simon) Rodia, an Italian tile setter who spent 33 years single-handedly building the towers. Rodia wired steel reinforcing rods together into a lacy structure, stuccoed them with cement, then studded the cement with broken bits of glass, tile, old dishes, pottery shards, cup handles, pebbles, and seashells. The strange assemblage sparkles in a multitude of colors in the sun.

His work completed in 1954, Rodia quietly left town, and the future of the towers became uncertain. Vandals broke the seashells and bottles, and the city decided the towers should be leveled because they represented a hazard to the general public. But the public became interested in preserving this forerunner of pop art. The fate of the towers was settled when the steepest one was subjected to a "pull test" before television cameras and didn't budge.

You can visit the towers at 1765 E. 107th Street daily from 11 A.M. to 5 P.M. A 75-cent donation (25 cents for children) contributes to maintenance and provides you with an informative booklet.

Hollywood Park Race Track

Just east of the San Diego Freeway (Interstate 405) in Inglewood, picturesque Hollywood Park features 50 days of thoroughbred racing from April to July, plus nightly harness racing from mid-September through December. The race track is famous for its beautifully landscaped infield.

Morning workouts from 7 to 10 A.M. begin a month before the racing season opens. Open to the public, they take place at the north end of the grandstand. Activities are described over the public address system by a racing expert. You can also take a bus tour of the stables and see a movie on racing. There is no admission charge.

Los Angeles International Airport

A few blocks west of the San Diego Freeway on Century Boulevard is one of the world's largest airports. It's served by every major domestic and international carrier. If you follow Sepulveda Boulevard through the tunnel underneath the runway, you may have the unusual experience of driving underneath a departing jet. You might enjoy dining in the elevated restaurant of the Host International theme building, distinctively rising in the center of the terminal complex.

Santa Sophia Cathedral

Though outside decoration is sparse, the Greek Orthodox Cathedral of Santa Sophia at 1324 S. Normandie, just south of Pico Boulevard, has the most richly decorated interior of any city church.

You'll especially notice the interior decoration of pure gold, 17 crystal chandeliers from Czechoslovakia, floors paved with antique marble, stained

Watts towers, *an amazing product of man's imagination, has been hailed as a folk art masterpiece.*

Exposition Park *displays elephants not behind glass, dinosaurs assembled without visible support.*

glass windows in rare colors depicting the 12 Apostles, and a mosaic-style painting of Christ that covers the dome.

Around the church is a tiny microcosm of Greek culture. About a half-block up the street on Pico Boulevard, the church-going crowds flock to C & K Importing Company for fresh breads brought in at

Fanciful *Brown Derby restaurant is a familiar sight on Wilshire Boulevard near Ambassador Hotel.*

9 A.M. daily, as well as for hundreds of other hard-to-find foods of Greece and the Mediterranean. It's a good place to assemble an on-the-spot picnic.

Next door is an importer of Greek gift items, and on the other side is a European record shop, offering Greek magazines and greeting cards.

FOLLOW L.A.'s FAMOUS STREETS

One of the best ways to see Los Angeles is to get off the freeways and drive its celebrity boulevards: Wilshire, Santa Monica, Sunset, and Hollywood. Each presents a different facet of city life. Almost every attraction in the western section of L.A. is on or near these thoroughfares. Two of them stretch from downtown Los Angeles to the ocean; one—Hollywood Boulevard—ends in the hills after taking you through the heart of Hollywood, filmland's one-time glamour spot. Moving from downtown outward, we'll point out some attractions along these boulevards.

Wilshire Boulevard

Stretching 16 miles from the city's center to the ocean, Wilshire Boulevard is one of the world's prestige streets, often compared to New York's Fifth Avenue. Launched in the 1920s with the opening of "Miracle Mile" (La Brea to La Cienega avenues), it soon began accumulating high-class shops, department stores, business firms, smart apartment houses, and plush restaurants. If you have time, you will want to stop at attractions along the way and explore interesting side streets. But even if you just keep driving, you will pass places closely identified with the growth of this city, along with some of the most interesting examples of new commercial architecture in the United States. Several well-known hotels have a Wilshire Boulevard address, starting with the downtown Los Angeles Hilton and including the farther-out Ambassador, Beverly Hilton, and Beverly Wilshire.

MacArthur Park, bisected by Wilshire Boulevard just west of Alvarado Street, was long known as Westlake, a country park at the westernmost edge of the city. Renamed for General Douglas MacArthur in 1942, the 32-acre park has a small lake and pleasantly landscaped grounds. Popular with the summer lunch group, it sports an open-air theater for Shakespearean and musical performances.

West of the park on the north side of the street is the Otis Art Gallery, open daily Tuesday through Saturday and on Sunday afternoons. A few blocks farther is Lafayette Park, another spot of welcome open space.

The Ambassador Hotel comes into view on the left soon after you cross Vermont Avenue. Set far back from ever-burgeoning Wilshire Boulevard amidst 27 protective acres of park like grounds, the venerable old structure has long been a Los Angeles landmark. Fresh appearing after an extensive face lifting, it still exudes an atmosphere of elegance.

Across the street is the "original" Brown Derby, tracing its origin back to 1926. The main dining room is in the center of this whimsically hat-shaped restaurant. Prices are less expensive here than at the other, more conventionally shaped Brown Derby on N. Vine Street, which has show business caricatures on the walls, or at the one on Wilshire in Beverly Hills.

Some of the best-looking buildings along this section of Wilshire are the insurance companies, banks, and churches. The Old World architecture of the Wilshire Boulevard Temple (with the largest Jewish congregation in the world) and the Masonic Temple contrasts sharply with the contemporary style of St. Basil's Catholic Church.

Miracle Mile, beginning at La Brea Avenue, actually stretches for several miles to La Cienega. You will recognize it by its median landscaped with palms. Although it does not seem quite as glamorous as the segments on either side, this section does have some outstanding attractions.

Hancock Park is one of the few remaining patches of greenery along Wilshire Boulevard. This is the site of the Rancho La Brea Tar Pits, where Pleistocene-era animals were trapped some 40 centuries ago. The collection of prehistoric animal skeletons that were found here is displayed across town in the Los Angeles County Natural History Museum in Exposition Park. In Pueblo days, the Spaniards used *la brea* (tar) from these pits to waterproof

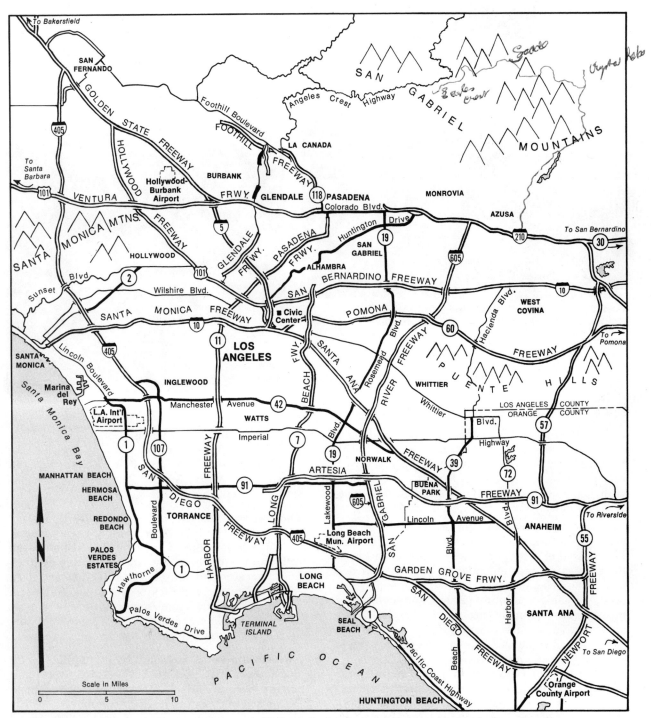

Los Angeles freeways *speed cross-city travel. Well-marked freeways allow rapid circulation of traffic, permit you to bypass congested areas, give easy access to all corners of L.A.*

their roofs. Not until 1905 was it discovered that the bubbly, black pits had entombed such creatures as mastodons, dire wolves, and imperial mammoths that came to drink at the ponds 13,000 to 40,000 years ago, only to be caught and trapped in the seeping tar. Today, a strange, life-sized scene of the recreated ancient animals — including fiberglass imperial mammoths with tusks 12½ feet long —brings a touch of prehistory to busy Wilshire Boulevard. At the observation building in the northwest corner of the park, you can see the asphalt-laden water still bubbling and some animal

Cornucopia *of domestic and foreign fruits at Farmers Market, W. Third Street and Fairfax Avenue*

Eye-catching models *of sinking mastodons at La Brea Tar Pits re-create drama of the past.*

bones still enmeshed in the tar. The building is open daily except Monday from 10 A.M. to 5 P.M. Scientists are still digging just south of the observation building, hoping to find small bones and microfossils overlooked in the original digs of 1906-1915 and perhaps new evidence of Ice Age man.

Los Angeles County Museum of Art is the largest art museum built in this country in over 30 years. It is housed in three gleaming pavilions on a 3-foot-thick concrete slab atop the tar pits in Hancock Park. The reflecting pool that surrounded it has become a major sculpture garden, dominated by a monumental Rodin bronze of Honoré Balzac. A latecomer in the art-collecting field, the museum has acquired some well-known works of art and is particularly rich in impressionistic paintings.

The Ahmanson Gallery, dominant pavilion in this imposing complex, houses the museum's permanent collections in separate galleries on four floors extending out from a lofty skylit central court. Collections, ranging from ancient treasures to futuristic experiments, are arranged chronologically.

On the upper level that connects the three buildings is the Norton Simon Sculpture Court, a popular meeting place featuring works of famous sculptors. You can lunch at the cafeteria in the nearby Leo S. Bing Center, which has facilities for films, lectures, concerts, and temporary exhibitions. The third pavilion, the Hammer Wing, is the home of changing exhibits.

Normally charging no admission fee, the art museum is open Tuesday through Friday from 10 A.M. to 5 P.M., from 10 A.M. to 6 P.M. on Saturday, and noon to 6 P.M. on Sunday. An admission fee is sometimes charged for special shows.

The Egg and The Eye, at 5814 Wilshire Boulevard across from Hancock Park, is more than a restaurant. It's a boutique, a curio shop, and more—an intimate place where you can see or buy contemporary crafts and museum-quality folk art from the world over, take a lesson on the making of an omelet, join a craftsmen's association, or simply dine on the balcony restaurant from a menu listing more omelets than perhaps you knew existed.

Farmers Market is keynoted by its familiar white clock tower that rises above W. Third Street and Fairfax Avenue and gives the busy neighborhood the air of a midwestern farming community. Words above the tower entrance read simply, "An Idea." The idea was to help farmers from the Los Angeles area during the worst years of the Depression by letting them use a vacant field at the edge of the city to market their wasting crops.

The Farmers Market idea not only helped the 18 original farmers but also grew into a giant market-restaurant-gift shop complex covering 20 acres and serving 20,000 visitors and shoppers daily year-round. Although tour buses pack the parking lots around noon, most people here are from L.A.

Studio audience, *technicians raptly monitor performer Carol Burnett at CBS-TV filming.*

Parabolic shape *lends distinction to savings and loan building at Wilshire and La Cienega.*

Some of the original farmers and their families are still associated with the market, maintaining their widespread reputation by selling fresh food from all parts of the world. Here you can enjoy a tray of delicious food from any one of the market's 26 kitchens serving food from six countries. This is also the place to go shopping without a list, letting impulse be your guide through the tempting displays. You can buy a puppy, a fish, or an exotic bird there—but leave your pet at home. No animals are allowed to roam the premises.

The market is open Monday through Saturday from 9 A.M. to 6:30 P.M. during the winter; it stays open somewhat later during the summer. Activity begins to slow down around 5 P.M. One restaurant offering varied entertainment is open until 2 A.M. For a map listing each merchant in the market, stop at the office just inside Gate No. 1. With the map, you can chart a course through the busy aisles that will take you past every stall and shop. With so many things to see and buy, a walk among the stalls takes about an hour. Allow plenty of extra time to visit the shops.

CBS Television City, at the corner of Fairfax Avenue and Beverly Boulevard, offers conducted tours through the studios, various program sets, equipment, and wardrobe departments. There is no admission charge, and parking is free. Tours begin on the hour from 1 P.M. to 5 P.M., Monday through Friday. For information, call 651-2345.

La Cienega Boulevard's loose Spanish translation, "the watering hole," is an apt one. Located about a mile past Fairfax Avenue, this is "Restaurant Row." The boulevard is more glamorous at night, when diners congregate in eateries on both sides of the street to enjoy some of L.A.'s best food.

Art galleries also abound on this fabled boulevard. The gallery row between Melrose Avenue and Santa Monica Boulevard hosts popular Monday evening promenades during which strollers can wander through shops or just gaze in the windows.

Beverly Hills comes into view when you cross San Vicente Boulevard. Though surrounded by L.A., it has never surrendered its identity. Notice the absence of billboards and the lower buildings. At the busy intersection of Olympic Boulevard and Beverly Drive is a "Monument to the Stars" who fought valiantly for the community's preservation when annexation to Los Angeles seemed likely.

Shop prowling is one of the city's main attractions. Beverly Hills is the place where New York stores open branches, imports converge, and dining is cosmopolitan. Perhaps because this is the center of the affluent community, variety seems wider and specialties more specialized. And more than elsewhere, the shops project a heightened sensual appeal; even the most appealing goods play second fiddle to imaginative display.

The big stores hold forth on Wilshire Boulevard. North from Wilshire, small high fashion shops mingle with delicatessens, coffee houses, and fish stores in a village atmosphere. Check with the Beverly Hills Visitors and Convention Bureau, 239 S. Beverly Drive, for maps and locations of shops.

Beyond Beverly Hills, Wilshire takes you past the exclusive Los Angeles Country Club, with two 18-hole golf courses on either side of the boulevard.

Westwood Village, mecca for college students and a rather quaint community in its own right, nestles at the foot of the University of California, Los Angeles campus. Stop for a walk through the village and explore its inviting shops and eating spots.

U.C.L.A. has grown in one generation from a cluster of five Romanesque buildings on a hilltop to a complete city of learning. The mammoth campus covers 411 acres of terraced hillside.

A major force in the city's cultural life, U.C.L.A. is a leader in drama, music, and the arts. The interesting architectural forms of the new buildings are complemented by an upside-down water fountain (presently turned off) in front of Franz Hall, outdoor sculpture, and landscaped gardens.

Areas of special interest include the wealth of art displayed in the Dickson Art Center's three galleries; the Franklin D. Murphy Sculpture Garden, a 4½-acre court containing one of the world's outstanding displays of 20th century sculpture; and the University Research Library.

Free campus maps are available at parking kiosks; parking is free on Sunday. You can reach U.C.L.A. by turning north from Westwood Village.

Palisades Park in Santa Monica is the terminus for Wilshire Boulevard. Stretching for almost 2 miles along the cliff top, the park offers perhaps the most beautiful and familiar view of Santa Monica Bay. On a clear day you can see the Channel Islands, and on almost any day you can see the Santa Monica Mountains reaching out into the ocean to form the northern crescent of the bay. This corridor of green lawn, flowers, and tall palm trees is a pleasant area for a stroll or a picnic.

Before you explore the park, stop at the Tourist Information Center on Ocean Avenue just south of Santa Monica Boulevard and ask for a brochure. It will point out such features of interest as the sundial, the camera obscura, the totem pole, some of the trees and memorial plantings, and the park's seven monuments.

Santa Monica Boulevard

Originating in Silver Lake, the district east of Hollywood, Santa Monica Boulevard parallels Wilshire Boulevard heading north for a stretch, then turns south and cuts through Beverly Hills and across Wilshire on its way to the ocean. Though not particularly noted as a scenic thoroughfare, it does pass some interesting sights. If you have driven out Wilshire Boulevard, it's an alternate route back to Los Angeles or on to Hollywood.

The Mormon Temple, a monumental white edifice high atop a hill on Santa Monica Boulevard (a few blocks east of the Santa Monica Freeway), is the largest temple of the Mormon faith (Church of Jesus Christ of Latter-day Saints). The gold leaf figure of Angel Moroni on top, once visible 25 miles out to sea, is now getting lost among the highrises. You can tour the grounds but may not go inside the temple. Movies shown at the Visitor Information Center take you on a tour of the interior. The center is open from 7 A.M. to 5 P.M. daily.

Century City—a panorama of broad thoroughfares, sky-reaching buildings, green parks, and plazas—is a super-city of tomorrow being built today on land owned yesterday by a major movie studio. Turn onto the Avenue of the Stars from Santa Monica Boulevard (just south of Wilshire) to visit this trend-setting city within a city.

Based on the master plan of architects Welton Becket and Associates, Century City seems slightly larger than life. Traffic within the giant blocks is

Strong Lipschitz *sculpture, "Song of the Vowels," is prominently displayed at U.C.L.A. Sculpture Garden.*

The Entertainment World of Los Angeles

Touring *Universal Studios, guests in bus caravan get a practical demonstration of how the parting of the Red Sea was brought about.*

Movie studios. The motion picture industry's sound stages are scattered over an area that includes not only Hollywood but also most of its neighboring cities. Many are in the San Fernando Valley, 20th-Century Fox is just outside the western boundary of Beverly Hills, and M.G.M. is in Culver City.

Only one film studio, Universal (Lankershim Boulevard just north of the Hollywood Freeway), offers elaborate tours, painstakingly explaining its operation to visitors. A million people a year enjoy a ride through the studio's 420-acre lot on guided, candy-striped trams that pass through many continents and centuries, T.V. and movie sound stages, false front sets, stars' dressing rooms, warehouses, and labs. Watch a flash flood, a torpedo explosion, a colonial mansion that burns on cue, and a re-created spectacle that even the Prince of Wales has enjoyed—the parting of the Red Sea.

The tram tour, main feature of the visit, takes almost 2 hours. Allow additional time for the shows: gasp at the stuntmen's performances; see how movie animals are trained; watch makeup being applied. During the summer, tours run daily from 9 A.M. to 5 P.M.; they operate from 10 A.M. to 3:30 P.M. the rest of the year. Tickets cost around $5 for adults, less for children. For specific information on schedules and prices call 877-1311.

Television studios. Today television is as much a part of the entertainment scene as movies have been. Many popular shows originate here, and you will be welcome in the audience of many programs if you first obtain tickets, offered free by most studios. Some studios can furnish tickets in less than a month, but others are booked up many months in advance. To arrange for tickets, you can call, visit, or write the studio. When you write, enclose a stamped, self-addressed envelope. These studios, listed by channel, invite the public to productions:

Channel 2 (CBS network, station KNXT). Address: CBS Television, 7800 Beverly Blvd., Hollywood 90036. Telephone Guest Relations, 651-2345.

Channel 4 (NBC network, station KNBC). Address: Tickets, National Broadcasting Company, 3000 W. Alameda Ave., Burbank 91523. Telephone 845-7000, Ext. 2481 (Guest Relations).

Channel 5 (KTLA). Address: KTLA, 5800 Sunset Blvd., Hollywood 90028. Telephone 469-3181.

Channel 7 (ABC network, station KABC). Address: (Name of show) Tickets, ABC-TV, 4151 Prospect Ave., Hollywood 90028. Telephone 663-3311.

Channel 11 (Station KTTV). Address: (Name of show) Tickets, KTTV, 5746 Sunset Blvd., Hollywood 90028. Telephone 462-7111.

Channel 28 (Station KCET). Address: KCET, 4400 Sunset Dr., Los Angeles 90027. Telephone 666-6500. (Educational TV station; few live programs).

Two large television studios offer conducted tours. At CBS Television City, 7800 Beverly Blvd., free tours start from the Artist Entrance on the hour Monday through Friday, 1 to 5 P.M. At NBC Color City, 3000 W. Alameda Ave., Burbank, tours start from the tour bungalow Monday through Saturday from 10 A.M. to 5 P.M. Admission price to NBC is around $2 for adults, half-price for children.

designed for the pedestrian; all parking on this 180-acre site is underground.

The land from which Century City rises was once the ranch of Tom Mix before it became the back lot of Twentieth Century-Fox Studio. In 1961 it was sold to the Alcoa Company for construction of a major new urban center in Los Angeles. Although the movieland sets were demolished, more than $1 million was invested in saving and replanting the unique studio tree collection.

Spread out like an oversized Japanese fan, Century City's crown jewel is the 800-room Century Plaza Hotel, designed by architect Minoru Yamasaki. Surrounded by landscaped grounds and resembling New York City's Rockefeller Center, it was the choice for the Presidential State Dinner honoring the first astronauts to reach the moon. The hotel, gardens, shops, and restaurants are well worth a look.

The Theme Center, across the street from the Century Plaza Hotel, is a rapidly developing entertainment complex. It features the large Shubert Theatre, a setting for Broadway productions on the West Coast, as well as for other legitimate theater performances. There are also two first-run cinemascopic theaters. Twin 44-story triangular office towers rise in the background. Shops, restaurants, and clubs complement the theaters and face the plaza.

Twentieth Century-Fox, one of the oldest and most prestigious movie studios in the industry, still exists on one corner of the Century City property. The studio is not open for tours because of restricted space. But work still goes on (television series and independent productions), and some sets are still standing. Part of the prop lot can be seen from some of the Century Plaza Hotel windows, but a better view of the *Hello, Dolly* set is from Pico Boulevard, the street on which the studio fronts.

On the north side of Santa Monica Boulevard, between Camden and Bedford drives in Beverly Hills, notice the city's comprehensive outdoor cactus and succulent collection, featuring specimens gathered from the deserts and jungles of the world.

Beverly Hills Thieves Market flourishes in a big red barn of a trading post topped with flying flags at 8549 Santa Monica Boulevard. In a carnival-church bazaar atmosphere, some 60 shops fan out from a central gazebo restaurant and circle a balcony loft, offering a potpourri of goods ranging from junk to gems, health food to wine and dried plants, apparel to environmental sculpture, antiques to handicrafts.

There are auctions at 8 P.M. Friday nights and fashion shows every Wednesday at noon. The market opens at 11 A.M. Wednesday through Sunday.

Hollywood Cemetery, on Santa Monica Boulevard between Van Ness and Gower streets, is the final resting place for some legendary Hollywood film stars. Silent film star John Gilbert is buried here, as are Douglas Fairbanks and many others. This is where the mysterious lady in black paid her annual visits to Valentino's grave.

Paramount Studios, one of the few still left in Hollywood, is south of the cemetery. It is not open for tours.

Sunset Boulevard

Gloria Swanson immortalized this street in the film *Sunset Boulevard*. She even lived on the famous thoroughfare (across from the Beverly Hills Hotel). Her home is gone, but other stars live nearby. Hawkers sell their addresses, and a few homes of the bygone great are open to the public.

There's still a magic to the name "Sunset Strip," although its character has changed. Even if you're not a star-gazer, Sunset Boulevard is an interesting drive. Beginning at the Plaza, it proceeds through Hollywood and wanders along the foothills of the Santa Monica Mountains for 25 miles to its intersection with the Pacific Coast Highway.

The boulevard intersects with the canyon roads that cut across the mountains to the San Fernando Valley. "Hideaway" homes are built along these winding roads. Perhaps the best known residential area is exclusive Bel Air.

Angelus Temple and Echo Park are just south of Sunset Boulevard on Glendale Boulevard. Although Angelus Temple is visually unprepossessing, in the 1930s it presented one of the greatest shows in Los Angeles—a nightly, slightly edited version of the life of Aimee Semple McPherson, complete with full cast and scenery. Aimee, a self appointed faith-healer, is gone, but the temple lives on.

South of the temple is Echo Park, a pleasant haven of greenery complete with a small lake for boating in a sylvan setting. It is notable for its lotuses which flower in July. Sometimes stocked with fish, it's the meeting place for small children.

The Hollywood Palladium, 6215 Sunset Boulevard, is usually the Saturday night home of "champagne musicmaker" Lawrence Welk. When he's in town, you can dine and dance (reservations required) from 8:30 P.M. on. It's a good idea to check (phone 466-4311) who is appearing at this entertainment emporium because other musical groups perform from time to time.

Almost across the street is the Aquarius, one of several Sunset Boulevard theaters—formerly Earl Carroll's theatre-restaurant. You can see and hear anything from rock opera to Shakespeare.

Schwab's Drugstore (Sunset Boulevard and Laurel Canyon) owes its reputation to the legend that Lana Turner was discovered sipping a soda here.

Roadside sale *of maps to movie stars' homes is example of media influence in Southern California.*

Filming *Warren Beatty's movie* Shampoo, *crew follows car along Sunset Boulevard.*

Although this was later denied by Mervyn Leroy, who cast her in a bit part, Schwab's became a gathering place for aspiring actors and actresses. More than a drugstore, it is still a place film personalities frequent. And you can get a very good meal here.

Sunset Strip in its heyday was one of the plushest stretches of the boulevard. Within this 20-block area was a trio of famous nightclubs: Trocadero, Mocambo, and Ciro's. Fans gathered here to watch the comings and goings of the movie colony. With the gradual demise of Hollywood as a film center, the Strip has exchanged its Rolls Royce culture for a Volkswagen one.

There's still action at night, but it centers on the young and hip strolling in and out of the numerous loud, gaudy lounges and glorified hamburger stands. The view over L.A. is still good, but people don't seem to notice; they're too distracted by the colorful costumes and the theatrical billboards.

Sunset Plaza is an oasis of delightful small stores just past La Cienega. You can buy and browse among boutiques and art galleries, eat at some very good restaurants, or sit at a sidewalk cafe and "people watch."

A mile past Sunset Plaza, you reach the end of Sunset Strip. Suddenly the towering buildings are replaced by the gracious green spaces surrounding the lovely homes of residential Beverly Hills in one of the most dramatic urban transitions to be seen.

The Beverly Hills Hotel (at Beverly Drive and Sunset Boulevard) enjoys a lush, green 16-acre setting across from a park. This pink palace, set back from a busy intersection (also the entrance to Coldwater Canyon), looks like a stage setting. Not camera shy, it has been used in films many times. It has also

been home to a multitude of famous personalities at one time or another. The hotel is well worth a stop, even if you only walk around the grounds.

"Where do the stars live?" is a frequently asked question here. Street-side vendors will provide you with addresses (not particularly accurate) for a price. You can also pick up a brochure on the stars' homes from the Sunset Plaza merchants or from the Southern California Visitors Council in downtown L.A.

Two homes are open for visiting: Lionel Barrymore's former home and garden is presently a health food restaurant at 8426 Sunset Boulevard, below the Strip. Harold Lloyd estate (1225 Benedict Canyon Drive), encased in 16 acres of lush gardens with spectacular fountains and a 100-foot-high cascading waterfall, was the playground of the stars of the 1930s. It is open on an on-again, off-again basis, and group tours are occasionally available; check with the Beverly Hills Visitors and Convention Bureau, 239 S. Beverly Drive. Inquire also about the castle on the hill above Sunset Boulevard and Doheny Road: Greystone Mansion, which cost Edward Doheny of Teapot Dome notoriety $4 million to build. Because of its tremendous size, the mansion later became a white elephant on the market. Eventually rescued by the city of Beverly Hills, it is now open to the public for weekend tours. The park that surrounds it is open seven days a week from 10 A.M. to 5 P.M. Tours of the house are conducted on Saturday and Sunday at 1 and 3 P.M., by reservation only. Tickets must be obtained in advance. Information is available at the Convention and Visitors Bureau, 271-1881 or 272-4049. The grounds are free; admission to the house is $1. Don't bring pets.

After leaving Beverly Hills, you soon get a good view of sprawling U.C.L.A. below you to the left.

Will Rogers State Historical Park will expose you to the wit and personality of humorist Will Rogers. At the main house (filled with mementos of the "cowboy philosopher's" busy life) of his Pacific Palisades estate, a curator is on hand to tell you about the paintings, Navajo rugs, lariats, saddles, and other objects.

In the stable area, you'll still find polo ponies in the corrals and exercising and roping rings. Riding and hiking trails circling the low hills above the ranch houses invite exploration. The park is open every day except major holidays. Admission is free; there is a small fee to see the main house (open from 10 A.M. to 5 P.M.). No picnicking or camping is permitted on the grounds. The entrance road to the park is located at 14235 Sunset Boulevard.

Self-Realization Fellowship Lake Shrine is one of the hidden treasures along this route. A small natural lake, fed by springs, it is set in a garden that almost succeeds in shutting out the traffic noise of busy Sunset Boulevard. Look for the shrine at 17190 Sunset Boulevard in Pacific Palisades, just up from the coast highway.

The fellowship is devoted to yoga. Its miniature park, dedicated to all religions, is open free of charge to everyone daily except Monday from 9 A.M. to 5 P.M. You walk a lakeside path past shrines, along garden slopes, and past a small houseboat, being rewarded with vistas of gazebos, a chapel in a windmill, and a waterfall.

J. Paul Getty Museum, beyond Sunset Boulevard, stands on the estate of perhaps the world's richest man. Turn west toward Malibu and you'll find the museum at 17895 W. Pacific Coast Highway.

Getty, an American industrialist, is known for having parlayed a small inheritance into a fortune in excess of a billion dollars. At least several hundred million dollars are represented in his collection of Greek and Roman statuary, Louis XV and XVI furniture, rare tapestries, and valuable paintings by Italian and Dutch masters. The museum building itself, a replica of the Villa Papyri (a large villa at Herculaneum destroyed by the eruption of Vesuvius in 79 A.D.), cost about $17 million to build.

The museum is open from noon to 5 P.M., Tuesday through Friday, and from 9 A.M. to 5 P.M. on Saturday. There is no admission charge.

Hollywood Boulevard

A comparatively short street, Hollywood Boulevard is perhaps the best known of all L.A.'s thoroughfares because it leads directly to the place most people visit first—Hollywood. Pedestrian-looking architecture? Perhaps. But Hollywood Boulevard still manages to retain a little of the sparkle of yesteryear.

Part of the boulevard is best explored on foot, especially the interesting mile and a half from Western Avenue to La Brea. You'll find book-browsing at its best here, along with some stores that would probably exist nowhere else.

Look underfoot. The bronze medallions studding the sidewalk mark the names of film, radio, and television actors.

Barnsdall Park, once the haughty stronghold of Olive Hill at Hollywood Boulevard near Vermont Avenue, ceased to be forbidden ground when the city of Los Angeles inherited it from the late Aline Barnsdall in 1927.

On the summit is the great Hollyhock House, one of Frank Lloyd Wright's early achievements. Pending restoration, it is not open to the public. Here also is L.A.'s handsome Municipal Art Gallery, first major art gallery to be built in the city since 1965.

Match your foot *size with those of the celebrities at Mann's Chinese Theater.*

Hollywood Bowl *provides sylvan setting for picnic during open-air concerts.*

Opened in 1971, it replaces a smaller pavilion also designed by Wright.

This two-story gallery designed by architect Arthur Stephens harmonizes well with the other buildings on the hill: Hollyhock House and the Junior Arts Center. The gallery does not have a permanent collection but presents a series of changing exhibitions. Films and dramatic and musical performances take place in the 300-seat auditorium. The gallery is open from noon to 5 P.M., Tuesday through Sunday. There is no admission charge.

For one week in the summer, an All-City Outdoor Art Festival exhibits sculptures, paintings, and other works of art.

Hollywood and Vine may disappoint you. At first glance it looks like any Main Street of any town. But look north on Vine Street at the Capitol Tower, a circular shaped structure appropriately resembling a stack of neatly piled records. If you make reservations three weeks in advance, you can take a 45-minute tour of the record-making facility, in addition to getting a peek at a recording studio. Write Capitol Tower, 1750 N. Vine Street, Hollywood 90028 for further information.

Also on Vine (just south of Hollywood Boulevard) is the Brown Derby Restaurant, where celebrity gazing competes for attention with the tempting cuisine. The Huntington Hartford Theater, among the best in Los Angeles, is at 1615 N. Vine Street.

The Hollywood Wax Museum, near Highland Avenue, has life-sized figures of movie personalities, presidents, and historical personages. In the Chamber of Horrors, you'll see the coffin used in the movie *The Raven* and a scene from *The House of Wax* with Vincent Price. A recent addition is the Oscar Movie Theatre, showing a film that spans more than 40 years of Academy Award winners and presentations. The accompanying sound track contains the best songs of each era. The theater is open daily from 10 A.M. to midnight (until 2 A.M. on weekends); admission is about $2 for adults and 75 cents for children over 6.

Grauman's Chinese Theatre still survives, despite a recent name change. Sid Grauman was a real showman. First he built the Egyptian Theatre, a replica of a palace in Ancient Thebes, on the south side of the boulevard. Then he outdid himself by creating the Chinese Theatre, a model of a Chinese temple with imported Oriental pillars, across the street (6925 Hollywood Boulevard).

The many hand, foot, hoof, and face prints, along with the signatures of well known stars imprinted in the concrete courtyard of this celebrated movie house (now Mann's Chinese Theatre), trace the history of Hollywood cinema since the theater opened in 1927.

Hollywood Boulevard's *Pickwick Bookshop is giant of the West, stocking over 150,000 titles.*

The Hollywood Bowl, built in a natural amphitheater in the Cahuenga Hills, grew from a simple bandstand in a weedy dell into an open-air concert theater with seating capacity of 20,000. The bowl's natural acoustics are responsible for its success; modern technology is trying for even better amplification. The "Symphonies Under the Stars," its noted summer series, features the Los Angeles Philharmonic Orchestra. The most notable annual event is the pre-dawn pilgrimage to the bowl for the memorable Easter Sunrise Service.

The bowl is on the west side of Highland Avenue, north of the Hollywood Boulevard intersection.

Mulholland Drive, within the city, then Mulholland Highway beyond, winds along the summit backbone of the Santa Monica Mountains, L.A.'s own mountain range. Driving its whole 55-mile length starting from the Hollywood Freeway in Cahuenga Pass is one of the easiest ways to get a view of the wilderness so threatened by urban pressure. The only longitudinal route along the Santa Monicas, this highway is one of the traditional scenic drives in Los Angeles. At the crest of the mountains, for more than half its length, the drive provides alternate vistas of the San Fernando Valley and the Los Angeles plain and then dips into canyons and small valleys. Eastern Mulholland Drive is residential; the older homes seem better suited to the mountains than the newer stilt houses.

At Topanga Canyon, you can follow winding Topanga Canyon Boulevard down to the ocean, emerging just east of Malibu, or continue on through the mountains, ending up at Leo Carrillo State Beach. You can also reach the sea on Malibu Canyon Road. The road past Topanga Canyon Boulevard is slow and the countryside almost wild.

You can get onto Mulholland Drive from the Hollywood Freeway in Cahuenga Pass, or you can avoid some of the tortuous course through residential areas by joining it farther west, at Laurel Canyon, Coldwater Canyon, Benedict Canyon, or Beverly Glen. Or enter Mulholland Drive from the San Diego Freeway.

GRIFFITH PARK

Griffith Park is a superpark, once the largest municipal park inside any city in America. Comparable in area with the cities of Beverly Hills and Santa Monica, on a fine weekend it may attain a population midway between the two (58,000).

Straddling the eastern end of the Santa Monica Mountains, the park was begun over 75 years ago with a gift to the city of some 3,000 acres by Colonel Griffith J. Griffith. The gift included a trust fund used since for the acquisition of more land and for building the grand old Griffith Observatory and Greek Theater.

Although rising to just 1,625 feet at the summit of Mt. Hollywood, the mountains in the park are steep and rugged. Such topography has helped to preserve nearly three-fifths of the land in a nearly natural state. Until the era of the bulldozer, it was simply too vertical for conventional city-park development. Most of the mountain heartland remains a sort of domesticated wilderness.

The perimeter of Griffith Park is very accessible. To the north is the Ventura Freeway, to the east the Golden State Freeway, and to the west the Hollywood Freeway. Both Western and Vermont avenues enter the southern park edge. Western leads to Fern Dell and the Nature Museum, Vermont to the Bird Sanctuary and Greek Theater; both reach the Observatory. Well-marked freeway exits lead to other points of interest.

Hiking, riding, and sightseeing are naturals here. There are 53 miles of hiking and 43 miles of bridle trails, allowing visitors to savor the untamed plant life, tree-shaded canyons, and wealth of birds and small animals. From twisting Mt. Hollywood and Vista del Valle drives, car-borne sightseers can get astonishing views on smog-free days of the San Fernando Valley, San Gabriel Mountains, coastal plain, and Santa Catalina Island beyond.

Griffith Observatory, high on a promontory, commands a vast panorama, spectacular at night. The observatory's large dome contains a planetarium; two smaller domes are for telescopes, and the halls display such things as a Foucault pendulum and a model of the moon's visible side. The observatory is open Tuesday through Friday from 2 to 10 P.M., Saturday from 10 A.M. to 10 P.M., and Sunday from 1 to 10 P.M. You can peer through the telescope

Shiny, live *miniature steam trains operate on the valley side of Griffith Park, attract rail buffs.*

from 7 to 10 P.M. every evening. Admission is free.

Planetarium programs are held at 3 P.M. and 8:30 P.M. daily, with extra shows on Saturday at 11 A.M. and 1:30 and 4:30 P.M. On Sunday, shows are held at 1:30 and 4:30 P.M. Admission is charged, and children under 5 are not admitted.

Greek Theater, an open-air stage set in a natural canyon on the way to the observatory, seats 4,000 people for drama, music, and dance performances. Check local newspapers and city guides to find out what's playing.

There are picnic grounds and tennis courts nearby. The Bird Sanctuary, once an aviary, is now the scene of Sunday afternoon nature walks.

Fern Dell is reached through the next canyon to the west, another access to the upland. Called Western Canyon, its road begins off Los Feliz Boulevard just east of the end of Western Avenue. You'll find Fern Dell to be a natural, spring-fed fern bower with a collection of exotic ferns. Here you can walk a half mile past waterfalls and terraced pools.

A good place to start exploring the park is the Fern Dell Nature Museum. Its exhibits describe plant and animal life in the park and some of the area's geological features. On weekends you can attend free showings of travel and nature movies in the museum. Its hours are from 1 to 5 P.M., Wednesday through Sunday; admission is free.

Griffith Playground means business. Intense recreational activity concentrates in the flatland along the eastern and northern edges of the park. The southeastern tip is one of the liveliest, at least when a soccer game is in progress. Here, along Riverside Drive south of Los Feliz Boulevard is Griffith Playground, which contains a swimming pool, tennis courts, playing field, and other activi-

Vest Pocket Touring

Twenty "Vest Pocket Tours" of Los Angeles and environs now makes it possible to sightsee on your own even without a car. A free brochure, published by the Southern California Visitors Council in cooperation with the Rapid Transit District, describes major attractions of 20 areas in and around Los Angeles, with suggested "tours" ranging from a half-day to one or more days.

In addition to visiting downtown L.A. and the Wilshire-Hollywood area, you can go to the ocean (Santa Monica, Los Angeles Harbor, Port of Long Beach, or the Manhattan-Hermosa-Redondo beaches), out to the San Fernando Valley, to Pasadena, or east as far as San Bernardino. Take half a day to visit Griffith Park, Forest Lawn, or the Arboretum in Arcadia.

One bus travels down to Orange County, making stops at Disneyland, Knott's Berry Farm, the Movieland Wax Museum and Palace of Living Arts, and other destinations.

Want to find out where the stars live? You can take a bus to Beverly Hills, get off, and walk past the homes of many of the great stars. For more star-gazing, there's a bus that takes you to Universal Studios and (with connections) on to the NBC Television Studios.

Even if you're planning to do your exploring by automobile, this handy little guide gives information on spots you might miss. The minibus route through the downtown area is shown on the back.

For your copy, stop by the Visitors' Council office or write to them at 705 W. 7th St., Los Angeles 90017. You can also pick up a brochure at the bus terminal at 6th and Los Angeles streets.

---

ties. Across Riverside Drive are the Cultural Arts Center and the Mulholland Fountain, a memorial to the father of the Los Angeles Aqueduct.

North of Los Feliz Boulevard, Riverside Drive becomes Crystal Springs Road. You pass the miniature train ride, a children's pony ring, and one of three 9-hole golf courses (another is directly across the river). Then you come to the big merry-go-round area. Listen to the band organ of the venerable 1926 Spillman four-abreast machine. Though a bit the worse for wear, it's still one of the best of its era. This is also the site of a new nature center and headquarters building. Call on the rangers for park information and for maps of the road and trail system. Beyond are two big golf courses and a driving range.

Los Angeles Zoo, at the northeast corner of the park, is marked by flying flags. The zoo draws more people than any other park attraction. First of its size to be built from scratch in modern times, it features the Theme Building in its center, 100 acres of attractive grounds, moats, and natural surroundings (instead of bars and cages) for zoo inhabitants. You can walk (it's mostly uphill) or take a tram to see animals that are grouped in areas resembling their native continents. The old Los Angeles Zoo is now a holding and recovery area for animals.

Happy Hollow, Prairie Dog Colony, The Mouse House, Tunnel Town, and the Baby Elephant Compound can be found in the Children's Zoo, where youngsters can see small animals at close range and, in some instances, even pet and feed them.

Open daily except Christmas from 10 A.M. to 5 or 6 P.M., the zoo is free for children 11 and under; there is a small charge for juniors and adults.

Continuing along the northern edge of the park, you pass Pecan Grove picnic area and the grounds of the Los Angeles Live Steamers Club. Here members work on their scale-model engines and track network, offering free rides on Sunday afternoons.

Travel Town, at the northwest corner of the main part of the park, is home for the West's largest collection of rail equipment. You enter through a restored rail depot, the station for a motorized antique streetcar that offers rides on a circuit of the grounds. The big attraction is the rolling stock: engines, streetcars, and train cars that invite climbing upon, and a dining car in which children's birthday parties may be arranged.

Riding stables front on Riverside Drive (in Glendale and Burbank, the park boundary is the Los Angeles boundary) and open into the park. Horse trailers also enter here, and weekend activity is intense. Riders cross the river by bridge and enter the park by tunnel under the Ventura Freeway.

On the Periphery of
Los Angeles

 An impressive dimension is added to Los Angeles by the array of beaches and mountains ringing the Los Angeles Basin.

Southern California beaches are hardly a discovery. If you've ever been caught in a coast highway traffic jam on a summer Sunday afternoon, you know that the shoreline of the Los Angeles city region is perhaps the greatest summer recreational resource in California. What is surprising is the variety of ways to enjoy the coastal area. Ranging in topography from wide, sandy stretches with gentle waves to narrow, rocky strips with explosive surf, the beaches invite every aquatic pleasure: swimming, boating, fishing, surfing, scuba diving, snorkeling. Although the shoreline is mainly urban, on a few stretches you can be amazingly alone.

Three high mountain ranges separate Los Angeles from desert lands to the north and east, forming an imposing backdrop for the teeming city. The San Gabriel, San Bernardino, and San Jacinto (pages 104-105) ranges rise abruptly to peaks over 10,000 feet. At low elevations, the frontal slopes of these mountains are closed because of fire danger from July 1 to the first rainfall (usually November). But in winter, residents head for the hills for snow fun: belly-thumping down the slopes on improvised sleds at such resorts as Lake Gregory, Lake Arrowhead, and Big Bear—easily reached from the valley floors—and near the ski runs.

A fourth mountain range, the Santa Monicas, marches right into the Pacific Ocean west of the city, its rocky tops forming the off-shore Channel Islands. Where mountains and beaches meet at Pt. Mugu, this chapter begins, tracing the metropolitan coastline first east, then south. Then the chapter shifts its focus to the attractions in or near the three mountain ranges surrounding Los Angeles.

Tossing a beach ball *at water's edge is a familiar pastime for many in-shape Southern Californians.*

Along L. A.'s Beaches

Southern California's beaches see action every month of the year. The huge Los Angeles population makes full use of the sea as a coolant when summer heat builds. Water temperature is around 67° from July until fall. Air temperature at Santa Monica will reach an average maximum of about 75°, even as the temperature in inland Pasadena rises ten degrees higher.

Winter weather is cyclic, with clear, warm air and a glassy sea often following a blustery rainstorm. Although few swimmers brave the 55° water for a dip, wet-suited surfers, surf kayakers, windsurfers, and lightweight-catamaran sailors turn out in force.

Here are some highlights of a coastal tour of Los Angeles County from Pt. Mugu in the west to Long Beach Harbor in the south.

FROM PT. MUGU TO SANTA MONICA BAY

The south slope of the Santa Monica Mountains drops abruptly to the sea on the first section of this east-west Los Angeles area beach tour. Its western half is rocky headlands and coves; it runs to good swimming beaches at the eastern end. Pt. Mugu to Malibu has the cleanest ocean along the metropolitan coast, offering clear water, healthy kelp beds, the best shore and offshore fishing and diving, and some very good surfing.

West of Santa Monica

Variety of activity and topography marks the beaches west of Santa Monica Bay. You can camp at two of the beaches, venture up into the hills, sand ski, and try your luck at soaring from bluff to beach. Facilities vary, but lifeguards are on duty during the summer.

Pt. Mugu State Park has about 3 miles of ocean frontage. The Big Sycamore Canyon section, making up the rest of this 6,500 acre all-purpose park, includes rather primitive campsites (closed temporarily after the 1973 fire), picnic grounds, and trails leading to peaks 1,500 feet and higher. There's a small fee for overnight camping and day-use in the canyon area.

What can you do? Hike, picnic, surf, rock fish, swim, beachcomb, or try sand skiing.

Leo Carrillo State Beach straddles the highway, about 12 miles from the nearest community, Malibu. Uncrowded for years, it started doing a land-office business when campsites were installed in 1960. Camping is in the canyon bottom inland from the highway. A few trails from the campgrounds in Arroyo Sequit Flat give access to the chaparral-covered foothills in the 1,200-acre park.

The 1¾-mile beach has beautiful sandy sections for swimmers and outcrops of rock for fishermen and wave watchers. Diverse underwater topography also produces fair to good surfing. Rest rooms, dressing rooms, and a concession stand mitigate the lack of a nearby town. A small fee is charged for parking and overnight camping.

It seems only fitting that this park is named after a movie star-parks commissioner since the park itself "starred" in all kinds of South Seas movies in the early days of Hollywood.

Zuma Beach, just west of Pt. Dume off State Highway 1, is L.A.'s largest county-owned beach. An excellent swimming beach (except for occasional summer riptides), it offers ample parking for about 2,500 cars (small charge) and modern facilities.

Dume, next door, is a long, steep-sided finger of sandstone pointing prominently to the south. Flocks of pelicans and cormorants perch on rocks a few hundred yards offshore; meanwhile, flocks of surfers are hurtling toward broad, sandy beaches or paddling away from them. Swimming is good; so are the tidepools.

Santa Monica Bay: home of surf and stars

Along this crescent-shaped bay, almost all the coast is sandy with wide beaches. About half of it is set aside for public use, and used it assuredly is: its total annual visitor count numbers about 50 million. Day-use parks usually offer excellent swimming, good surfing, sunbathing, and beach play. Hang gliding is good at two spots: Dockweiler and Torrance beaches. (The latter discourages the sport during the crowded summer season.) Although the beaches are fairly similar with sandy stretches below high bluffs, facilities differ. Some charge admission; others do not. Lifeguards are generally on duty during the peak season.

Paradise Cove, a private beach, charges admission. You can fish from the pier (with a license), buy bait

Omnipresent media *emphasis in Southland brings camera crew to Marina del Rey.*

Standing room only *at Marineland as crowd watches dolphin ballet in pool above Pacific Ocean.*

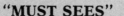

Beach scavenging *never gets boring along Southern California's productive beaches.*

"MUST SEES"

J. PAUL GETTY MUSEUM (Malibu)—ancient Roman villa replica houses priceless statuary, furniture, and paintings

QUEEN MARY (Long Beach)—fabled British ocean liner; tour decks and shops; visit Cousteau's Living Sea museum

PALOS VERDES SCENIC DRIVE—15 miles of varied spectacular marine and mountain views; view Wayfarers' Chapel

MARINELAND (Palos Verdes Peninsula)—world's largest oceanarium; watch whales, seals and dolphins perform

MAGIC MOUNTAIN (Valencia)—new 200 acre family amusement and entertainment center; top summer-night music

BUSCH GARDENS (Van Nuys)—take a boat ride through lush gardens; amusement rides and bird shows; tour brewery

PASADENA—City Hall, Art Museum, Gamble House, Pasadena Historical Museum, Pasadena Center, Rose Bowl

HUNTINGTON LIBRARY (San Marino)—also art gallery ("Blue Boy," "Pinkie") and botanical gardens on former estate

L.A. STATE AND COUNTY ARBORETUM (Arcadia)—ride tram through outstanding plantings and historic buildings

MISSION INN (Riverside)—celebrated landmark hotel (now private apartments); peek into interior courtyards

RAMONA BOWL (Hemet)—California's early history lives in spectacular pageant *Ramona;* late April in natural amphitheater

RIM OF THE WORLD DRIVE (San Bernardino Mtns.)—scenic route to Lake Arrowhead and Big Bear resort areas

and tackle, go out on a sportfishing party boat, launch your own boat, water-ski, or swim. It's open from 6 A.M. to 5 P.M. daily.

Corral-Solstice and Las Tunas beaches, to the east, are typical of most of the beaches in this area: sandy stretches for swimming, roadside parking.

Malibu Lagoon, a 35-acre beach with a ⅔-mile ocean frontage, incorporates Surfrider Beach (known to surfers world-wide). Except for the area reserved solely for surfers, the beach offers good swimming. You'll find rest rooms, concessions, and parking along the highway.

Malibu Pier (private) offers fishing (with a license), sportfishing boats, an excursion boat, bait and tackle shops, and a restaurant open daily.

Malibu has long been known as a "getaway" spot for movie and TV stars. Houses block the sea view along the highway for several miles and perch precariously on cliffs above the road.

Will Rogers State Beach, at the intersection of the coastal highway and Sunset Boulevard, is beneath the Pacific Palisades (so close beneath them that slides have forced several relocations of the highway a few feet south, into some badly needed parking lots). Lifeguards and rest rooms are provided on the beach, and restaurants line the highway nearby. It is the scene of the lifeguards' annual December games.

Santa Monica

At Santa Monica the shore turns southerly for a splendid sweep of 20 miles of almost wholly acces-

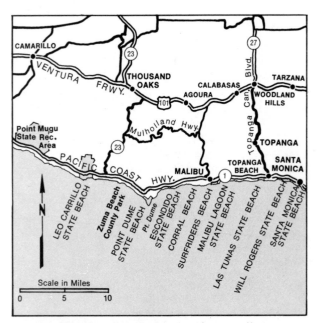

Bountiful beaches *line the Los Angeles coastline from Pt. Mugu to Santa Monica, luring sunlovers.*

sible, broad, sandy beach encompassing eight public beaches, five fishing piers, and two small craft harbors. Then it rounds the Palos Verdes Peninsula for 15 rocky miles as the road rides high above the cliffs before losing itself among the channels of two big harbors—Los Angeles and Long Beach.

The swimming and boating are very good but the fishing only fair because now the first massive pollution—from storm drains and industrial, sewage, and steam plants—begins to pollute water from here on down the coast.

Santa Monica State Beach, adjacent to Ocean Avenue, has been the most popular of the bay beaches from the point of numbers since the 1860s. It has picnic tables, fire rings, and playground equipment and is handy to restaurants.

Some 3.2 miles of broad beach are marked by a series of parking lots between buildings on the highway. Two small surfing areas lie just northwest of the pier.

Santa Monica Pier is at its peak when warm weather, inland smog, barefoot beachgoers, and more fully clad land people mingle. It may not be pretty, and it's mostly commercial, but colorful throngs and a variety of activities turn the pier, the esplanade below, and the clifftop park above into a lively scene. Some things are free: fishing from the pier or watching volleyball players, surfers, and practicing acrobats at what was once called Muscle Beach. You can also take out a fishing party boat. The rest is old-time carnival: a classic merry-go-round, amusement concessions, games of skill, souvenir stands, fish markets, and restaurants.

The pier extends Colorado Street out over the water to a turnaround at the end. If you can find a space, you can park on the pier. To avoid weekend traffic jams, park elsewhere and walk.

Venice—California's answer to Italy

Perhaps one of the most unusual beachfront communities in the West, Venice-by-the-Sea was the dream of Abbot Kinney, a wealthy Easterner, who, in 1892, induced the Santa Fe Railroad to extend its tracks to these 160 acres of sand dunes and salt marsh, where he built his dream city with homes, hotels, interconnecting canals plied by a fleet of gondolas, amusement halls, and a large Chautauqua auditorium. Unfortunately, engineering mistakes caused the canals to deteriorate. Venice began to decline, and oil developments ended the dream. All that remains of a glamorous past are a few bridges over some weed-grown canals.

But, though it is old and run down, Venice has 3 miles of desirable beach and a good municipal fishing pier, both of which are being eyed jealously by affluent developers to the north and south.

The Venice pier, at the foot of Washington Street,

What's he doing? *He's dredging surf for sand crabs to use as bait on pier above.*

Surf and sand *create perfect conditions near Newport Pier for lively sport of skimboarding.*

is thoughtfully designed and organized for round-the-clock fishing. Bays at short intervals expand its perimeter (about 400 yards long), and concrete pilings centered beneath it minimize line snags. At the seaward end is a refreshment stand. Fish cleaning facilities are a respectful distance away.

Marina del Rey

It's easy to believe that Marina del Rey, home port for more than 6,000 boats, is the largest man-made pleasure boat harbor on Pacific Coast.

One of the most dramatic waterfront scenes in the world is the huge armada of boats of all types heading out to sea or parading placidly up and down the main channel.

New shopping centers abound in Marina del Rey; new motels and hotels face beach and waterfront.

Harbor cruises leave Fishermans' Village — a Cape Cod collection of shops, restaurants, and art galleries — every hour. The harbor cruise aboard the "Marina Belle" gives you a close-up look at many celebrities' boats, as well as Chinese junks, catamarans, antique and classic craft, and old, square-rigged Scandinavian schooners.

Large public launching ramps allow boat owners to truck or trailer in their boats. Power and sail-boat rentals are available for Marina cruising and offshore deep-sea fishing.

The famed Marina del Rey waterfront restaurant row is one of the largest concentrations of casually elegant eating places in Greater Los Angeles area.

At the Undersea Gardens, the main waterfront attraction, you descend 1½ fathoms to view marine life through submerged windows. Scuba divers hand feed some pretty exotic fish close to the windows so you can watch. Open daily until 10 P.M., it charges a modest admission fee.

Dockweiler State Beach, next in line, sits beneath the takeoff pattern of Los Angeles International Airport. It's the first beach going south on this stretch that has fire rings (about 1,000) where you can bring your dinner and roast marshmallows until midnight. Swimming is good and surfing is fair. There's room to park for a small charge.

El Porto County Beach, a few miles south of Dockweiler, has more than two miles of sandy beach-front. Parking is somewhat limited.

Manhattan State Beach, with a public fishing pier, is farther south, located between Manhattan and Hermosa beaches to the south. You'll find more youthful beach *aficionados* per square yard than almost anywhere else along the coast.

Hermosa Beach also has a municipal pier at the foot of logically named Pier Avenue, off the Coast Highway a few blocks south of Artesia Avenue. Much like other piers in the region, it has a bait and tackle shop, rest rooms, and a snack bar for the comfort of anglers.

Redondo State Beach adjoins a marina complex (King Harbor) of restaurants, motels, yacht clubs, and boat facilities. Next to it are the shops and restaurants that line two piers out over the water, giving a good view of the 1½-mile beach. Access to the parking structure at the piers' landward end is from Torrance Boulevard.

Torrance County Beach is the last beach before the sand gives way to the rocky bluffs of the Palos Verdes Peninsula.

FROM PALOS VERDES TO LONG BEACH

Following the scenic drive around the Palos Verdes Peninsula is a pleasant alternative to continuing on the coast highway. You pass several interesting tourist attractions, as well as many ocean overlooks. You're on your way to the busy ports of Los Angeles and Long Beach. Attractive seaside shopping, good fishing spots, a marine museum, and the imposing *Queen Mary* are only some of the oceanfront attractions. You'll also find some historical surprises.

The plush Palos Verdes Peninsula

Below Pt. Conception the most prominent projection on the coastal map is the Palos Verdes Peninsula, about 15 miles of rocky shore with a few sandy beaches. Informal access at several points has been made by tidepool probers, rock fishermen, skin divers, and surf scanners. A spectacular scenic drive through this area has been a traditional attraction of the Los Angeles region.

Less frequented is the relatively isolated seacoast 100 feet below the cliffs. Since accessibility to this shore is limited by tides, all of the beach areas are hard to explore in one day. Newspapers publish exact times of tides for each day. Fires and overnight camping are prohibited.

For a view of the shore and cliff base from the sea, take a boat ride from Marineland. From offshore, you'll see manmade landmarks of the peninsula, as well as the great tidal-bore caves of Portuguese and Inspiration points.

The Scenic Drive through the peninsula follows the rugged cliff top for 15 miles. Few roads in the area offer such varied or spectacular marine and mountain views. The route on Palos Verdes Drive W. and S. starts in park-like Palos Verdes Estates and ends in the park at Pt. Fermin in San Pedro.

Winding through beautiful residential areas and flower fields, the drive has several ocean view turnouts. It passes such points of interest as the Pt. Vicente Lighthouse (open Tuesday and Thursday afternoons); Marineland oceanarium; and the Wayfarers' Chapel overlooking Abalone Cove. You can picnic and enjoy the views at Pt. Fermin Park, which looks out toward Catalina Island. The Old Pt. Fermin Lighthouse (built in 1874 out of wood and lumber brought around Cape Horn) is presently undergoing restoration.

From this end of the drive, take Gaffey Street to the Harbor Freeway and Pacific Coast Highway.

Royal Palms State Beach, 2 miles northwest of Pt. Fermin off Paseo del Mar (extension of Western Avenue), offers one of the few places to swim on the south coast of the peninsula. Space and facilities are limited.

The Wayfarers' Chapel *is a landmark atop the Palos Verdes Peninsula.*

Its shoreline *artistically carved by the sea, the Palos Verdes peninsula is hilly.*

Wayfarers' Chapel

This small chapel built of glass walls and redwood beams sits on a hill at Portuguese Bend, overlooking the ocean and Palos Verdes Drive S. Its towering white-rock campanile holds a gold cross. Many plants mentioned in the Bible grow on the grounds. Sunday morning service is at 11 A.M., but the church is open daily to visitors. Swedenborg Reference Library and Museum is located just east of the chapel.

Architect Lloyd Wright (son of Frank Lloyd Wright) designed the unique chapel for the Church of the New Jerusalem as a memorial to Emmanuel Swedenborg, but it is intended as a place of worship and meditation for people of all faiths.

Marineland of the Pacific

Marineland, a water zoo at the southwest tip of the peninsula, is actually a four-ring sea circus. Though the aquariums and sea collections are impressive, entertainment is the first purpose of this well-known Palos Verdes show place. Here's a rare opportunity to see a "killer whale" leaping 18 feet out of the water to grab a fish from the teeth of its trainer, a dolphin jumping through a fire-ringed hoop, or a sea lion crooning a tune.

One ticket admits you to the Oceanarium and all the shows and exhibits. Parking is free. Marineland opens at 10 A.M. every day and closes at sunset. Shows run in repeating cycles so you can enter at almost any hour and not miss a performance. Marineland is on Palos Verdes Drive S., midway between San Pedro and Redondo Beach. If you are not already on the scenic drive, the best approaches are Western Avenue and Hawthorne Boulevard south from Pacific Coast Highway.

The Sky Tower, a circular elevator ride up 344 feet above the sea, offers a panoramic view along the coastline and out to sea for some 20 miles. Admission is included in your Marineland ticket.

Boat rides give a different view of this fascinating coastline. Offered hourly every day during the summer and weekends year-round, the 50-minute boat cruises of the peninsula start at noon. Cost is moderate. To reach the boat, take a small tram just outside the Marineland gate down to the pier.

Los Angeles Harbor: an aquatic freeway

The Port of Los Angeles and the Port of Long Beach share the world's largest manmade harbor. Its maze of channels, inlets, and islands covers 50 miles of developed waterfront, shielded by a 9-mile breakwater. Newest of major western ports (started in 1889), Los Angeles is a leader in tonnage and modern handling techniques. It is the center of

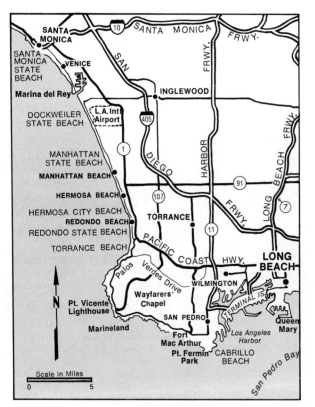

From Santa Monica *to Long Beach stretch some of L.A.'s heaviest-use beaches.*

the country's seafood canning industry. The Port of Los Angeles includes the Terminal Island, San Pedro, and Wilmington districts.

Soaring 185 feet above the main channel in the harbor is the Vincent Thomas Bridge, replacement for a former auto ferry. This handsome suspension bridge (25 cent toll), painted green, connects San Pedro with Terminal Island, where most of the harbor's large shipping berths and warehouses are.

Sport fishermen who like to get out on the open seas for big fish can find plenty of party boats at the 22nd Street landing and at San Pedro Sportfishing next to Ports of Call. This harbor is also the jumping-off point for cruise ships to Mexico, Hawaii, and the world. But primarily it is industrial. Except for Cabrillo Beach, there is little shoreside activity. Visitors can watch such everyday shoreline action as net mending and unloading catches.

Fort MacArthur, in San Pedro near the harbor entrance, once helped protect the harbor. Now it is headquarters for the 47th Artillery Brigade and an important air defense center.

Cabrillo Beach, just south of the fort, is usually crowded with people, cars, and boat trailers. You'll find picnic tables and barbecue pits. In addition to a still-water beach inside the breakwater, there's a surf beach on the ocean popular with fishermen.

Two Princesses and a Queen

Where do great passenger ships go when they retire? If you answered, "The coast of Southern California," you'd be right. For three vessels have left the high seas to become landlocked tourist attractions here:

S. S. Princess Louise, Terminal Island. Built in 1921 as Canada's premier luxury liner, the Princess Louise is now a spacious floating restaurant with seven elegant rooms for dining and dancing. Replicas of the Crown Jewels of England, the Captain's Quarters, and the Nautical Museum are added attractions. Permanently berthed off Terminal Island in Los Angeles Harbor, she is open daily for dining.

S. S. Princess Louise, Redondo Beach. Sister ship to the famed Port of Los Angeles Princess Louise, this new floating restaurant recently opened in the Redondo Beach Marina. The elegant luxury liner, overlooking its own peaceful lagoon, is open daily for lunch and dinner from 11 A.M. It's located off North Harbor Drive in Redondo Beach.

R. M. S. Queen Mary. Dwarfing her "sisters," the world's most famous ship is now open for tours of her five decks. Visit the Queen Mary Museum, Jacques-Yves Cousteau's extensive Living Sea exhibition, and the upper levels of the luxury vessel. The Queen Mary, permanently moored in Long Beach, gives visitors the unique opportunity to view areas never seen by passengers on the famous Cunard luxury liner. You can visit the suite once occupied by Winston Churchill or inspect the Daimlier limousine that was used by Queen Mary in the 1930s. A portion of the ship is now a floating hotel. Open from 9 A.M., there is a 50 cent "boarding charge" before 5 P.M. for those visiting only the restaurants and shops. There are admission charges if you wish to take the tours. The Queen Mary is at Pier J (the end of the Long Beach Freeway) in Long Beach.

Adding new glamor *to Long Beach waterfront is the black, white, and red Queen Mary, now a hotel, restaurant, tour site, and home of Jacques Cousteau's Living Sea exhibit.*

On the harbor side is a public boat launching ramp and a fishing pier paralleling the breakwater. The Cabrillo Beach Marine Museum, 3720 Stephen White Drive, tells about Los Angeles Harbor and maritime lore in general, in addition to displaying sea shells, ship models, marine specimens, and navigation equipment. Offering free admission, the museum is open daily from 10 A.M. to 6 P.M.

Two extensive shopping complexes (Ports of Call and Whaler's Wharf) face the main channel of the harbor at Berths 76 and 77 on Harbor Boulevard. Restaurants, import shops, and craftsmen combine with harbor tour boats and nautical memorabilia of every size, including the ancient San Francisco Bay ferry *Sierra Nevada.*

Banning Park is located on the coast highway two blocks east of Avalon Boulevard. General Phineas Banning, founder of Wilmington and a fabled host, built a 30-room colonial showcase in 1858 and landscaped it with beautiful gardens a few years later.

Now the mansion is a museum, exhibiting furnishings from the last century. The home and grounds are open to the public from April to mid-October, 1 to 4 P.M., for a very small fee.

Not far away, at 1053 Cary Avenue, is the Drum Barracks, the only remaining building of a Civil War military post that eventually will be restored.

Long Beach

Long Beach is important as a naval base, a major port, a manufacturing center, and a resort and recreation area. Next to Los Angeles itself, it is the largest city in the area, with a population of more than 370,000. Long Beach is linked with Los Angeles, 21 miles to the north, by the Long Beach Freeway. The Pacific Coast Highway and San Diego Freeway cut east and west through the city.

One of the main attractions is a 7-mile arc of white sand beach. Because it is inside the harbor breakwater, there's almost no surf, making it attractive to swimmers and sunbathers. Along the beach are dressing rooms, showers, and rest rooms. Lifeguards are stationed at frequent intervals. The Belmont Fishing Pier protrudes from the approximate center of this beach, between Redondo and Park avenues. Adjoining it, on shore, is the Belmont Plaza Olympic Pool.

West of the beach are launching ramps for a popular water ski area. At the east end is a sizable yacht basin. Off toward the west end, a mile-long area, formerly known as Nu-Pike and now called Queen's Park, rambles along Ocean Boulevard. The old carnival area still has a roller coaster.

Alamitos Bay and the Long Beach Marine Stadium (in the southeast corner of town) are the last of the beach areas in this section. Here are three marinas with berthing capacity for 2,000 boats, restaurants, motels, yacht clubs, and the Seaport Village shopping complex. There's a public launching ramp (north of the Second Street bridge across Marine Stadium, on the east side), city-operated sailing classes, a swimming beach on the bay, and water skiing. Marine Stadium is reserved for power boats and shell racing. At adjacent Colorado Lagoon, you can swim and picnic (fire rings are available), and parking is free. Just south are the San Gabriel River Channel jetties, favorite places for fishing and watching the boats going in and out of the bay.

The Queen Mary still reigns in Long Beach. Just why a retired Cunard Liner should be parked at Long Beach may still puzzle some people, but no one can question that the *Queen Mary* is a popular attraction. Purchased by the City of Long Beach, she arrived here in 1967 after a 14,500-mile journey around Cape Horn. The venerable lady is now open for tours, dining, or you can sleep on board in staterooms run as a hotel.

Long Beach's *Belmont Pier invites strollers to explore its wings jutting out into the Pacific.*

For further information, see "Two Princesses and a Queen," page 40.

Art and history in Long Beach present many contrasts. The new combines with the old, the commercial with the artistic. The following are a few examples of today's art and yesterday's past in this coastal city:

● **California State University at Long Beach** is a place to view some provocative works of sculpture —results of an international sculpture symposium held here a few years ago. Nine sculptors of seven nations executed the massive outdoor art. Main entrance to the college is on Seventh Street just east of Bellflower Boulevard. Visitors may park in an area near the intersection of E. Campus Boulevard and Seventh.

● **Long Beach Museum of Art,** a small, attractive building at 2300 E. Ocean Boulevard, has a permanent collection of modern art (emphasizing Southern California artists) and a sculpture garden. Open Tuesday through Friday from 10 A.M. to 5 P.M. and from 1 to 5 P.M. on weekends, the museum is closed Monday. Admission is free.

● **Rancho Los Cerritos,** built in 1837 in typical Spanish architectural style, is one of the finest of the restored adobes in the Los Angeles area. The building style of that time—thick walled, shaded by wide verandas, formed around a central patio— was so suited to the Mediterranean climate of Los Angeles that it is still being copied in home design today. Once surrounded by acres of rolling hills and lush grazing land, the adobe is now adjacent to the grounds of a country club at 4600 Virginia Road.

One of the most delightful things about the large place is the original garden, with trees over a century old and vividly colored flowers in spring and summer. Los Cerritos is open Wednesday through Sunday from 1 to 5 P.M. with no admission charge.

• **Rancho Los Alamitos** has become a city museum-park, where you can drive to the top of its knoll and step back a century. Though the trees have grown thick and the rancher and cowhands have gone, time seems to have stopped within the seclusion of the rambling red and white ranch house. The Bixby family (donors of the property) left the house equipped with family possessions that span many generations.

Headquarters for the Bixby ranch, which once covered parts of Long Beach, Seal Beach, and Garden Grove, this was a working cattle operation until 1953. Today, ranch house, barn, stables, and sizable gardens occupy the last 8 acres. The original adobe, built around 1806, was once owned by Jose Figueroa, then governor of California; the Bixbys owned the ranch from 1878 to 1968.

You can take a free, hour-long, guided tour of the house between 1 and 5 P.M. Wednesday through Friday and from 10 A.M. to 5 P.M. Saturday and Sunday. The gardens and barn are also open.

To get there, take Palo Verdes Avenue south from the San Diego Freeway. At the intersection of Anaheim Road is a "private road" sign, but you may continue one block to Bixby Hill Road and turn left to the entrance.

Catalina Island: a nearby getaway

Once a hideout for buccaneers and smugglers (though only 21 miles from shore) and the site of an unusual aquatic gold rush, Santa Catalina Island has been a popular visitor destination ever since 1887, when the resort town of Avalon was opened and steam service started from the mainland. Except for Avalon, the 21-mile-long island consists of mountainous wilderness and calm coves.

Crossing the sea to Catalina, California's only offshore island resort, offers travel experiences available nowhere else on the coast: a nostalgic old steamer, stubby amphibians, sleek turbojet planes, and modern excursion boats.

Most depart for Avalon from the San Pedro district of the Port of Los Angeles—on the main channel right under the Vincent Thomas Bridge. Go south on the Harbor Freeway, taking the Harbor Boulevard exit. The terminal has parking.

Long Beach-Catalina Cruises make two trips year-round (three on Friday) with additional summer departures. The terminal is the Magnolia-Navy Landing, 330 Golden Shore Boulevard, Long Beach. Go south on Long Beach Freeway almost to the end; take the first Downtown exit, then the Golden Shore exit.

Summer cruises from Newport Harbor to Catalina start in June. Daily trips leave from Davey's Locker at the old Balboa Pavilion on the peninsula. Flying to Catalina takes only 20 minutes; planes leave from both Catalina Terminal (at San Pedro) and Long Beach.

The sea voyage is still best experienced on the stately Big White Steamer, the 50-year-old *S. S. Catalina*. Her two-hour summer excursions offer open-air and indoor benches, music, snack stands, and plenty of time to observe the horizon. Once you land, though, you'll only have about three hours to explore (if you take other lines, you'll have somewhat more time ashore). Reservations are needed for any crossing during peak season.

At the present time, boat trip prices are between $8.50 and $9.50 round-trip for adults. The seaplane is around $10 one way. Airline tickets are about $17.50 round-trip; children under 12 are half-price.

Avalon, though still chiefly geared to the pedestrian, is acquiring some motor traffic; tour vehicles line up to greet debarking steamer passengers. Shops and restaurants along Crescent Avenue offer good window shopping. An open-air trailer train running along the avenue offers an inviting ride for the foot-weary.

Still the landmark to visitors arriving in Avalon Harbor is the fortress-like Casino, really a movie theater topped by a vast and unobstructed ballroom. On the first floor is the Catalina Museum.

Exploring the island can be a short or long-term experience. The 4-hour visit allowed day steamer passengers lets you stroll the bustling waterfront and pier and have lunch. You can also take motor tours that give you a glimpse of Catalina's interior and boat trips to the seal colony and undersea gardens. Those staying for a long day or overnight

Period atmosphere *of the Casino overlooking Avalon's harbor persists in updated Catalina.*

Bicycling on Beachside Paths

Two new bikeways along Southern California beaches lead cyclists past colorful piers, lively crowds, and beach vistas unseen by automobile travelers. Running next to the sand's edge, one of the paths leads you along Santa Monica Bay; the other stretches along the Newport Beach Peninsula.

The South Bay trail, along Santa Monica Bay, goes from Playa del Rey to Hermosa Beach and continues from King Harbor to the Palos Verdes bluffs. The total distance is 18 miles, but most cyclists take shorter jaunts. Favorite short stretches are the Santa Monica, Venice, Manhattan Beach, and Hermosa Beach areas.

A broad concrete bikeway, the trail is wide enough for two cyclists in each lane, but beware of oncoming cyclists since there is no center divider to separate lanes. Wandering off the path heads a cyclist for a soft landing in the sand. Except for two traffic bottlenecks (Lincoln and Culver boulevards), riding is automobile-free.

While pedaling along the route, you might want to stop at the Fisherman's Village complex of shops and restaurants at Marina del Rey. Watching the multitude of sailboats and pleasure craft coming and going from the harbor is a favorite view while biking along the waterfront.

When you are near Torrance Beach, you may be treated to the thrill of watching hang glider pilots launching themselves off the low bluffs nearby.

Newport Beach Peninsula sports a 2.2-mile stretch for bikers along the beach's edge. Beginning just off the northwest end of Balboa Boulevard on 36th Street, the pathway ends at E Street, five blocks southeast of the Balboa Pier. Bikers along the route share the sidewalk with pedestrians.

On the way to the beach you can watch fishermen bringing in the day's catch around midmorning as you pass by Newport Pier and the Dory Fish Market. Stop for a picnic on the grass at the foot of Balboa Pier or relax along the sandy stretches of beach.

By riding five blocks farther on, you can hop the ferry to Balboa Island's shops and restaurants. The channel crossing fare is 15 cents each way.

Arriving back on the peninsula, continue along the bikeway to E Street. Here the pathway ends, but by jogging inland to Ocean Boulevard, you can then bike the short distance to watch the "Wedge." Wave action caused by the angle of the harbor entrance jetty to the beach created the Wedge. The waves sometimes reach gigantic proportions and are a magnet for expert bodysurfers. Spectators often gather to watch.

Venice bikeway *is bordered by greenbelt of lawns and palms. Weekday traffic is light.*

(have advance reservations) will have time to explore the island's coastline or interior.

Catalina is a great place for horseback riding. Transportation to stables is available from Island Plaza. Biking, fishing, and diving are also popular sports; rental equipment is available at modest prices. Nature lovers will enjoy seeing the buffalo and a thoroughbred Arabian horse ranch in the interior, as well as a botanical garden.

In the summer a 1-hour night boat cruise will take you to observe hundreds of the biggest and highest flying of the world's flying fish. Aroused by the boat's searchlight, they sometimes fly right over the boat; occasionally one will land on board.

Around L. A.'s Mountains

Our tour of the mountains encircling Los Angeles and the valley towns at their base covers the area from the San Fernando Valley in the west to the Upper Santa Ana River Valley in the east. We begin with the westernmost Santa Monica Mountain range, move on to survey the San Gabriel Mountains and their environs, and end by exploring the recreationally rich San Bernardino Mountains.

Along the way you'll find many diverse parks, gardens, resort areas, and landmarks, as well as some of Southern California's most famous smaller cities. In or near these mountain chains are such familiar names as Griffith Park, Burbank, Pasadena, San Marino, Mt. Wilson, Pomona, and Lake Arrowhead.

In these mountains, sportsmen can hike and ride over hundreds of miles of trails, try their luck in the stocked streams of national forests, and hunt for various wildlife. Motorists and sightseers can take scenic walks, picnic, explore a wilderness area, or drive through picturesque thoroughfares. Angeles National Forest, a giant preserve in the San Gabriel Mountains, includes nearly a fourth of the area in Los Angeles County.

SANTA MONICA MOUNTAINS

Los Angeles has a mountain range in its midst. Even those who have never heard of the Santa Monicas by name probably know Griffith Park, Mulholland Drive, and Sunset Boulevard, all within or bordering this island of emptiness that reaches into the heart of L.A.

The Santa Monicas are unusual among American mountains in that they run east and west: 47 miles from the Los Angeles River to the Oxnard plain. Some of the best beaches in the northern section of the Los Angeles coast lie at their foot.

In a drive through the Santa Monicas, you can see Griffith Park; three great canyons (Sullivan, Rustic, and Topanga); the Santa Monica state park project; the Claretian Seminary (former palatial estate of King Gillette of razor blade fame); Tapia County Park beside Malibu Creek; spectacular rock and gorge formations at the old Century movie ranch, now a state park (due to open in 1975); Lake Sherwood (one of six impoundments of Malibu Creek and tributaries open to the public for a fee); and Malibu Canyon and Pt. Mugu on the coast.

Public access to the scenic richness of the Santa Monicas will increase markedly in coming years as the extensive Santa Monica Mountain park projects progress. More than 7,000 acres are scheduled for development. Now opened are Trippet and Will Rogers State Historical parks, with access from Sunset Boulevard; planned for the future are Los Liones and Topanga. Opening in January, 1975, will be the Century ranch park project—2,600 acres of hiking room in the scenic canyon beside Triunfo Creek; access is from Las Virgenes Road.

Two parks mainly for hikers and equestrians are slated for improvements. They are 13,000-acre Pt. Mugu State Park (access from the coast highway), with beach camping and hiking trails in mountains, canyons, and meadows; and 400-acre Charmlee County Park (access from Encinal Canyon Road), offering surprise upland meadows, oak groves, and a view of Malibu beaches. (Parks may close often during the summer fire danger season.)

Griffith Park now has the most extensive system of hiking and bridle trails. Inquire at the park ranger office on Griffith Park Drive. Will Rogers State Historical Park also has trails for horses and hikers that ascend to good viewpoints. Cyclists can enjoy happy trips on lightly traveled roads off Mulholland Highway.

San Fernando Valley

The San Fernando Valley section of Los Angeles (220 square miles bounded by the Santa Monica, Santa Susana, Verdugo, and San Gabriel mountains) only 60 years ago comprised open wheat fields, farms, and a few small towns. Since the area was annexed by the city of Los Angeles, it has grown to a population of a million. Despite the valley's tremendous growth, there are charming remnants of its past and some appealing oases of the present. From downtown Los Angeles you can reach the valley easily on the Hollywood Freeway. From the north you enter on the Golden State Freeway (Interstate 5) or from the west on the Ventura Freeway (U.S. 101).

Famous landmarks to explore

Much of the history of Southern California has been preserved in and near the valley. You'll find the original San Fernando Valley mission, some famous stage stops, and, to the north, the site of

The horsey set *flocks to rural Calabasas in the Santa Monica mountain range.*

Unspoiled, *unexpected mountain meadow vistas open up in Charmlee County Park.*

Bear Creek, *in San Gabriel Wilderness, is mostly a tree-lined, friendly passage.*

Southern California's gold discovery.

To the east in the hills separating the San Fernando and San Gabriel valleys are one of the first museums devoted to history of the native Indians and the home of its founder, now a state park. Nearby is the beginning of the preservation of the Victorian era, Heritage Square.

To simplify the location of these historical landmarks, we have organized the section from west to east. It starts where you would arrive in the valley on the Ventura Freeway, from the west, and on the Golden State Freeway, from the north; continues through the middle of the valley; and ends in the Arroyo Seco foothills.

Calabasas, a century ago, was a stage stop, two days out from Los Angeles on the road to Monterey. Fifty years ago it was the last stop in the San Fernando Valley for motorists heading west on U.S. 101. Today it is bypassed by the Ventura Freeway, and its visitors are those who deliberately seek it out. And they do, for this tiny hamlet has a

kind of unfabricated charm rare in Los Angeles: rickety old stores and houses containing a diversity of shops where you can see craftsmen at work, a restaurant (chief meeting place for town people), a tavern (the former general store, moved here in 1908 and newly outfitted with pioneer furnishings), and a publishing office for the country weekly.

The gem of Calabasas is the Leonis Adobe. Tucked away among tall trees, this ranch house is a monument to Miguel Leonis, a contentious Basque land baron who played a colorful part in the region's history. Restored and furnished, it is open from 1 to 4 P.M. on Wednesday and weekends. A small donation provides maintenance.

Calabasas bustles during the annual Pumpkin Festival in October. Take Mulholland Drive-Valley Circle Boulevard exit from the Ventura Freeway.

Placerita County Park and Nature Center all started six years before the Sutter's Mill gold strike in 1848 when a weary shepherd named Don Francisco Lopez stumbled into gold when he stopped

Guided boats *take the visitor through the convincingly tropical lagoons lacing Busch Gardens.*

for a nap under an oak tree near what is now Newhall. Lopez, so the story goes, dreamed of gold as he slept. On awakening, he was hungry and grabbed a handful of wild onions nearby. Gold nuggets clung to the roots, the first glimpse of what was eventually discovered as an $80,000 deposit.

The gold is all gone, but the tree—now called the Oak of the Golden Dream—is still there in this small park about 5 miles east of Newhall, off U.S. 14. It is a pleasant place to picnic.

Los Encinos State Historical Park (16756 Moorpark Street, Encino) is the starting point of the valley's recorded history over 200 years ago. The Portola party stopped here by an Indian settlement around a spring that is still flowing. Here, all the bustle you left on the boulevards seems far away. Embraced by antique olive trees and tall grevillias are the Osa adobe of 1849 and turn-of-the-century sheep ranch buildings. Some of the rooms in the Osa adobe are furnished; recorded voices describe their contents. Los Encinos is open Wednesday through Sunday from 10 A.M. to 5 P.M. Expect a small admission charge.

Mission San Fernando is the focal point of the valley's oldest settlement. Founded in 1797 by Father Lasuen, the 17th mission was known for its hospitality (it was a Butterfield Stage stop) and its fine cattle. The mission subsequently served as headquarters for Governor Pico and later for Colonel Fremont during the Mexican-American War. Allow at least an hour for the well-marked walk through extensive mission buildings and grounds. Located on San Fernando Mission Boulevard between the San Diego and Golden State freeways,

the mission is open daily from 9:30 A.M. to 5 P.M. A 50 cent donation is requested.

Across the street in Brand Park is the Memory Garden, with a statue of Father Serra. Then go south on Columbus Avenue two blocks to the YMCA field for a look at the Andres Pico Adobe. Its exterior shows how a typical adobe house grew. Its oldest portion built about 1834 by ex-mission Indians, it acquired lean-to rooms and a second story during its long career.

Southwest Museum (off the Pasadena Freeway) at 234 Museum Drive is somewhat east of the valley in the hills cut by the Arroyo Seco. This museum has one of the country's outstanding attractions of colorful Western Indian artifacts. Of particular interest are the Indian portraits and the large collection of basketry.

Though there is a hillside parking lot above the building, it is more interesting to park below the museum and enter through the tunnel that is lined with interesting dioramas of American Indian life. An elevator whisks you up through the hill to the museum building and exhibits. Open daily except Monday from 1 to 5 P.M., the museum is closed from August 16 to September 16. Admission is free.

Lummis Home, or El Alisal, is the name for the two-story "castle" of Charles Fletcher Lummis, founder of the Southwest Museum. Never completed, it is the work of his own hands, with help from his sons and an Indian boy or two when he had funds to pay. Its rocks were hand-hauled from the Arroyo Seco river bed. It sits on 3 acres of land near the Avenue 43 exit of the Pasadena Freeway.

A native of Massachusetts, Lummis was always a follower of his own beliefs (he created the slogan "See America First") and walked over 3,000 miles to get to Los Angeles where he became the first City Editor of the Los Angeles Times. Two plaques on the walls of El Alisal list his achievements; one seals the crypt containing his ashes. Now a state park, it is open every afternoon except Saturday.

Heritage Square (across Pasadena Freeway at Avenue 43) is the beginning of the city's Victorian home preservation and restoration. Two Victorian houses now stand on the square: the Hale House and the Valley Knudsen Garden-Residence; in the future, others will be added. The houses are open to the public for special events.

Parks and gardens to visit

Varied is the word for the parks and gardens in the San Fernando Valley and surrounding area. Two of them are built around industries; one is a family amusement park, another the home of a former film star; one, perhaps the strangest, is a cemetery.

Once again, we have listed the attractions in this section from northwest to southeast, starting just north and west of the San Fernando Valley limits and ending in the foothills to the east of the valley.

William S. Hart Park, northwest of the valley, at the junction of Newhall Avenue and San Fernando Road in Newhall, was the ranch of William S. Hart, Western star of silent screen days. He left Horseshoe Ranch (a 253-acre estate) to the people of Los Angeles County to be preserved as a park.

The original ranch house at the bottom of the hill contains mementos of the star's motion picture career and is flanked by a corral filled with gentle livestock for the delight of children. Shaded picnic areas are nearby. Hart's home atop the hill, a Spanish-Mexican style mansion called *"La Loma de Los Vientos"* (Hill of the Winds), houses historical weapons, American Indian artifacts, Western art items (including paintings by Charles Russell and Frederic Remington) and other relics of Western Americana. A herd of bison roams the hills.

The ranch is open from 10 A.M. to 6 P.M. daily except on major holidays; the museums are open from 10 A.M. to 5 P.M. daily except Saturday. There are no admission charges. A free shuttle service brings visitors from the park entrance.

Magic Mountain, located just off the Golden State Freeway near Valencia, features "white-knuckler" thrill rides, gentle rides, top-name entertainment, and other attractions. You can take a bouncing, splashing dash through a log-flume water course that climaxes with a 90-foot plunge into Whitewater Lake. Try riding a runaway mine car that roller coasters around and through narrow passageways or a water-jet boat called "El Bumpo." A petting zoo brings young ones into contact with an animal farm, complete with a quaint Pennsylvania Dutch barn. All this is part of a 200-acre family amusement park, the Southland's newest. One-price fee ($6.50 for adults; $5.50 for children 3 to 11) includes unlimited use of rides, attractions, and entertainment (food, games, and shopping not included). Open daily from 10 A.M. to midnight (closes 10 P.M. Sunday) during the summer, the park is open weekends only during fall and spring.

Chatsworth Park, a section of oak country set aside for recreation, occupies a corner of the valley that still has some rural flavor. This area of green lawn among the oaks is at the base of the Simi Hills, located west on Chatsworth Avenue off State 118 in the town of Chatsworth. Children will enjoy climbing on covered wagons, a stockade, tepees, and log horses; rock scramblers can climb the hills.

Busch Gardens has risen out of the flat land of central San Fernando Valley to become one of the show places of Los Angeles, a *tour de force* of tropical and mountain landscape linked by waterways. Your visit may start with a 10-minute monorail tour of the Anheuser-Busch brewery. Then you'll move along to see the gardens on foot, by boat, and on another monorail which passes through an enormous aviary. The boat glides gently through gorges forested with pines, refreshed by cataracts and enlivened by rare and exotic birds. Refreshment pavilions that seemingly float on the water offer drinks but no food; no picnicking is allowed in the park. A bird show, magic show, and other entertainment take place in a roofed amphitheater several times daily.

In 1972, a 5-acre addition increased the park to more than 22 acres. The new section includes an exciting barrel flume ride; a huge, walk-through flight cage; a magic show; a special show place for otters; penguin and sea lion programs; and an individual boat ride popular with young skippers. The gardens are open daily except Christmas and New Year's. Summer hours are 9 A.M. to 6 P.M.; winter hours are 10 A.M. to 5 P.M. One moderate admission price covers all rides, attractions, and shows; parking costs 50 cents. The location is 16000 Roscoe Boulevard, immediately west of the San Diego Freeway in Van Nuys. You'll find the gardens crowded on weekends and during summer.

Forest Lawn in Glendale, east of Griffith Park, is the first of the extraordinary Forest Lawn Memorial Parks (open to visitors from 8:30 A.M. to 5:30 P.M. daily). These superbly landscaped 206 acres form what is probably the best known, most visited, and most controversial cemetery in the world. Here there are no tombstones but instead an unusual collection of statuary, memorials, shrines, and replicas of famous churches. The collection includes reproductions of Michelangelo's sculpture and the famous "Last Supper" stained glass windows. The entrance to Forest Lawn is on Glendale Avenue, northeast of the terminus of Glendale Boulevard at San Fernando Road.

Lawry's California Center, at 568 San Fernando Road, is a garden oasis by a freight yard. Expanded from offices and a seasoning preparation plant (which you can tour), Lawry's handsome shopping complex includes antiques, cookware, pottery, and plants. You can eat indoors or out—all in a setting of trees, flowers, fountains, and lawn. Lawry's is open weekdays only. Shop hours are from 9 A.M. to 5 P.M.; lunch is served from 11:30 A.M. to 2:30 P.M. Half-hour plant tours are conducted at 11:30 A.M. and 1:30 and 2:30 P.M.

Burbank—where entertainment begins

Satirized for years as "beautiful downtown Burbank" on a television show, this city is really the center of the movie and television industry. Film studios are based here and stars live nearby in the Toluca Lake area. The Hollywood-Burbank Airport is one of the busiest in Southern California, and even the formerly drab downtown section has become a delightful shopping mall.

Burbank is one place where you can tour the studios (see "L.A.'s Entertainment World," page 25). Both Universal City, largest studio in the world, and NBC Television Studios offer guided tours. The Disney studio, behind NBC, is not open to visitors.

SAN GABRIEL VALLEY

The San Gabriel Valley is certainly the most lush, in terms of greenery, and the most plush, in terms of money and architecture, of the three Los Angeles area valleys. It contains the oldest valley settlements in the L.A. region, some of the area's finest museums and estates, and some of the oldest architecture and gardens.

The stately city of Pasadena

Pasadena, the *grande dame* of the area, is perhaps best known for the colorful Tournament of Roses Parade and Rose Bowl game held on New Year's Day. But primarily it is an attractive residential community with stately trees and old buildings at the base of the San Gabriel Mountains. Driving through the quiet streets, you'll find many places of architectural interest, including the Gamble House at 4 Westmoreland Place, one of the best known works of architects Charles and Henry Greene. The house is open to the public free of charge on Tuesday and Thursday from 1 to 4 P.M.

The Pasadena Historical Society Museum, at 470 W. Walnut St. (across Orange Grove from the Gamble House), is another example of the gracious mansions that once lined the streets. Guided tours are from 1 to 4 P.M. Tuesdays and Thursdays; admission is free.

The Pasadena Library, grand-manner City Hall, and Civic Auditorium are all set in a line along a short stretch of Garfield Avenue. All were built between 1925 and 1932 to become the heart of a formal civic center, a plan which never materialized. Around the remodeled Civic Auditorium, the Pasadena Center, with its shops, meeting rooms and landscaped gardens, provides a focal point for access to the civic center. The park across from City Hall is a good place to relax or lunch.

For those who like to explore on bicycle, an officially designated 10-mile bikeway in Pasadena runs north along the Arroyo Seco from Columbia Street, past the Rose Bowl, and up across Devil's Gate Dam to Oak Grove Park.

The Pasadena Art Museum (at Orange Grove and Colorado boulevards), one of the most important new museums of modern art in California, symbolizes the new architectural look coming to Pasadena. The cornerless, tile-clad museum baffles design critics, but most admit that its positioning and classic setting are superb. A permanent collection of 20th century art and a highly selective Oriental collection of art are on view, as well as changing exhibitions of painting, sculpture, graphics, and photography. Purchased by Norton Simon in mid-1974, the Art Museum will be closed for repairs until the spring of 1975.

The Pacificulture Asia Museum at 46 N. Los Robles Ave.(one-half block north of Colorado Boulevard) is housed in a tiny palace that has been a landmark for some 50 years. Now it is a lively showcase for Pacific and Asian art and architecture. Some of the ethnic art is for sale. It's open Wednesdays and Friday through Sunday from 1 to 5 P.M.; admission is free.

Brookside Park and the Rose Bowl in its center cover more than 500 acres in Arroyo Seco Canyon. You'll find picnic areas, playgrounds, hiking trails, a swimming pool, and a municipal golf course, in addition to the famous Rose Bowl. Seating 100,000, the stadium is the home of a climactic intersectional football game played every New Year's Day. During the rest of the year, it is the site for other football games, political rallies, and civic events. A Football Hall of Fame inside the stadium is open daily from 8 A.M. to 4 P.M. Main entrance to the stadium is on Rosemont Avenue. On the second Sunday of every month, the Bowl is the scene of a mammoth swap meet (flea market).

Descanso Gardens, at 1418 Descanso Boulevard in La Canada, was formerly a private estate and is now 165 acres of magnificent beauty any time of the year. From late December through March, the vast collection of camellias is in bloom. A Japanese tea pavilion is nestled here in a camellia forest. Camellia shows are held here annually, as are shows of other special interest flower societies.

The beautifully landscaped historical rose garden features species planted in chronological order to demonstrate the development of modern hybrid tea roses. Peak of the blooming season is May and early June. Through the archway opposite the historical roses are group plantings of each of the All-American Rose Selection winners chosen since the inception of the program in 1940. Unlike many of the old roses, these specimens bloom from May until December. Descanso Gardens is open from 8:30 A.M. until 5:30 P.M. daily. Guided tram tours are given from 1 to 4 P.M. weekdays and from 10:30 A.M. to 4:30 P.M. Saturday and Sunday.

Huntington Library and Art Gallery

Many superlatives have been used to describe the Huntington Library, Art Gallery, and Botanical Gardens at 1151 Oxford Road north of Huntington

Drive in San Marino. The home and 200-acre estate of Pacific Electric tycoon H. E. Huntington were willed to the public, so you may visit them without charge. The Art Gallery in the mansion is composed of seven large and fifteen small galleries. The 18th century British art collection exhibited here is acknowledged as the best in the country. It has some of the world's most celebrated English paintings: "Sarah Siddons as the Tragic Muse," "Blue Boy," and "Pinkie."

In the library (a large, white classical building), you'll see selections from the outstanding collection of half a million volumes of rare books and 5 million manuscripts, some as old as eight centuries. Among the fascinating works are a Gutenberg Bible, a "First Folio" of William Shakespeare's plays, Benjamin Franklin's hand-written autobiography, and George Washington's genealogy in his own hand. Many of these priceless treasures are attractively displayed.

The acres of rural and formal gardens on the estate have a number of highlights: the desert garden, the palm garden, two types of Japanese gardens, the circular Shakespearean garden with a bust of the poet and flowers and shrubs mentioned in his works, the herb garden, the first commercial avocado grove in Southern California, and an orange grove—but not a producing one.

Huntington is open to visitors Tuesday through Sunday from 1 to 4:30 P.M. It is closed Monday, holidays, and during October.

The Old Mill, west of the Huntington Gardens (follow Euston Road to the park), once ground grain for the San Gabriel Mission. Built in 1810, it was fully restored in 1920. Today, as you walk through the dark rooms with their low ceilings, it is not hard to imagine the rasping of millstones. The water that turned the stones was channeled through the lower story of the mill and down into Wilson Lake, now a small wooded area called Lacy Park. Part of the Old Mill is now the southern office of the California Historical Society. It is open daily, except Saturday, from 1 to 4 P.M.

Mission San Gabriel, fourth mission to be dedicated in California (1771), was moved to its present site 9 miles east of L.A. in 1775. Its location at the crossroads of three well-traveled trails (now 534 Mission Drive in San Gabriel) made it a busy place. It was once known for its extensive vineyards and winery, the oldest and (at one time) largest in the state. The mission's winery helped to finance the Plaza Church in the Pueblo of Los Angeles.

Architecture of the church is unlike that of other missions: the facade is on a side wall, and there are Moorish-capped buttresses and long, narrow windows, reminiscent of a cathedral in Cordova, Spain, where the mission's main builder received his training. Notable attractions include the Indian paintings of the Stations of the Cross hanging in

Arching bridge *gracefully punctuates the Japanese Garden on Huntington Library's exquisite grounds.*

the museum west of the sacristy, along with a 300-year-old painting of the Virgin Mary. The tradition-minded Claretian Fathers restored the mission and maintain it today, conducting masses every Sunday. Mission San Gabriel Archangel is open to the public daily from 9 A.M. to 5 P.M.

Whittier (southeast of San Gabriel) is the home of Pio Pico, Mexico's last governor. Before fleeing the country, he began seizing mission lands and selling them to unscrupulous politicians. San Gabriel was one he sold before his departure, but the sale was later declared invalid. His hacienda, now a historical monument, gives a fairly complete view of life among the wealthy of 19th century Mexican California. Only part of the house is "original"; Pico himself tacked on additions as the need arose and as whimsy moved him. Located at Pioneer and Whittier boulevards, the home is open from 9 A.M. to 5 P.M. Wednesday through Sunday.

Flowering in Whittier is Rose Hills Memorial Park (3900 Workman Mill Road), site of the Pageant of Roses Garden, where most of the petals for the famous parade are gathered. Peak bloom is in April and May, September and October.

Los Angeles State and County Arboretum, at 301 N. Baldwin Avenue, between Huntington Drive and Colorado Boulevard, contains thousands of plants grown in every continent of the world. The Demonstration Home Gardens, jointly sponsored by the Arboretum Foundation and *Sunset* Magazine, display take-home ideas in garden design. Hours are from 8:30 A.M. to 5 P.M. daily.

Santa Anita Race Track is just across Baldwin Avenue from the arboretum. During the thoroughbred horse racing season from December 26 to mid-April (with a special meet in October), throngs of racing fans jam the 500-acre track. Well-landscaped grounds include nearly one million special Santa Anita pansies in peak bloom for the season. Track entrance is on Holly Avenue. Gates open at 11 A.M.; general admission: $2.25; small parking fee.

SAN GABRIEL MOUNTAINS

Stretching from seaward slopes to the Mojave Desert, the San Gabriel Mountains form the northern border of the Los Angeles area. The most accessible of high mountain ranges near Los Angeles, these mountains have been called the city's mountain playground, offering back country hiking and riding, camping, picnicking, wilderness areas, and short walks to scenic waterfalls.

Among the popular destinations are Mt. Wilson, Mt. San Antonio ("Old Baldy," the highest peak in the range at 10,064 feet), Mt. Baden-Powell, Crystal Lake, and Big Pines. All but Baldy and Crystal Lake are reached from the Angeles Crest Highway (State 2) from La Canada; State 39 from Azusa is the access to Crystal Lake.

You can see some of the high country by car, but the best is seen on forest trails leading to the heights. The middle high country (or mid-range) is reached by the Angeles Crest Highway, the eastern high country by San Antonio Canyon Road. Both are within an hour's drive from the edge of L.A.

The front ranges make easy walking, revealing what the motorist would never expect: a surprising wealth of cascading streams, rocky gorges, and fragrant woodland behind a facade that looks rugged and austere from the plain below and even from the mountain roads. Short hikes lead to scenic waterfalls, old gold mines, and Indian trails. Westernmost peak of the front range, Mt. Lukens (5,074 feet), is the highest point in the city of Los Angeles and presents its climbers with a rewarding view of the vast area below. Access is from Big Tujunga Canyon Road to the Stone Canyon trail.

Little Santa Anita Canyon holds the biggest surprise of all: half a dozen waterfalls and some of the greenest forest found in the front range, now set aside as the Sierra Madre Historical Wilderness. Through this canyon runs the Mt. Wilson Trail of 1864, the first trail made by explorers in this area. To reach the canyon, park near the intersection of Miramonte Avenue and a street named Mt. Wilson

Dizzying swirl *of the International Rotunda in Mission Inn draws tourists.*

Anglers *line sandbars near main river and East Fork above San Gabriel Reservoir.*

Trail in Sierra Madre; a trail into Santa Anita Canyon joins this one near the top.

Angeles Crest Highway, State 2, originates in La Canada and connects the most popular sites and activities in the San Gabriel Mountains. At Vista, one of the picnic areas on the range crest, you may catch sight of bighorn sheep. Many climbers move up to this higher country when fire season closes the front range. Of the crest peaks, Mt. Williamson and Mt. Islip are the shortest hikes from the highway and the two easiest to climb. Vincent Gap, 5 miles from Big Pines, is the starting point of popular hikes to the old Big Horn (an introductory walk of 3 hours with very little climbing) and Mt. Baden-Powell, a steep, 4-mile trip each way, second perhaps only to Old Baldy as a worthy climb.

Mt. Wilson Observatory, reached by the Mt. Wilson road which leaves State 2 at Red Box, is world renowned for the 100-inch, 100-ton Hooker telescope camera and its magnificent views. The observatory is open free of charge from 10 A.M. to dusk daily. It lies beyond Mt. Wilson Skyline Park, which has an eating pavilion, picnic area, and children's zoo. Admission is $2 per car.

San Gabriel Wilderness, an area set aside to preserve the wild, rough mountain country, requires accomplished hiking skill and good maps to explore. Automobile sightseers can sample the flavor of this area on a drive of about 70 miles from La Canada to Azusa on State 2 and 39. You will enjoy panoramic rim views (especially at Jarvi Memorial Vista) across to rugged Twin Peaks and down into awesomely steep Devil's and Bear canyons.

Pomona-Walnut Valley

Along the base of the San Gabriel and San Bernardino ranges is a valley usually designated as Pomona-Walnut by weather forecasters. Vineyards are losing out to urban pressures in what was once one of the great wine-producing areas. You can still see about eight of the wineries in the Cucamonga-Guasti area. Most are on or south of Foothill Boulevard off the San Bernardino Freeway. Don't miss Thomas Vineyards, oldest commercial winery in California and second oldest in the nation, now an historical landmark. Photogenic Guasti (adjacent to the Brookside Winery) is a quiet town, its silence broken only by jets from Ontario International Airport, a quarter-mile away, and the Ontario Motor Speedway, across from the airport.

The Pomona Valley provides a handsome setting for a unique cluster of colleges in Claremont: Pomona, Claremont Men's College, Pitzer, Scripps, Harvey Mudd, and Claremont Graduate School. Each retains its individuality and sets its own requirements; yet all share common library, research, laboratory, and entertainment facilities.

Pomona is a center for horses and higher education. South of Claremont, Pomona is the site of the huge Los Angeles County Fair every September. Largest county fair in the nation, it underscores an often overlooked fact: the urbanized Los Angeles area is still a significant agricultural producer.

Every Sunday afternoon from mid-March through July, you can watch an Arabian horse show at Cal Poly near Pomona. Shows began in 1925 when the campus was still part of the Kellogg ranch. Show time is 2 P.M. Take the Kellogg Drive exit south from the San Bernardino Freeway and follow the signs. There's a small admission charge.

Padua Hills Theater, founded in 1923 on a wooded hilltop behind Claremont, has been attracting visitors with a varied blend of activities ever since. Enjoying a play in its small theater is the main event, but visitors can dine to the sound of Mexican music, shop for imports or pottery made on the premises, or stroll in the olive-shaded setting. Plays offering glimpses of life in Mexico or early California change every seven weeks. Dialogue might be in Spanish, but you can follow the action without understanding the language. Performances are scheduled Wednesday through Saturday at 8:30 P.M.; matinees are on Wednesday, Saturday, and Sunday at 2:30 P.M. After the play, enjoy the fiesta in the patio. From the San Bernardino Freeway, take Indian Hill Boulevard exit and drive north to Foothill Boulevard. Turn right (east), then left (north) on Padua Avenue.

Rancho Santa Ana Botanic Gardens, on Foothill Boulevard just west of the turnoff to Padua Hills, is devoted exclusively to native California plants. A short, well-marked nature trail, beginning near the giant sequoias west of the administration building, takes you past a cone collection, home demonstration garden, and through woodland, rock, dune, and desert areas. Try to see it in the spring when the California poppy is in bloom. It is open daily from 8 A.M. to 5 P.M., except on major holidays; admission is free.

The San Bernardino County Museum shouldn't be missed. You'll see a mixture of animal, vegetable, and mineral exhibits, as well as the largest egg collection in the United States. At publication time, the museum was being moved from Bloomington to a new, larger facility on California Street beside Interstate 10 near Redlands.

Redlands and Yucaipa share historical honors. Just west of Redlands on Barton Road is the *asistencia* of Mission San Gabriel with two museums. At Yucaipa is the Sepulveda Adobe (oldest house in San Bernardino County), now restored and open from 1 to 5 P.M. daily except Monday. The Mousley Museum, also in Yucaipa, has everything from Kachina dolls to sea shells.

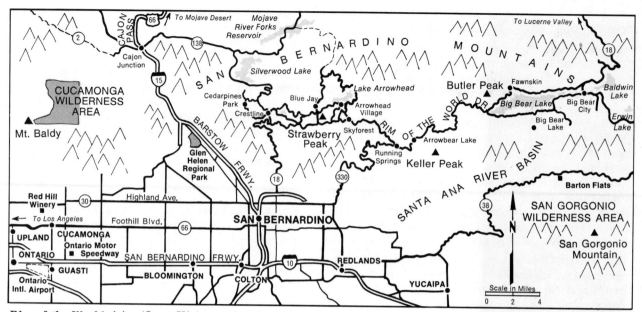

Rim of the World *drive (State Highway 18) takes you on a famous winding route through the scenic San Bernardino Mountains. Climbing as high as 7,200 feet, the road reaches resorts.*

Historical countryside

If you drive from L.A. to the mountains or desert through Riverside, Perris, and Hemet, expect to see some historical countryside. Allow time along the way for such attractions as California's first navel orange tree, the famous Mission Inn, and Mt. Rubidoux—site of an annual Easter sunrise pilgrimage.

Riverside is the birthplace of California's multimillion dollar navel orange industry. One of two original trees brought from Brazil in 1873 is still bearing fruit (corner of Magnolia and Arlington streets); the other, transplanted to the courtyard of the Mission Inn by President Theodore Roosevelt in 1903, died in the late 1920s, but the trunk is still preserved.

The Mission Inn, modeled after the California missions, is a stunning sight. Begun as an adobe cottage in 1875, it grew to become one of the showplaces of the countryside. Covering a square block bounded by Sixth, Seventh, Main, and Orange streets, this one-time resort hotel houses many treasures, including the Patio of the Fountains, the Garden of the Bells, and the St. Francis Chapel. One-hour tours leave the lobby daily at 11:30 A.M. and 2:30 P.M.—adults, $1; under 12, 50 cents.

Orange Empire Trolley Museum resurrects a form of transportation that is all but extinct in most American towns. In Perris, the trolley car is still alive and running. The legendary days of John Henry come alive as visitors ride to the clickety-clack of steel on rails and the nostalgic whine of electric motors. On exhibit in the museum are rail-

road equipment and mementos of the past, stretching from the trolley-car era to the age of electric railroading—a period of over half a century. Open weekends from 11 A.M. to 5 P.M. (except July, August, and September), the museum is located at 2201 S. A Street (1½ miles south of Perris). Admission is free; there's a small fare for trolley rides.

Ramona Bowl focuses on Indian history in the Hemet and San Jacinto area, where the local residents have been staging California's greatest outdoor play, *Ramona*, since 1923. It is generally held on three successive weekends starting in late April. Early reservations are recommended; you can make them after January by writing to the Ramona Pageant Association, Box 755, Hemet 92343. Tickets range in price from $3 to $5.

Adapted from Helen Hunt Jackson's 1884 novel about Ramona and her Indian lover, Allesandro, the play is presented in a natural amphitheater in a canyon on the slopes of Mt. San Jacinto. An entire mountainside is the stage, and more than 350 people take part in this spectacular drama.

From Riverside to the Ramona Bowl, take State 60 and 79 through San Jacinto or U.S. 395 and State 74 through Hemet. Allow plenty of time for heavy traffic. Parking is free, but you will have quite an uphill walk to the amphitheater entrance.

Maze Stone Park, nestled in boulder-studded, chaparral-covered mountains 3 miles off the Perris-Hemet Highway, is one of the finest prehistoric Indian petroglyphs in Southern California. The drawing is so clear it almost looks new, but its age is unknown. Most archeologists agree it is the work of ancestors of the Indians whom the Spaniards encountered here in the 1700s; others claim it is similar to glyphs found in Tibet and was made by Buddhist missionaries a thousand years before the arrival of the Spaniards. The small park (picnic tables, water, and rest rooms) makes a fine place for a picnic break.

SAN BERNARDINO MOUNTAINS

Highest of the mountain ranges surrounding Los Angeles, the San Bernardinos are another part of the mountain barrier between coast and desert. Past them are two major automobile routes: Cajon Canyon north to the Mojave Desert and San Gorgonio Pass east to the Coachella Valley. Peaks are high: Mt. San Gorgonio (called Old Grayback because of its high expanse of naked granite) is 11,502 feet; many peaks on the south face reach over 10,000 feet. The San Bernardinos are rich in history, scenery, and recreation.

For detailed information on hiking, camping, fishing, touring, and a good map of the mountains, write the San Bernardino County Economic Development Department, 175 W. Fifth Street, San Bernardino 92415, or visit one of the Forest Service offices in San Bernardino, Lytle Creek, Skyforest, Fawnskin, or Mill Creek.

From Interstate 15 you can get into the mountains on scenic Rim of the World Drive; the interstate also provides an easy "back door" to both the San Bernardino and San Gabriel Mountains.

West of Interstate 15, via State 38 and the Angeles Crest Highway, is Wrightwood, an all-year resort in the San Gabriels. Snow is usually not quite as good as in the San Bernardinos, but a few small resorts with ski schools flourish.

Silverwood Lake Recreation Area, reached via State 138 east of the interstate, provides 13 miles of shoreline for fishing, swimming, waterskiing, and boating. Picnic sites scattered among trees and bluffs overlooking the area offer a beautiful view of nearly a thousand acres of blue water. Popular with local residents (only 30 miles from San Bernardino), it has ultra-modern facilities including lifeguards, a concession stand, boat rentals, and sinks for cleaning fish. Overnight camping facilities are available at Mojave River Forks Regional Park, a few miles east.

Rim of the World Drive (State 18) is the famous route leading to the best-known locations in the San Bernardino Mountains. The scenic road winds up to elevations of 5,000 to 7,200 feet. As you start your ascent from San Bernardino, note the "arrowhead," a natural landmark on the mountain face.

For spectacular views along your way, take short side roads up to fire lookout stations on top of Strawberry Peak (most accessible), Keller Peak, and Butler Peak. Rim of the World Drive takes you near Crestline, Lake Gregory (site of an old Mormon settlement and today a favorite swimming destination), Blue Jay, Lake Arrowhead, Running Springs, Arrowbear, Big Bear Lake and other small mountain resorts. It also passes large ski resorts and snow fun areas. Ski lifts often run for sightseers in the summer.

Lake Arrowhead is a manmade recreation lake and all-year resort, offering water sports, along with beautiful scenery. A marina has water-ski instruction, boat rentals, and swimming and fishing areas. You'll find a golf course, theaters, abundant restaurants, motels, stores, and private cabins. At the south end of the lake, the resort center village is a picturesque, Alpine-style town but also contains a bit of bustling civilization, especially on weekends. The resort is open in the winter for skiers. Nearby Blue Jay has an outdoor skating rink.

Big Bear Lake, further east, is another resort development and scenic spot for water activities. In the village on the west end of the lake are motels and restaurants, many with lake views. Staying in the village, you can walk to theaters, a bowling alley, and an ice rink. South of Big Bear, manmade Cedar Lake, complete with an old waterwheel and mill, was the locale for the first technicolor movie and today is used by movie and television crews.

Nearby Snow Summit ski resort runs its lifts in the summer for views of the lake and mountains at an 8,300-foot elevation. Good ski areas abound in the area; most are along the south shore. From the mountain ridge south of the lake, you can look across Barton Flats to the vast white dome of San Gorgonio, summit of a snowy wilderness that is a goal for rugged hikers and backpackers.

Holcomb Valley, hidden away on the far side of the hills north of Big Bear Lake, enjoyed a brief heyday in 1860 when it was Southern California's richest gold and silver field. Rich in folklore and artifacts, its mining buildings still stand, and gold-seekers still try their luck. Easiest access is through Polique Canyon, just east of Fawnskin on the north side of the lake. For more extensive tours, start from Green Valley Lake at the west end or from the Doble Mine overlooking Baldwin Lake at the east end. Dirt roads are easily handled by any car, and there are four campgrounds.

San Gorgonio Wilderness can be reached from Big Bear by taking State 38 (part of the California Scenic Highway system) through Barton Flats and Mill Creek. During gold rush days, this was the first trail into Bear and Holcomb valleys. Heart Bar State Park is one of the jumping-off places into the wild area. It is unique in having facilities for both horses and people (advance reservations required).

Orange County

 Once little more than a sleepy agricultural county scented by orange blossoms, Orange County was transformed by the magic wand of Walt Disney in the 1950s into one of the largest tourist meccas in Southern California.

Today, Orange County possesses the greatest aggregation of manmade amusements to be found anywhere. In addition to renowned Disneyland, there are three major parks and seven specialty museums. The area has become a sort of spread-out, continuous world's fair.

But there's more. There's the great Golden Coast—extending from north of Huntington Beach (surfing capital of the world) through the seaside communities of Newport and Balboa and the art colony of Laguna south to San Clemente. Along this generous stretch of beach world are produced many of Southern California's famous golden tans.

Among the rolling hills on the former Irvine Ranch is the newest University of California campus, part of a dynamic master-planned community. You'll also find remains of mission days at San Juan Capistrano (even the swallows return annually to visit).

Visitors return again and again to Orange County. There's always some new addition to the amusement parks or new restaurants and shops to browse through. You can't see it all in a day or even several days. You'll find many attractive, moderately priced hotels and motor inns clustered around the inland amusement parks and also along the beach highway.

During the summer—peak tourist season—most places you visit will be crowded. Summer temperatures are usually in the high 80s and up inland; at the ocean it's much cooler, but beach space is often at a premium. In winter you'll have plenty of elbow room, but amusement park hours are shortened and it's likely to be cold along the shore. Still, this is the county in which oranges thrive; and so should you.

You enter Disneyland's *imaginative Fantasyland across a moat and through Sleeping Beauty's Castle.*

A MECCA FOR DIVERSION

The possibilities for adventure in Orange County are unlimited: peer from inside your car as a lion climbs aboard the hood to examine you, eat a slice of boysenberry pie while strolling the streets of a ghost town or listening to Wagon Camp music, gaze at crocodiles squirming in their mud baths, or watch Dorothy and her friends tread the "yellow brick road." This is only a sampling of the many attractions centered in this region. And, most surprisingly of all, none of the adventures mentioned above happens in the world of Walt Disney's "Magic Kingdom," a major amusement area that by itself would bring fame to any county.

Threaded by freeways, the area is accessible from anywhere in Southern California. You can drive, take a bus, or fly directly to Orange County.

By car from Los Angeles, take the Santa Ana Freeway (Interstate 5) or the San Diego Freeway (Interstate 405), which joins Interstate 5 south of Lion Country. North and southbound freeways (Long Beach, San Gabriel River, Orange, and Newport) connect with the coast highway and freeways north of Orange County.

The easiest route from the east is along Interstate 15 (San Bernardino Freeway) to the Riverside Freeway (State Highway 91).

Bus transportation is both national and local. Orange County is served by Continental Trailways and Greyhound, which operate with national schedules. Continental has a terminal in Santa Ana and Laguna Beach. Greyhound has stations in Santa Ana, Anaheim, Newport Beach, Laguna Beach, and Fullerton for through, not local, traffic. (You can't take Greyhound from L.A. to any Orange County town closer than San Clemente.)

The Southern California Rapid Transit District has direct service from its main Los Angeles terminal (located at Sixth and Los Angeles) to Disneyland, Knott's Berry Farm, and the Movieland Wax Museum.

Airlines serve Orange County from major California cities. You can take commuter flights on Golden West Airlines from Los Angeles International Airport to Orange County Airport in Santa Ana and to Fullerton Airport. (The Golden West terminal is between the Western Airlines and TWA satellites.) The flight takes about 25 minutes.

You can also fly directly to Orange County on Air California from San Francisco, San Jose, Oakland, San Diego, and Palm Springs. For further information, see your travel agent or airline representative.

Helicopters fly from Los Angeles International Airport to some local airports; an airport coach service makes scheduled daily stops at the area's major hotels.

Once you're there, check with your hotel or the Anaheim Convention Center about the numerous sightseeing services which also provide transportation between amusement spots.

Orange County has one of the best transit systems in Southern California. Buses cover every area of the county, and booklets with maps are distributed widely. Any city hall, large hotel, or civic center will have them. You can also pick them up at the Convention Center in Anaheim.

TOURIST WORLD

Consider time and money when you plan a foray into Orange County's amusement centers. You'll need both.

Five major attractions are clustered around Buena Park, 20 miles southeast of Los Angeles, and only a tempting 5 miles from Disneyland. Even if you have unlimited stamina, you'll never see them all in one day. You'll also want to visit the lion park (farther south), several interesting car and plane museums, and an alligator farm. In this entertainment mecca, a weekend will allow you only to scratch the surface.

To give you an inkling of the cost, we have computed a "typical family" admission at each place for a family with two children ages 11 and 15 (including general admission and a basic ticket book where there are separate charges inside the gates). Most places are open from midmorning to late afternoon.

Knott's Berry Farm and Ghost Town

Knott's (typical family admission: $12), on Beach Boulevard in Buena Park, is the oldest of the amusement parks. Deliberately more countryish than the others, it really began in 1920 as a berry farm with a little roadside shed where the Knott family sold their produce. As a restaurant in the early '40s, it attracted such crowds that founder Walter Knott decided to provide them with amusements while they waited.

From these humble beginnings, the farm has grown into a 200-acre combination of "ghost town," restaurants, specialty shops, and entertainment center—still operated as a family enterprise.

Everything is designed for family enjoyment, from the vaudeville show in the Calico Saloon (where the strongest drinks served are sarsaparilla and boysenberry punch) to the village of Indian tepees and real Indian Chiefs. Gaiety and nostalgia combine in the music of the organ grinder and the tinkling of the nickelodeons. The tooting of a calliope announces a performance at the Birdcage Theater, where you can cheer the hero and hiss the

Disneyland's *futuristic monorail passes its 1890 railroad station.*

Enjoying the warmth *of a car hood is this mellow citizen of Lion Country.*

You can scramble *in and out of antique planes at Movieland Air Museum.*

"MUST SEES"

DISNEYLAND (Santa Ana Freeway to Anaheim)—six "lands" of make-believe; fireworks display summer evenings

KNOTT'S BERRY FARM (State Highway 39, Buena Park)—200-acre, one-time berry farm turned entertainment center; old-time nostalgia, rides, shows, music

LION COUNTRY (Moulton Parkway off San Diego Freeway)—take a safari from your car through the "African plains"

MOVIELAND WAX MUSEUM & PALACE OF LIVING ART (State 39, Buena Park)—good collection of Hollywood stars in wax

IRVINE CAMPUS, UNIVERSITY OF CALIFORNIA (Santa Ana Freeway to Irvine)—preplanned university campus programmed to year 2000

SAN JUAN CAPISTRANO (off Interstate 5)—home of "Father Serra's Chapel" in California's seventh-established mission

BALBOA PENINSULA—colorful community of shops and homes; Balboa Pavilion, famous landmark now restaurant and gift shop; Balboa ferry—10-cent ride between Balboa Island and peninsula; dory fleet of fishermen go to sea daily in rowboats

LAGUNA BEACH (on Pacific Coast Highway south of Newport Beach)—Southland's prominent art colony, summer resort, lovely beach

DANA POINT HARBOR (Dana Point)—the only Southern California marina landscaped as a park; picnic facilities, bicycle trails, restaurants, still-water beach, small fishing pier

Judy Garland *and her fanciful friends from Oz help to populate Movieland Wax Museum.*

villain of an old-time melodrama. At Knott's you'll be able to ride on a burro, stagecoach, cable car, merry-go-round, steamboat, in an ore car through a mine, or on a "log" down a flume. The passengers on the real, smoke-belching Denver and Rio Grande narrow-gauge train are properly affrighted when gun-firing bandits enter the cars.

Most of the attractions are concentrated inside the Ghost Town enclosure, but some spill across Beach Boulevard to an area with lagoons and a full-scale reproduction of Independence Hall, built with handmade bricks and cracked Liberty Bell.

At the Fiesta Village, scene of an unusual Mexican fireworks display during the summer at 10 P.M., you can shop and watch Mexican craftsmen.

Newest features include a Roaring '20s theme area and the Knott's Good Time Theatre, a 2,150-seat, air-conditioned showcase for top stars.

The park stays open late on summer weekend nights, and the Wagon Camp features country and western music programs. Parking is free.

California Alligator Farm

Reptiles in residence are one of Southern California's most venerable tourist attractions at the California Alligator Farm (typical family admission: $6.75). Moved in 1953 to its present location in a 2-acre, junglelike park across La Palma Avenue from Knott's, it houses more than a hundred species representing all five orders of reptiles, with an emphasis on crocodilians.

Alligator and snake shows are held daily during summer (on weekends only the rest of the year).

Movieland Wax Museum and Palace of Living Art

Just a few minutes drive north from Knott's and the California Alligator Farm (at 7711 Beach Boulevard, Buena Park) is the Movieland Wax Museum, featuring over 125 wax likenesses of Hollywood stars in scenes from memorable movies and television shows. Here you'll find more glitter and glamour than in Hollywood and encounter more stars than on the busiest day at any studio lot: Judy Garland and friends in *The Wizard of Oz;* Sophia Loren in *Two Women;* Clark Gable and Vivien Leigh in *Gone with the Wind.* One warning: Don't get carried away and touch any of the figures. If you do, you'll trigger an alarm system.

Next to the wax museum is the Palace of Living Art, where famous sculptures and paintings are brought to life, some in wax. Faithful replicas of Michelangelo's works are, like the originals, carved from Carrara marble, and artists are shown at work with their models on famous masterpieces: *Mona Lisa, Blue Boy, Odalisque.*

Because the rendering here is done in meticulous

"Watch out for bandits!" *is warning given passengers on Knott's Berry Farm train.*

detail, these are probably two of the most interesting museums you'll ever see. Your admission fee (typical family: $8.25) is good for both museums. Both museums stay open into the evening all year.

Cars and planes

Automobile and airplane buffs will find it hard to pass up the next four attractions, all devoted exclusively to these subjects.

Movieworld Cars of the Stars (see admission charge under *Planes of Fame* following) displays 100 antique, classic, motion-picture automobiles at 6920 Orangethorpe Avenue, Buena Park (just north of the Santa Ana Freeway). In an inventory of more than 700 cars you'll probably see "Ma Barker's" 1930 Cadillac, Al Jolson's 1929 custom-built Mercedes-Benz, and Fatty Arbuckle's Pierce-Arrow —all in historical settings with costumed mannequins, painted backdrops, and related artifacts.

Planes of Fame (typical family admission: $8.45 for both car and plane attractions) traces the history of aircraft from the Wright brothers' era to the space age. The collection includes over 30 planes, many of them one-of-a-kind aircraft, such as the World War I Hanriot Scout flown by French ace Charles Nungesser. Other notable planes include the Japanese "Zero" fighters and the Flying Tiger.

The Briggs Cunningham Automotive Museum (typical family admission: $6.25) is west of Orange County Airport at Baker Street and Redhill Avenue. One of the nation's superlative collections, it houses 100 automobiles notable in the history of automotive development. Lovingly cared for, most are in running order and are occasionally exercised.

Open daily in season, the museum is closed Mondays and Tuesdays during the winter.

Movieland of the Air (typical family admission: $4.75) is on the other side of the airport, off Campus Drive and south of the terminal. It contains a collection of about 22 aircraft, all but a few in flying condition and most of them veterans of films. Myriad dents attesting to its popularity, a World War II bomber is on hand for patrons to kick. Free movies run continuously, and rides in the open-cockpit "barnstomer" are a magnetic attraction.

Lion Country Safari

Extending the range of the tourist-park district southeastward is Lion Country Safari (typical family admission: $11.25), a 500-acre wild animal preserve where people are "caged" in automobiles while animals roam free. You ride in a safari through country populated by one of the world's largest assemblages of African animals, all roaming loose in natural surroundings. Eight preserves separate incompatible beasts.

Independence Hall *at Knott's Berry Farm is an exact replica of the original in Philadelphia.*

A lonely alligator *is a rarity at the Alligator Farm, one of Orange County's compelling sights.*

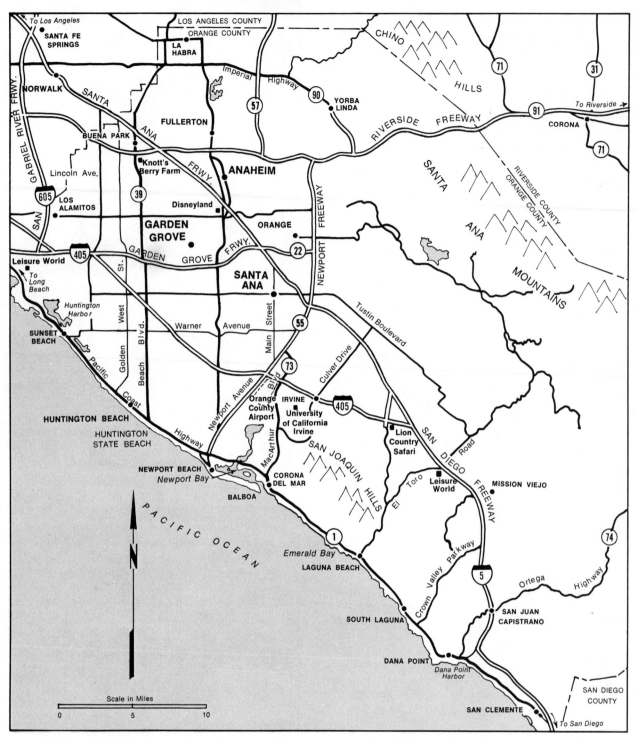

Orange County *stretches from above Sunset Beach to just below San Clemente along the coast. Its beaches below Corona del Mar are lovely; its inland tourist attractions are plentiful.*

The drive is not long, but you will want to park and watch the animals—including almost 22 lions—so allow 1½ hours.

Both rare and more common species of animals breed better here than in the wild because they are safe from predators. Several years ago, a senile lion named Frazier put Lion Country on the map with stories of his capacity to sire cubs.

Other denizens of the plains include a herd of now-rare white rhinoceroses, 17 species of hoof-and-horn animals, a flock of ostriches, chimpanzees, cheetahs, giraffes, and elephants.

The safari ends at an entertainment center, offering bird shows in an amphitheater and a junior jungle where children may pet small exotic animals and play in a tree house. On the jungle river boat trip, you'll see exotic birds close at hand and an island full of chimps; another jungle ride takes children past animated animals. You can also rent a hippo pedal boat for a ride on Lake Shanalee.

The park is open every day from 9 A.M. until sundown. Convertibles are banned from the preserve; you can rent an air-conditioned car for the safari. You can also rent a tape-recorded tour and player. Animals are most active during the cooler hours and at feeding times.

Adjacent to the San Diego Freeway at the Moulton Parkway offramp, you'll see no-nonsense signs giving would-be gate crashers this terse warning: "Trespassers will be eaten."

Disneyland—the best-known park of all

The father of "theme parks" springing up around the country, Disneyland has been world-renowned for almost 20 years because of its combined use of technology and imagination to control the environment and achieve illusion. It's at its best in creating a three-dimensional illusory experience you move through, most masterful of which is the Haunted Mansion. A disembodied head speaking from inside a glass sphere, a ballroom full of transparent dancers, and spirits perching on the back of your moving chair are all part of the experience.

In Disneyland, an enjoyable ride becomes a trip into history, space, fantasy, or a foreign land. An entire area becomes a reproduction of a well-known fairy tale.

Disneyland even undergoes marked seasonal changes outdoors with only subtle changes in weather, producing Easter blooms in spring, flashing autumn colors after Labor Day, and displaying brilliant poinsettias at Christmas time. The park has truly become what Walt Disney intended: a place enjoyed by adults as well as children, actually drawing more of the former than the latter.

On your first park visit, consider the 2-hour guided tour in small groups which will introduce you to all six "lands" in the Magic Kingdom. The tour price will increase your "typical family" cost (from $10.25 for admission only to $22.30 for admission plus 15 attractions), but the tour does include the entrance fee and admission to several park attractions. If you prefer to explore the park unguided, you will save money by buying ticket books—but be prepared to spend more once inside.

Your first experience within the park is Main Street 1890 in Home Town, U.S.A. Here you may encounter the colorful Disneyland Band (known for its showmanship as well as its musicianship) marching in front of the nostalgic old ice cream parlor and silent movie house or in the Town Square and depot, where the Santa Fe and Disneyland Railroad embarks on its tour of the park.

• **"Adventureland"** provides a jungle boat ride and safari in alligator, gorilla, and elephant territory; the opportunity to climb the treehouse of the shipwrecked and industrious Swiss Family Robinson; and a visit to the "enchanted" Tiki Room.

• **"New Orleans Square,"** with the Blue Bayou Restaurant, exciting Pirates of the Caribbean ride, and the eerie Haunted Mansion, evokes the glamour of the French Quarter of this Louisiana city.

• **"Bear Country,"** Disneyland's newest, features a Country Bear Jamboree with such characters as Liverlips McGrowl and offers canoes you can paddle along the rivers of America.

• **"Frontierland,"** the haunt of Tom Sawyer and Davy Crockett, is your target for a ride on the riverboat "Mark Twain," which passes Tom's island. Or you can take a raft across the river and explore Fort Wilderness.

• **"Fantasyland"** — that make-believe, now-believable world of Peter Pan, Alice in Wonderland, and Winnie the Pooh—is reached by crossing a moat and entering Sleeping Beauty's Castle. One of the most popular rides in the park is here: zoom down the 14-story Matterhorn in a bobsled.

• **"Tomorrowland"** has to be continuously renovated as today catches up with tomorrow in the exciting world of science. It now offers a Submarine Voyage, Flight to the Moon, Adventure through Inner Space, and People-Mover.

Each land has restaurants and refreshment stands, shops, services, and free exhibits. You won't see all of Disneyland in a day, so either return again or plan ahead, being very selective for your only visit. Disneyland changes continually—whenever inspiration and imagination ignite. Even a yearly visit would reveal new surprises.

Open daily from 8 A.M. to 1 A.M. from mid-June to mid-September, the park is closed Monday and Tuesday during the rest of the year. Winter hours are from 10 A.M. to 6 P.M. Wednesday through Friday and from 9 A.M. to 7 P.M. on weekends. Take the Santa Ana Freeway to the Harbor Boulevard exit in Anaheim. There is a parking charge.

Daytime or evening can be equally engrossing in Disneyland. In the summer, music of the Dixieland band is prominent in the night air, and name bands entertain. Multicolored fireworks light the sky at 9 P.M. every night. You'll spend a large amount of your time waiting in lines to see such popular evening attractions as the Electric Parade.

Disneyland is less crowded in winter (as well as in the fall and early spring). Lines are shorter, and streets offer you more strolling room. It's also cooler, but there's less entertainment.

The Disneyland Hotel, across the street, is the largest hotel in the county. It's connected to the park by a fast monorail from Tomorrowland. Your ticket lets you stop off in the park for a visit.

Water World, a freshwater marina in the backyard of the hotel, is well worth a look. Stroll along a seawall, docks, pedestrian bridges, ramps, and viewing pavilions. Along the way you may inspect boats and other recreation craft, look in on craftsmen's booths, see a display of large marine equipment, watch swimmers basking on the sandy beach around a manmade pool. In the evening, the lighted fountains become a Dancing Waters spectacle.

You can have lunch or dinner in a restaurant overlooking the water or get out on the water in a paddle boat. And you may fish for trout (Wednesday through Sunday), paying $1 for each.

Anaheim Convention Center, directly across from Disneyland, might make a good first stop for your Orange County tour. Here you can get free information on restaurants, lodging, and sightseeing.

Baseball, car, bike, and horse racing

There's no lack of sporting events in Orange County. Home of baseball's California Angels and football's California Sun is Anaheim Sports Center at 2000 South State College Boulevard, just north of the Santa Ana Freeway.

In Irvine, the Orange County International Raceway is a drag strip for autos, motorcycles, and go-carts. Drag racing is on Saturdays, motorcycle racing on the first Sunday of each month. Head north off the Santa Ana Freeway at Moulton Parkway. Motorcycles race every Friday evening at the Orange County Fairgrounds in Costa Mesa, and midgets compete at the El Toro Speedway, 23001 S.E. Valencia.

Quarter horse races are held nightly (except Sunday) from June to September at Los Alamitos Race Course, 4961 Katella Avenue, Los Alamitos. Harness races take place in the winter, often in February.

THE PRESENT ...

The northwestern section of Orange County is crowded; you'll find little evidence of the bean fields that once flourished for miles. As urban sprawl spreads southeastward, "instant cities" sprang up, land sites decreased, and people began to fear this once-beautiful countryside would suffer the fate of surrounding areas. Irvine Company—owners of an 83,000-acre ranch representing one-fifth of the area of Orange County—retained William L. Pereira in 1960 to prepare a broad, general development plan of its land, designed to stop or at least to integrate the urban sprawl. Within this framework, the Irvine Company planners, working with other consultants, prepared a more detailed plan. The plan, a comprehensive look at the total environment, established building and population density limits and provided greenbelt areas, effective traffic flow, and aesthetic balance. Billboards, overhead power lines, and TV antennas were forbidden. Both shopping centers and wildlife preserves were included in this mountains-to-ocean master plan. Still being modified to conform with state and regional planning commissions, this plan is a model for the rest of the country.

The University of California at Irvine enjoys the unique advantage of being developed within the master plan. Its 1,500 acres (over twice the area of U.C.L.A.) are the focal point of the city of Irvine, which one day will incorporate some 53,000 acres of the ranch. By the turn of the century, the community is expected to have 100,000 people, the university 27,500 students.

Buildings that now stand give a strong indication of the future development planned for the Irvine campus. The heart of the plan is a central campus formed around a ring with six major quadrangles shooting off like spokes, each devoted to a distinct academic field. With cars relegated to remote parking pastures, circulation is by foot, bicycle, or elephant train. Connecting the quads is an underground utility channel, carrying heat, light, air-conditioning, and television cables. Planners have taken full advantage of the commanding site of the campus, being landscaped with connecting parks.

...AND THE PAST

Where are all the orange trees? Many are gone, though a few groves survive on the Irvine Ranch and some still hold out around San Juan Capistrano. And faint traces of a distant past still linger among the mission ruins at San Juan Capistrano and at an adobe standing on land once owned by one of Portola's corporals. There are other historical attractions, too, and looking for them is part of the fun.

The Charles W. Bowers Memorial Museum, in Santa Ana, offers a look into Southern California's past. The mission-style structure has galleries devoted to natural history, archeology, early and contemporary California art, and artifacts of the Southwest. Here you will find an extensive collection of early Spanish and Mexican documents, among them deeds to area ranchos.

In the museum patio, leaning against a wide-spreading pepper tree, is a large *metate*—its pocked

Thousands of acres *of undeveloped land in Orange County are part of Irvine Ranch site.*

Tourists join swallows *in wanting to return to Mission San Juan Capistrano, a cool retreat.*

surface a mute testimony to the work of long-vanished Gabrielino Indian women, who gathered around its rim to grind acorns.

The Bowers Museum, at 2002 N. Main Street, is just south of the Main Street offramp from the Santa Ana Freeway. Hours are from 10 A.M. to 4:30 P.M. Tuesday through Saturday (also from 7 to 9 P.M. Thursday) and from 1 to 5 P.M. Sunday. It's closed on Monday; admission is free.

Diego Sepulveda Adobe, 1900 Adams Avenue in Costa Mesa, is a California Historical Landmark. Once part of a mission *estancia* (ranch), it stands on old Indian grounds. Excavations have uncovered several Indian burials and bits of broken shell. After secularization of the missions, this property became part of Rancho Santiago de Santa Ana. The adobe, once the home of Don Diego Sepulveda and still bearing his name, later became a ranch house. In 1963, the adobe and surrounding 5 acres were given to the city of Costa Mesa as a memorial to the early settlers of the area.

From Costa Mesa, take Harbor Boulevard north to Adams Avenue and west to Mesa Verde Drive W. The adobe is open on Saturday and Sunday from 1 to 5 P.M. and on weekdays by appointment only. Telephone (714) 834-5302 for an appointment.

San Juan Capistrano is venerable

The village of San Juan Capistrano has been a favorite stop for travelers ever since its mission was founded in 1776, the year of American independence. About midway between Los Angeles and San Diego, it is bypassed by Interstate 5. Even so, its streets fill up on weekends and holidays with people who come to see the picturesque mission, shop, eat, or break up a longer journey.

The town is small enough to cover on foot. Horseback riders from nearby rural communities and cyclists in from the lightly traveled old highway are part of the traffic. On the street you still hear the Spanish language, and you see the influence of Mexico in the restaurants, the craft and fashion shops, and the building design.

The sweep of California history is displayed in the architecture of San Juan, from the mission and adobes of the Spanish and Mexican eras to the Egan house and the railway station dating from the 19th century. Nondescript buildings remain from the time San Juan was a farm town with a main highway running through it. Now, with architectural controls in the mission district, some handsome new structures are appearing.

Most of the adobes are on the main street, south of the mission. All are labeled, but none is open as a museum. A restaurant absorbed two, and two more contain shops; the other four are private.

You will get a glimpse of how one colorful 19th century figure lived in the grand old Richard Egan house, open on weekends, when its restorers put out the welcome sign (a small tour charge contributes to upkeep).

ORANGE COUNTY   **63**

Southern California's Bird Men

Successful hang gliding *requires some earnestness, much tenacity, and a good measure of luck.*

A new sport has hit Southern California.

Recently, bird watchers have reported sighting a strange new type of bird. These large, brightly colored creatures have up to a 20-foot wingspan and range from bright red to blue and yellow.

If you should happen to sight one or more of these creatures, you'll find that they are actually men, suspended from manmade kites. Their sport is sky-sailing, or hang gliding, and enthusiasts are rapidly filling the hillsides and skies of Southern California.

By running off of a high hill or ocean cliff, the flyer, hung in a leather seat strap under the kite, launches himself. He banks and dives gracefully downward, landing easily on his feet. Sky sailors, depending on their skill, soar from hills as high as 2,000 feet or more and perform turns up to 360° with amazing precision.

You might enjoy bringing your picnic lunch and making an afternoon of "bird watching"; if you do, you will probably see many other fascinated onlookers sitting on the roadsides or hillsides. Main centers for sky-sailing enthusiasts are in Escape Country, Trabuco Canyon, Playa del Rey (foot of Imperial Highway), Elsinore (inland from San Juan Capistrano), Norco (near Riverside), Sylmar, Pacific Palisades, and Torrey Pines (north of San Diego).

At the fountain opposite the four adobes, you enter a landscaped shopping center where you can have breakfast or lunch outdoors in the Coffee Garden. Open Tuesday through Friday from 10 A.M. to 3 P.M., it is staffed by Family Service women.

Toward the center of town, you can shop for both old and new: antiques and bric-a-brac, gifts and crafts, pottery and stitchery materials.

Mission San Juan Capistrano is the great attraction of San Juan Capistrano. The mission was founded in 1776 by Father Junipero Serra. The seventh in the California mission chain, it was completed in 1806 after a decade of work, but much was destroyed in an earthquake only 6 years later.

A small donation will take you through the gates so that you may walk at your leisure through legendary ruins and lush restored gardens. Fluttering white pigeons splashing in the mossy fountain are so used to visitors that they may eat out of your hand. Past the fountain, the broken, ivy-covered walls are lone remnants of a stone church that was once the most magnificent in the mission chain. Today, the ruined walls hold the mud nests of the legendary swallows of Capistrano.

Four bells, saved when the original bell tower collapsed, today ring out in a campanile. Behind the campanile is a small tranquil garden, a fountain, and the mission museum.

Having survived the rigors of neglect and time, the modest mission chapel is believed to be the oldest church in California. The adobe chapel, called "Father Serra's church," is the only remaining place where he is known to have said Mass. Inside, the 300-year-old giltwork *reredos* from Spain was added during the mission's restoration in the 1920s.

Outside you may stroll through a shady arcade (a remnant of the original mission) and along flower-bordered paths past ivy and rose-covered walls. Other buildings and excavations of tallow vats and working parts of the mission are open to visitors. The mission grounds are open from 7 A.M. to 5 P.M. daily.

The legend of the swallows of San Juan Capistrano is known through stories, songs, and poems. Supposedly, the swallows return to their nests every year around St. Joseph's Day; actually, the majority of cliff swallows do return on March 19, but some of the group also arrive a little earlier or later. The swallows leave their mission nests for an unknown southern destination around October 23 (date of the death of the patron saint of the Mission, St. John of Capistrano).

Starr-Viejo Regional Park

Another bit of old California, this park is reached 7 miles in from San Juan through the lovely pastoral land beside the Ortega Highway (State 74). Here the county has set aside a 5,500 acre former ranch as a wilderness preserve. You can picnic free beside the highway or in a meadow farther into the park for 50 cents, or you can camp for $2.

Starr-Viejo is a hiker's and horseback rider's park, with almost no development, including water —so bring your own. You walk beside the creek of Bell Canyon—which flows in winter—through grassy meadows, into oak and sycamore woodlands, up through chaparral to low ridges for a view of the mountains and the sea.

Tucker Wildbird Sanctuary, just past the charming old town of Modjeska (named for the great actress who lived nearby), is a beautiful oasis of trees, flowers, plants, and wildlife, operated by California State University at Fullerton. You can walk along a lovely stream and listen to the birds sing. The home is open from 9 A.M. to 4 P.M. daily except Mondays; a 50 cent donation is requested for upkeep.

SOUTH COAST

Orange County's coast has two faces. The shore of the Los Angeles plain, as far south as the Balboa Peninsula, has the heaviest-use beaches. The picturesque bluff coast begins at Corona del Mar with a rocky shoreline along which the beaches are mainly small coves. It is the summer resort capital of this populous part of the country, with most activity centering around the county's north end (on beaches that are not the most attractive part of the coastline).

Seal Beach abuts the Los Angeles County line and is just south of Long Beach. Along the inland side of the highway, the coastal route from this point south almost to Huntington Beach bears the constant reminder of the oil industry—operating pumps, refineries, and storage tanks. But modern technology has enabled the beach towns and parks to continue serving the populace with no greater inconvenience than a lingering odor of petroleum.

Seal Beach and Sunset Beach (next door and to the south) are beach towns in the full sense of the word. The coast highway follows along just behind the rim of sand, lined on either side with refreshment stands and places offering any kind of beach gear for sale or rent. At Seal Beach, surfing between the pier and jetty area occurs only during the summer in the early morning or late afternoon.

Sunset Bay has a marina (reached from the coast highway) and an aquatic park (west on Edinger Avenue from Bolsa Chica Road), as well as a launching ramp and space for parking car trailers.

Bolsa Chica State Beach, a 3-mile-long strip between the ocean and the highway, is lined with bodies in the summer and on warm weekends year-round. An extension of the general shoreline, which is a 300 to 360-foot-wide strand of sand adjacent to the highway, the beach has fire rings (common to several beaches in this region), rest rooms, and lifeguards. Exclusively a day-use park, it closes at midnight. Watch your driving along these beaches, for cars park wherever there's an available inch of space, and it's not uncommon to see a horizontal surfboard with legs below dashing across the highway between traffic.

Huntington Beach

In 1901 Philip Stanton organized and helped settle a townsite on the coast of Shell Beach. The new town, named Pacific City, was intended to rival Atlantic City on the East Coast. In 1902, Henry E. Huntington of Pacific Electric Railway bought a controlling interest in the project and renamed the community.

The beach is famous today, but not for the same reasons as its East Coast counterpart. To intrepid surfers world-wide, it's "the capital"—home of the summer international surfing competition—where they can tackle some of the greatest combers along the coast. Most of the surfing activity centers around the Huntington Pier (at the foot of Main Street), which reaches several hundred feet out into deep water on tall, concrete legs. Early in the morning or later in the evening (after the swimmers and sunbathers have gone), you can hang over the edge of the rail and get a bird's eye view of man and board.

You won't be alone, even on a foggy morning, for here flock the fishermen, outfitted with folding stools, tackle boxes, and lunch sacks, to settle in for a long peaceful day. When the weather is less calm, a good place to fish is at the flood control levee of the Santa Ana River.

The state beach, stretching for 2 miles south of the pier, is spectacular on summer nights, when its 500 fire rings are ablaze with bonfires.

Newport Beach and Balboa

The opulent homes, handsome yacht clubs, and mast-studded harbor you see here would appear to have little connection with Newport's salty past, when the town was literally a "new port" between San Diego and San Pedro. Yet some of its original character still remains, or is being recultivated, if you look carefully.

In 1863, Captain S. S. Dunnels pushed the sidewheeler *Vaquero* past the mud flats into the harbor at the mouth of the Santa Ana River, unloaded lumber from San Diego, and picked up a cargo of produce from the inland fields, marking the beginning of a prosperous trading era. James and Robert McFadden bought that boat and landing in 1888, contracted for another steamer, built a long wharf on Newport Bay, and laid out a townsite. This was the beginning of Newport Beach.

Balboa Peninsula no longer boasts of sidewheelers, but thousands of boats still use the harbor. Pleasure craft of every description are anchored in channels dredged from former flats on land created by the dredging and planted with homes. It's the biggest yachting harbor on this section of the coast, berthing some 8,000 boats. Whatever land is left sells by the square foot—perhaps one of the reasons this area is called the Gold Coast.

Most of the tangible glimpses of yesteryear are on Balboa Peninsula (on the ocean side of Newport), a long skinny sandspit stretching out to sea, the tip of which is called Balboa.

If you turn south on Via Lido at the north end of the peninsula, you cross a humpbacked bridge leading to Lido Isle, a posh residential area dredged up from the harbor's bottom. Almost every waterfront home has a boat at its back door.

On the peninsula is the site of McFadden's Pier (west of the intersection of Balboa and Newport boulevards). The original pier was destroyed by

fire and rebuilt as a fishing spot with tackle shops at its foot. But many buildings around the area date back to the original waterfront days and are now being restored as Old Town (or Cannery Village), a charming conglomeration of boutiques, restaurants, boatyards, and antique shops. One cleverly converted warehouse, The Factory, has over 30 tiny shops under one roof.

The dory fleet which works from the beach adjoining the pier is the last of its kind on the West Coast. Each day at dawn, fishermen shove off in their small wooden boats, working alone 5 to 10 miles out at sea to set trawl lines with thousands of baited hooks for rockfish, halibut, mackerel, flounder, sea trout, and sand dabs. With luck, the fishermen head for shore by midmorning, helping one another through the surf onto the beach, where the area quickly turns into one large, open-air fish market. To the delight of camera-clicking customers, this picturesque fleet has now been designated an historical landmark.

The Newport beach, extending 5¼ miles, is narrow at the northwestern edge and broadens farther south and east. There are fire rings near Balboa Pier, farther out on the peninsula. The largest parking areas are at Palm and Balboa boulevards and at 26th Street. Surfing is popular in the morning in the Newport Pier area, in late afternoon from 30th Street west, and all day at the mouth of the Santa Ana River.

Balboa Pavilion, focal point for the Newport Beach playground area for nearly three-quarters of a century, once was the terminus of the big red streetcar line, Pacific Electric, from Los Angeles. It also served as a bath and boathouse for stylish bathers in ankle-length bathing togs. Since then, the venerable pavilion, with its much-photographed cupola, has been the scene of many "firsts," including the first Surfboard Riding Championship Races in the U. S. in 1932. The Tournament of Lights yachting celebration, held in December, began here in 1908.

When the Big Band sounds echoed across the nation, the pavilion resounded to thousands of dancing feet as the Balboa Peninsula became known as the place that gave birth to a dance that swept the nation—the Balboa Hop.

Redecorated in 1962, the pavilion still preserves its original look of 1902. It has a restaurant, gift shop, and banquet room and also serves as the Newport terminal for Catalina tours, whale-watching cruises, and harbor excursions. At the nearby dock, you may rent all types of water craft and make arrangements for a fishing boat.

Harbor cruises are perhaps the best way to see Newport Bay. You won't get a look at all of Newport's 13 square miles (two of which are underwater), but you will see its small islands and bluff-

Shops in Balboa Island's modish shopping district offer smart leather goods, custom-made bikinis.

Biggest bargain in the West: the car, bike, and people-ferry from mainland to Balboa Island.

top subdivisions. Harbor cruises leave from the "Fun Zone Dock" near the ferry landing—about 20 daily in the summer, fewer on weekends the rest of the year. On a 45-minute narrated cruise (moderate charge for adults and children), you'll see waterfront homes of motion picture and television stars and many of the boats berthed in the area. The *Pavilion Queen* leaves her dock near the pavilion for an evening cocktail cruise, complete with dancing and live entertainment.

Balboa Ferry, operating since 1919, has little three-car ferries (the last on the southern coast), which have been transporting residents and vacationers between the peninsula and Balboa Island (20 cents for cars; 15 cents for bicycles; 10 cents for passengers). Brought into being by a petition signed by the entire island population (26 strong), the ferries are still the most interesting way to get to Balboa, connected now by a two-lane bridge and road from the coast highway.

Balboa Island has an artsy-craftsy shopping center with a European flavor crunched into about three short blocks. Parking is almost impossible on summer weekends. For exploring, your best bet is to park on one of the side streets lined with small wooden houses and walk.

The island's jetties supposedly tamed what was once considered some of California's best surf. But

a rock extension of the jetty created a phenomenon called The Wedge, where large breakers are further amplified into a maelstrom. Expert body surfers challenge the waves even during the winter; for others, it's best as a spectator sport.

Just across the bridge separating the upper and lower harbor is the *Reuben E. Lee*, replica of an old-time riverboat, now a three-deck, floating restaurant.

Overlooking the ocean and bay to the south is Newport Center (on Irvine land)—a vast shopping, business, professional, and financial complex. Fashion Island, one of the largest and most tastefully designed shopping centers in the West, features interrelated malls and plazas, one equipped especially for children.

Upper Newport Bay, just south of the bridge crossing the upper bay arm on the east side of the coast highway, has a park within a bay. A commercial enterprise called Newport Dunes Aquatic Park, it offers numerous ways of getting out on the quiet, warm waters of the 15-acre lagoon. For a small entry fee, you can use the beach, dressing rooms, playground, wading pool, fire rings, and launching ramp. You can also rent paddleboards, kayaks, sea cycles, and sailboats. It's an attractive overnight camping spot for trailers and campers.

The water skiing and speedboat area of Newport

Harbor is on Upper Newport Bay (not connected with Newport Dunes).

For a real surprise in the midst of all the resort hubbub, take Backbay Drive, off Jamboree Boulevard. It leads you along the east shore of upper Newport Bay—a vast estuary scarcely touched by man and nearly invisible except from here because of bluffs all around. It is islands and channel at low tide, a minisea at high tide. There are always birds in action, but in fall it swarms with ducks, geese, and other users of the Pacific Flyway. The area is on its way to becoming a wildlife preserve.

Corona del Mar State Beach, just south of the breakwater, is operated by the city of Newport Beach. Wide and sandy with palm trees, its ½ mile total frontage is divided into two parts. Big Corona is at the east jetty; Little Corona is around the point to the east. The beach is very popular year-round; there's a charge for parking. To get there, turn west off the coast highway on any of the streets named for flowers in Corona del Mar between Orchid and Iris. Look for attractive shops and restaurants along the coast highway in Corona del Mar. Development is taking place on the hills to the east of the highway, and your view to the sea is often blocked by exclusive residential development. The topography has changed from low, lagoon-backed seashores to a continuing rank of steep bluffs. Irvine Ranch properties account for a considerable stretch of empty shore between Corona del Mar and Laguna Beach, the next town south.

Laguna Beach offers more than sand

Long known as an art colony, Laguna Beach is now a city aware of its French Riviera setting, as well as its problems. Not the least of these is traffic. To follow the coast highway through town on a summer weekend is to experience an interminable series of starts and stops. There are a number of stores where you'll want to pause and take a look.

Painters' galleries are numerous throughout the town. An art lover's first stop might be at the Laguna Beach Museum of Art, 307 Cliff Drive. Open daily from 11:30 A.M. to 4:30 P.M., it provides an ever-changing variety of media.

The ceramics industry was pioneered here, and many other types of crafts now compete for space with galleries. Often you can watch artisans creating handcrafted pottery, jewelry, clothing, leather goods, rugs, or other articles.

Remote and inaccessible, Laguna Beach was discovered in the 1890s. First-comers built summer homes on the hills, which were followed by more pretentious residences. The colony's boutiques, galleries, little theaters, and coffee houses that sprang up were popular long before Greenwich Village began attracting attention.

Unlike many beach resorts which hibernate during the winter, Laguna holds a Winter Festival in February and March, as well as its famous Festival of Arts and Pageant of the Masters in the summer. Since 1932, thousands have gathered annually to see the local residents don costumes and become living pictures. So professional is the performance that it's hard for visitors to believe these "paintings" are really alive.

Laguna has less than a mile of public beach, its use limited by the scarcity of street parking. The main beach is along the coast highway in the center of town; it has become a beguiling "window to the sea" park, now that a number of buildings that blocked it have been torn down. To the north are Crescent Bay, Divers Cove, and Heisler Park (with bluff-top fire rings and picnic tables); to the south are Woods Cove and Victoria Beach. Surfers congregate at St. Ann and Cress streets before 11 A.M.

In South Laguna is Aliso Beach Park, a ¾-mile frontage with lifeguards, a few fire rings, and a handsome fishing pier. Adjacent Camel Point and West Street beach, to the south, have another similar ½ mile of beach.

Dana Point, once a cliff over which cowhides were thrown to waiting traders (see references to Point San Juan in Richard Henry Dana's *Two Years Before the Mast)*, subsequently became a lonely cove frequented by abalone hunters, a park, and now the site of a luxurious marina with accommodations for 2,000 boats.

A manmade harbor created space for boats and yachts; Mariner's Village, a deliberately rustic complex, offers shopping and restaurants; and some of the prime ocean fishing grounds are combed by the Dana Wharf Sportfishing boats. There's a 15-lane launching ramp and a still-water swimming beach with a small fishing pier and a camper parking area at the marina. Perhaps one of the most popular amusements is simply boat watching.

Doheny State Beach is next door. Popular and crowded, Doheny offers camping combined with a safe beach and good surfing. The lagoon on San Juan Creek at the north end of the park is a wild bird habitat. Surf fishing (once better than it is now) and a fair grunion run are attractions.

The park is near the junction of State 1 and Interstate 5 at Capistrano Beach in Dana Point.

San Clemente State Beach is really a dual-purpose park, similar to Doheny. Campsites perch on the edge of a bluff, shaded and separated with mature trees and shrubs. Because it is extremely popular, camping reservations are important. For information, write to Orange Coast State Parks, 3030 Avenida del Presidente, San Clemente 92672.

Well-established footpaths lead from the cliffs to the beaches below; don't stray off the trails, for the

Laguna Beach is an Art Festival

Attractive gourds *used as decorative holders are among many craft items at the summer Laguna Sawdust Festival.*

Laguna Beach is a city created by artists. Attracted by her curving bay setting, one of the most picturesque sections of the Pacific coast, they came to capture the magnificent, unspoiled beauty of the sea and land on canvas and remained to form the nucleus of a town. From their first humble art shows has grown one of the oldest and most exciting spectacles in the state—the Festival of Arts and Pageant of Living Masters. Launched out of Depression desperation, the show now attracts some 300,000 spectators annually.

From mid-July to late August, the entire city is alive with art. In addition to the more famous exhibition, you can browse among three other art shows, all running simultaneously: Art-Affair (500 block on South Coast Highway), a more traditional exhibit of arts and crafts; Sawdust Festival (Laguna Canyon Road), an unstructured, unjuried, and uncensored crafts show; and Discovery Festival, displaying arts and crafts.

The Festival of Arts and Pageant of the Masters at Irvine Bowl is an ambitious cultural festival. From noon until 11:30 P.M., daily visitors stroll through a tree-shaded park among booths displaying works by local artists in all media. Children can take a fling at creativity in an art workshop—smocks, paints, and canvases are provided. A marionette show plays in a little theater. At 8:30 P.M. the Pageant of the Masters begins. Masterpieces of painting, sculpture, and tapestry are recreated by living models in a 2-hour tableau. Staging, lighting, costumes, and commentary add to the effect.

So popular is this evening performance that tickets are sold out months in advance. You can get an application form for next year's show while you're there or write (several months in advance to be sure of tickets) to Festival of Arts, 650 Laguna Canyon Road, Laguna Beach 92651. Prices range from $3 to $7 and include the admission fee to the grounds (50 cents; children under 12 free).

Parking is limited, so plan to arrive early. Park along Laguna Canyon Road or (for a fee) in a lot across the street from the grounds.

bluffs are crumbly. Swimming is good (lifeguards are on duty), but watch for occasional riptides.

San Onofre State Beach (formerly part of the Camp Pendleton Marine Corps base) was opened for public use in 1971. The beach is not visible from Interstate 5. Take the Basilone Road exit off the highway and follow signs past the nuclear power plant. Campers and trailers occupy the bypassed old coast highway, and three trails lead about ¼ mile down to a usually broad beach.

San Diego
& Across the Border

 San Diego is constantly changing and consistently charming. At first glance, the city's modern facade belies its old age. But California's oldest town is ever mindful of her rich Spanish-Mexican heritage. Monuments report it and buildings preserve it. A legacy of place names, graceful architecture, and a relaxed life style reflect San Diego's pride in her past.

California's history began here when Juan Rodriguez Cabrillo landed at Point Loma in 1542. Sixty years later, Sebastian Vizcaino also reached the bay he named San Diego. But the West Coast's first settlement was not established until 1769, when Father Junipero Serra, a member of Portola's expedition, founded Mission San Diego de Alcala on Presidio Hill. The village became the anchor point for Spanish domain in California and a terminal point of the famous El Camino Real (the King's Highway), now U.S. Highway 101.

Thanks to a splendidly natural setting, equable climate, and thoughtful planning from the days of her forefathers, this once sleepy little seaside community is now the third largest city on the Pacific Coast. Constant sea breezes keep the air clear and fresh. An average temperature and humidity in the mid-60s make San Diego an all-year city.

Water-oriented San Diego also owes her growth to a great harbor. Vast, natural, and almost landlocked, San Diego Harbor is one of the world's best deep water anchorages. Host to ships from all ports, it is also home of the 11th Fleet, the Navy's largest.

Up the coast are gems of seaside villages, colorful flower fields, and wide, sandy beaches. The interior, or back country, holds a wealth of surprises, ranging from San Diego's new Animal Park to the old-fashioned mountain mining village of Julian.

Across the border lies the fascination of another country—Mexico. The chapter reports on what to see in several Mexican towns that are a convenient drive from San Diego.

San Diego's greatness *stems in large part from its splendid harbor setting and its salubrious climate.*

San Diego Has Sparkle

San Diego offers plenty to see and do. Many inexpensive recreational activities are easily accessible; some of the finest attractions are free. San Diego County claims more good public bathing beaches (70 miles) than all the rest of California. Boating centers around the harbor and Mission Bay to the north. In the heart of the city are Old Town (the original village) and Balboa Park, location of the San Diego Zoo—largest collection of wild animals in the world.

A sports center, San Diego has major league football, basketball, baseball, hockey, a stadium, and an International Sports Arena. You can play tennis, soar, skin dive, deep-sea fish, or sail any time of the year. Golfers will find that one of the 66 courses will suit them to a tee.

Moving around is easy to do in San Diego. The International Airport (Lindbergh Field) is near downtown; a network of freeways, ringing the city, can take you anywhere within minutes. In about 20 minutes, you've crossed the Southern California border into Mexico or driven up the coast to Del Mar. For the most part, hotels and motels are clustered around the harbor, Mission Bay, Mission Valley, and downtown. Close to major freeways, they are easy to locate. Campers will find a wide selection of sites; one campground will rent whatever you forgot to bring—including the camper.

Visitors can receive specific information by writing to the San Diego Convention and Visitors Bureau, 1200 Third Avenue, San Diego 92101. The bureau publishes a 52-mile motor tour guide to the most interesting attractions. Start anywhere along the route; just follow the yellow and blue road signs bearing a white sea gull.

Biking enthusiasts have a choice of several scenic routes marked by signs along the ocean and through the Presidio and Balboa Park. A new bike trail is under development south along San Diego Bay from the Naval Training Center estuary.

THE WATER WORLD

San Diego should be viewed from the water. The beautiful harbor is a notable exception to the rule that waterfronts are ugly and conceal the fascination of great ships. San Diego's provides both visual and recreational amenities for people against a colorful backdrop of commercial and naval vessels. It offers parks where you may stroll and play, a pier and embankments for fishing, boat launching, a small beach, and places to watch the big ships go by or take a closer look at yachts, tuna clippers, oceanographic crafts, and an antique sailing ship. And it offers thriving complexes of marinas, hotels, shops, and restaurants oriented to a water view.

Harbor Tours

The best way to get your bearings is on a harbor excursion. Both 1 and 2-hour cruises loop close along the shoreline, exposing a full range of air, surface, and undersea craft and harbor activity otherwise hidden from sight. The shorter cruise takes you as far west as Shelter Island and downbay almost to the San Diego-Coronado Bay Bridge. The longer one takes you to the sea at Point Loma and down as far as the Navy's mothball fleet—a 25-mile loop.

Boats leave from the well-marked dock on Harbor Drive at the foot of Broadway. In summer, short cruises leave at 45-minute intervals; 2-hour cruises leave at 10 A.M. and 2 P.M. Prices range from $2 to $3 for adults, half-fare for children. Schedules change during winter months.

Embarcadero

North of the excursion boat dock is the former square-rigger *Star of India*, probably the oldest (1863) iron-hulled merchantman still afloat. Go aboard for a hint of sea life over a century ago. Now painstakingly restored, the ship is moored as a maritime museum. Especially interesting are the captain's and passengers' quarters, grouped around a skylit saloon, and a between-decks museum. It's open daily; there is a nominal admission fee.

Walk north to see some picturesque action on weekdays at the net yard on the seawall dock for long-range tuna clippers. You must stay outside the fence to watch the fishermen mending huge nets.

Don't miss Broadway Pier—San Diego's unique park-on-a-pier—where a lot of net handling takes place and sleek cruise ships are often berthed.

Sport fishermen can board a catamaran out of H & M Landing at the municipal pier (over next to Shelter Island) for half-day trips to the Coronado

Graciously landscaped *San Diego pier brings parklike quality to the commercial waterfront.*

Some bears *beg, some don't at famous zoo.*

Sprawling *in all its Victorian splendor, Del Coronado Hotel is a San Diego landmark.*

"MUST SEES"

BALBOA PARK (downtown San Diego)—setting for museums, galleries, theatres, and zoo

SAN DIEGO ZOO (Balboa Park)—world's largest animal collection in 128 acres. Children's Zoo, Skyfari, and guided bus tour

EMBARCADERO (foot of Broadway)—waterfront activity, tuna clipper net handlers, square rigger and other vessels, a park on a pier, seafood mart, and start of the harbor tour

OLD TOWN (central San Diego off Interstates 5 and 8)—State Historic Park gives views of yesteryear San Diego. Restored adobes; shops and restaurants

MISSION SAN DIEGO DE ALCALA (Interstate 8 to Mission Valley)—oldest of California's missions. Museum with Father Serra's handwritten records

MISSION BAY PARK (Mission Bay)—model city marina containing Sea World, 80-acre

water happening: aquatic shows, exhibits, rides, Japanese pearl-divers, performing killer whale

CABRILLO NATIONAL MONUMENT (tip of Point Loma)—commemorates California's discovery. Lighthouses, museum, major whale-watching point

DEL CORONADO HOTEL (take San Diego-Coronado Bridge)—West's Victorian-style architectural wonder, now a State Historical Landmark. Public tours

TIJUANA (15 minutes south of San Diego on Interstate 5)—gateway to Mexico. Shopping, jai alai, bullfights

TORREY PINES (north of La Jolla, off U.S. 101)—only natural grove of rare pine trees, alive when Cabrillo discovered California

WILD ANIMAL PARK (30 miles north of San Diego off U.S. 395)—animals roam freely in spacious habitat; visitors view from monorail

Islands. Boats leave at 4:30 A.M. and 12:30 P.M. for a 6½-hour fishing cruise. Fares are about $10 for adults, half-fare for youngsters under 13.

Waterfront dining is good along the Embarcadero. A new Mediterranean-style seafood complex offers visitors a choice of buying fresh fish to take home or dining on seafood delicacies. A nearby nautical gift shop posts the tides; the sunset water view from this end of the Embarcadero is one of the town's finest. Try waterfront dining at the nearby foot of G Street, too. In a Latin American gift shop, you can watch a Guatemalan weaver working.

Shelter Island and Harbor Island

Two manmade vacation "islands" in San Diego Bay accommodate boaters, sailors, sportsmen, and atmosphere-seekers. Though they once were mud and sandpiles built up by dredging operations in the bay, Shelter and Harbor islands are now attractive resort areas studded with forests of boat masts.

Shelter Island offers a fishing pier, attractive marinas, boat launching ramps, restaurants, and hotels. Tropical blooms, torches, and "Polynesian" architecture give a South Seas flavor. Winding paths provide good strolling, biking, and bay-watching sports. Friendship Bell is here, the gift of Yokohama, San Diego's sister city in Japan. Really a peninsula, Shelter Island is connected to Point Loma by a salty causeway with marinas, a chandlery, and an art gallery.

Harbor Island, located opposite the San Diego International Airport, can be viewed from a peaceful vantage point in Spanish Landing Park on Harbor Drive. The island features high-rise hotels, restaurants (one a floating riverboat replica with a grand view), and marinas. On the western tip of the island, a Spanish-style building houses a combination lighthouse and restaurant.

The Navy

San Diego is home to the large 11th Naval District, as well as to many other military installations. Though no longer known primarily as a Navy town, San Diego is still influenced by the activities that the Navy brings.

The Naval Training Center Museum, with models, paintings, photographs, and maritime paraphernalia, is open to the public from Monday through Friday. It can be reached by following Interstate 5 to Rosecrans Avenue; use Gate 3. Naval vessels moored at the Broadway or Navy piers on Harbor Drive also hold open house on weekend afternoons once a month.

Parade watchers can attend a full-fledged, colorful military review any Friday afternoon in San Diego at either Naval or Marine centers. Parades begin about 2:30 P.M. at the Naval Training Center and at 3:30 P.M. at the Marine Corps Recruiting Depot, located off Pacific Highway; go southwest on Barnett Avenue and enter Gate 4.

Coronado

Coronado's relative isolation gives it the flavor of an island. Actually it's connected to the mainland by a long, scenic sand spit and a graceful bay bridge. Low guard rails on the sweeping span open up a panoramic view reaching from San Diego skyline south into Mexico.

Coronado was a sterile, wind-blown peninsula, populated with jackrabbits, coyotes, and occasional wildcats, when Elisha Babcock and H. L. Story bought the 4,100 acres (including North Island) in 1885. Babcock's dream — to build a hotel that "would be the talk of the Western world" — came true in the form of the striking, red-roofed Hotel del Coronado, still operating as the focal point of this area and now a State Historical Landmark. Distinguished guests over the years have included several United States presidents, Thomas A. Edison, Henry Ford, and Robert Todd Lincoln. Legend has it that here the Duke of Windsor met the Duchess when she was Mrs. Wally Spencer, wife of the commanding officer of North Island, and he was the Prince of Wales.

Tours of this Victorian-styled, wooden wonder begin at 2 P.M. every Saturday. From the lobby, a guide leads you through intricate corridors and cavernous rooms. The hotel resembles an ocean liner in its complexity. You'll see basement kitchens big enough for a small city, rooms rich in handcrafted wood joinery and carving, and a gilded openwork elevator, as well as the Hall of History and interior garden court. The hotel rests almost entirely upon massive rain cisterns used during World War II to protect a treasure of antiques. A new 7-story addition, fronting on the ocean, also houses a large convention center.

Across from the hotel, a picturesque boathouse (now a restaurant, designed to match the Victorian architectural style of the hotel) sits at the edge of Glorietta Bay, a small boat harbor that contains a public launching ramp. Adjoining it is a municipal golf course and a public bathing beach (caution: watch for stingrays early in the season). At the north end of the peninsula is the Naval Air Station, one of the oldest in existence.

Silver Strand State Beach, one of America's finest day use beaches, occupies almost the full length of the long sand spit that connects the tip of the peninsula to the mainland at Imperial Beach.

Millions of tiny, glittering seashells gave their name to this 5-mile-long ocean beach. There is some clamming, fair surf fishing, and a notably good grunion run.

The sand is dotted with nearly 400 fire rings and picnic units; the parking lot has space for almost 2,000 cars, and the climate is almost always very good.

Pedestrian underpasses cross beneath State 75 to the bay side, where there is quieter water, good for swimmers and water-skiers.

Point Loma

The high promontory that shelters San Diego Bay from the Pacific Ocean offers a great view of the harbor. On a clear day you can see a panorama reaching from the mountains of Mexico to those far beyond the mesa of La Jolla and from the

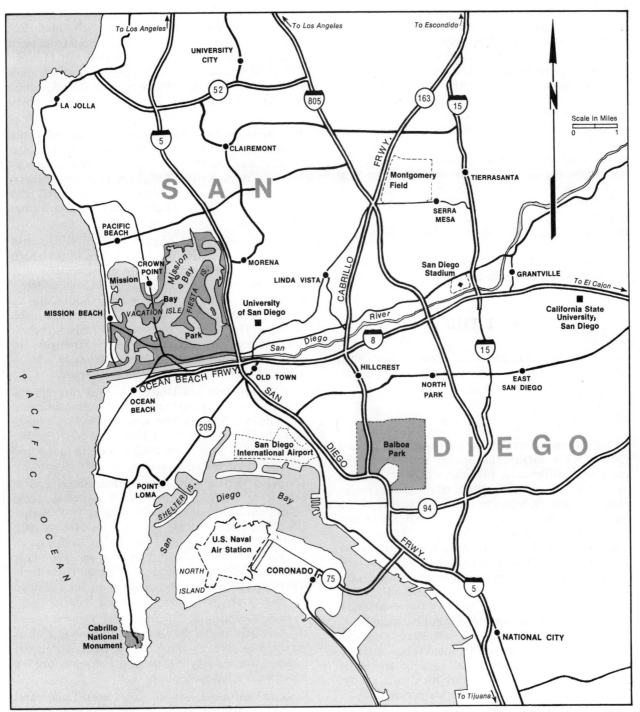

This San Diego area map *reveals much about the city: its long coastline; generous recreational areas (Mission Bay, Balboa Park); major north-south (I-5) and east-west (State 8) freeways.*

sprawling city of San Diego to the Coronado Islands and out to sea.

At the tip of Point Loma is Cabrillo National Monument, one of the smallest, most historic, and most visited monuments in this country (outdoing even the Statue of Liberty).

Cabrillo's statue, a gift from Portugal (homeland of the great navigator), faces his actual landing spot at Ballast Point, and the nearby Visitor Center explains the discovery and events following it. On the high bluff, a lighthouse built in 1854 appears just as the lightkeeper left it years ago. This is one of Southern California's great whale-watching points in winter and early spring.

The monument has a nature trail, a surprisingly unique plant community, and some of the best tide-pools left in Southern California (marine biologists invite you to look but not touch). It is open daily from 9 A.M. to 5:15 P.M. To reach the monument from San Diego, go southwest on Rosecrans Street and follow the signs; from Mission Bay, take Sunset Cliffs Boulevard to Catalina Boulevard.

A drive through residential Point Loma takes you past the U. S. Navy reservation and through Fort Rosecrans. Near the military gate at Silvergate Avenue and Rosecroft Lane are the famous Rosecroft Begonia Gardens, in bloom from June to October. Admission is 25 cents.

A LOOK AT THE PAST

As California's first link with history, San Diego preserves and celebrates her past so that it remains alive in a modern metropolis.

Old Town

In 1769, Father Serra chose a hill site overlooking the bay for a mission that would begin the settlement of California. A presidio was also built to protect the mission; this site is now called Presidio Hill. Soon a town began to sprout at the foot of the hill, with a plaza, a church, and the attractive tile-roofed, adobe homes of California's first families.

Spanish, Mexican, and American settlements thrived here; buildings and relics of these periods survive, some being restored or reconstructed with adobe bricks shaped at the same site which furnished the original bricks. Much of the restoration is within Old Town San Diego State Historic Park, an area of 6½ blocks bounded by Wallace, Congress, Twiggs, and Juan streets. Old Town is bordered by old residential areas and two modern freeways, Interstates 5 and 8. Its streets are for strolling only; leave your car in a lot at the park's perimeter.

Old Town is no sterile museum display; shops and restaurants are often housed in existing build-ings and patios. Shopping, once confined mainly to San Diego Avenue, has been broadened by the addition of Bazaar del Mundo, a cluster of shops remodeled from a former Mediterranean-style motel that faces the plaza. Set around a garden, these shops are of better than usual quality. You can eat in a Mexican restaurant or visit a delicatessen in the Farmer's Market for cheeses, wines, and picnic makings. Here, visitors will rub shoulders with shopping San Diegans.

Walking is the best way to savor the historical flavor. Do it on your own or take a tour from park headquarters on Wallace Street (daily at 11 A.M.; 2:30 P.M. on weekends). Historical Society tours depart from Whaley House on San Diego Avenue at 1:30 P.M. Saturdays. Both tours are free. These are some of the Old Town sights you'll see:

El Campo Santo, at San Diego and Linwood, is the easternmost landmark in Old Town. This adobe-walled, Mexican Catholic cemetery (1850-1880) was the final resting place for many founding fathers, as well as for a few bandits. It's hard to tell how many were buried here because so many headstones are missing.

The Whaley House, corner of San Diego and Harney, is the oldest brick structure in Southern California. The American-style mansion, the only one of its kind in San Diego, served as a dairy, funeral parlor, theater, saloon, courthouse, and as the city's first Sunday school. It is reputed to be haunted. The restored house and premises, including such historical relics as a yellow streetcar, are open Wednesday through Sunday from 10 A.M. to 4:30 P.M. A small admission fee is charged.

The Derby-Pendleton House (entered through the Whaley House) is perhaps the first prefabricated building in California. The New England-style home was shipped around Cape Horn and put together with wooden pegs. Now a museum, its hours and admission fee are like those at Whaley House.

Chapel of Immaculate Conception, San Diego at Conde, was Old Town's first church, converted from an old adobe house and dedicated in 1858. Father Ubach, in charge of the parish from 1866 to 1907, brought the first organ to San Diego. Well known for his work with the Indians, he was reputedly the original "Father Gaspara" of Helen Hunt Jackson's novel *Ramona*—he claimed to have known the characters in the story and their families.

Casa de Altamirano, San Diego and Twiggs, site of the first printing of the San Diego *Union* in 1868, is restored as an early day printing office. Originally a home, the building was used as a store before the newspaper's location there.

Casa de Pedrorena, San Diego between Twiggs and Mason, is a large, restored adobe that is now a popular Mexican restaurant with a courtyard.

Is Whale Watching your Cup of Tea?

Off Point Loma, *an experienced boat captain steers close to southbound whales. Note (at left) giant tail flukes of a submerging whale.*

California's great gray whales cruise close to the Southern California coast each winter on their way from the Bering Sea to calving grounds in the Gulf of California, a 6000-mile migration. Watching the 40 to 50-foot creatures (weighing about a ton a foot) swimming steadily along at about 4 knots is an exciting experience.

The best place to watch on land is at Point Cabrillo National Monument on Point Loma in San Diego. During the season (December to early February), you'll see them pass by in "pods" of two or three within a half-mile of shore. At this exposed location, an observer can track a single whale for an hour or more. At the lookout station, you can see a whale display, listen to a recorded message telling the story of the migration, or use a coin-operated telescope. In the Visitor Center, a film is shown several times a day.

A good pair of field glasses is a whale-watcher's best friend at this vantage point or at Point Dume, the Palos Verdes Peninsula, Laguna Beach, or La Jolla.

For a closer look, take a charter boat trip from San Diego, Mission Bay, Dana Point, Newport Harbor, San Pedro, Marineland, or Redondo Beach. Call in advance for trip information, for their schedules follow the whales.

After you spot a whale's tail, watch next for the spout, a vapor exhaled from the animal's lungs. From three to five successive spouts usually signal a dive that will cover about 1,000 feet of horizontal distance in about three or four minutes; more spouts signal a longer dive.

Casa de Estudillo, east of San Diego on Mason, built of logs and rawhide on a lot granted by the governor, was the home of Captain Jose Estudillo, commandante of Monterey and San Diego. The first Spanish *casa* to be constructed on the plaza, it was robbed of roof tiles and reduced to ruin after the family left in 1881. Extensively restored, the house and garden afford a glimpse of how a comparatively wealthy rancher lived.

Casa de Bandini, at Mason and Calhoun, originally a one-story adobe, had its second story added when it became a stagecoach station in the 1860s. Built by wealthy Don Juan Bandini (known for his lavish fandangos and dinners), the house was Stockton's headquarters during the American occupation in 1846. Kit Carson also visited here.

Plaza Vieja, or San Diego Plaza, was the center of town. A comfortable and verdant stop for walkers today, it was once the noisy scene of bullfights and other entertainments. Among the lacy pepper, eucalyptus, and graceful palm trees stands the flagpole that has flown Spanish and Mexican flags for two centuries; the American flag was added in 1846.

Casa de Machado, San Diego between Wallace and Mason, was built in 1832 as the home of a Spanish Army soldier and his wife. Scarcity of wood required use of adobe in most of the early homes, and here you can see some of the original bricks, formed and placed by the good soldier Machado.

The Mason Street School, west of San Diego on Mason, was San Diego's first public school building. When replaced, the quaint one-room schoolhouse became a tamale factory. Now back at its original location, it displays mementos of the early San Diego school system.

The Machado-Steward House, on Congress between Wallace and Mason, was built by Jose Manuel Machado for his daughter, who married John C. Stewart, a shipmate of Richard Dana. Dana describes his visit to the house in 1859 in *Two Years Before the Mast.* In contrast to the Estudillo residence, this small clapboard adobe displays how a man of moderate means may have lived.

The Seeley Stable and barns, corner of Juan and Twiggs, is Old Town's newest attraction. A replica of the stables of Albert Seeley, stagecoach-line operator circa 1869, the stable will serve as the Roscoe Hazard Museum, housing a collection of horse-drawn vehicles and Western artifacts.

Casa de Lopez, a longtime local favorite sometimes called Flynn's House of 10,000 Candles, is a State Historical Landmark at the deadend of Twiggs Street. Walk-through tours are conducted daily.

Visitors will find the flavor of Old Town one of its fascinations: bread baking in the outdoor oven behind the Machado house on Saturday, brick making, candle dipping, wool spinning, and horse-and-buggy rides (for a slight fee).

Presidio Hill

Just five years after Father Junipero Serra and the Spanish soldiers set the Royal Standard, raised the cross, and dedicated the first mission in California, the site was already too small for the mission's growing members. Because of the need for fresh water and in order to be closer to Indian settlements, Mission San Diego was moved in 1774 from Presidio Hill 6 miles east up Mission Valley. The presidio and the old American garrison (Fort Stockton) have long been covered over. Their foundations are outlined in the mounds of grass on the hill. Diggings in the area are archeological excavations.

The birthplace of California is now the home of handsome Serra Museum, a Spanish Colonial structure; lush Presidio Park; and the Serra Cross, made of bricks from Spanish ruins and marking the site of the original mission chapel.

Standing prominently at the head of the hill and gleaming white in the sun, the Serra Museum exhibits the area's history from mission days through pioneer times. Although the museum is only open daily from 10 A.M. to 5:30 P.M. (except Monday), sunrise or sunset is a beautiful time to walk about the subtly shadowed walls and take in the view of Mission Bay, Point Loma, Mission Valley, and Old Town.

At Presidio Park a wonderfully green, scenic place to picnic and relax is either on top of the hill or in the palm canyon next to it. From the canyon, hiking trails wind to the top of the historic hill.

Mission San Diego de Alcala

The San Diego Mission was the first in the long line of missions built in Alta (upper) California.

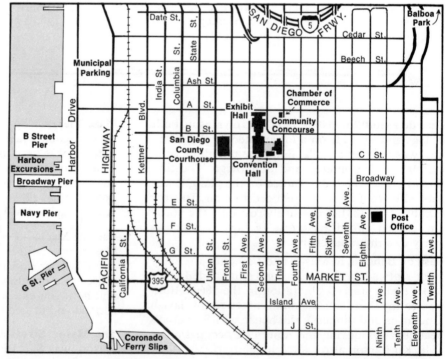

Downtown San Diego is compact—an efficient mix of business, governmental, and cultural buildings.

The restoration of the "Mother of the Missions" retains the graceful and simple facade of the original mission and is characterized by a strikingly graceful campanile. Here you'll discover a museum, containing original mission records in Father Serra's handwriting; a reconstructed Indian village; and olive trees from the original grove planted at the early mission.

Sunday services are still held in the original chapel. The mission is open to the public from 9 A.M. to 5 P.M. daily; guides are available.

California's dramatic heritage is no better depicted than in the impressive missions representative of Spanish religious and colonial fervor. Four such monuments to the early Franciscans exist in San Diego County: Missions San Diego and San Luis Rey and their *asistencias* (branches), Pala and Santa Ysabel. San Diego Mission is best reached on Interstate 8 to Murphy Canyon Road; watch for mission exit signs.

DOWNTOWN SAN DIEGO

Once a collection of tattoo parlors, saloons, and pawn shops, downtown San Diego is gradually being restored and rebuilt. As the city's skyline grows upwards, restaurants are being opened atop buildings to take advantage of the view.

Although many large stores have moved out to Mission Valley, the central part of the city is cleaning up its stores, streets, and parks and creating new pedestrian malls.

Walking in downtown San Diego is the best way to get the feeling of this changing city. Central City Association, 631 Home Tower Building (Broadway at 7th) offers a free pictorial map.

Horton Plaza (bounded by 3rd, 4th, Broadway, and E streets) is a good place to start. A green oasis, it is home for open-air art shows, soapbox orators, and people-watchers. You can catch a bus to Tijuana from here. A visitor information booth is open during the day to answer questions or provide material about the city and the surrounding area.

The Plaza is the center for a 15-block restoration project, designed to help facelift San Diego. Adjacent to this redevelopment is a projected 8-block Gaslight Quarter, which will eventually be a major tourist attraction. Across the street from the Plaza is the U. S. Grant Hotel, one of San Diego's oldest and best known.

Any walking tour should include a look at the ornate calendar clock in front of J. Jessop & Sons. It won a design award in 1905.

The Charles C. Dail Concourse (formerly Community Concourse) is one of the major attractions in the downtown area. The concourse covers more

Mission San Diego de Alcala, *the first in the California mission chain, has simple, graceful lines.*

than a full city block (bounded by A and C streets and 1st and 3rd avenues). It includes a Convention and Performing Arts Center, as well as the City Administration Building. The 3,000-seat Civic Theatre is home for the San Diego Symphony and San Diego Opera Company and host to hundreds of dramatic and musical events throughout the year. A huge car parking facility tops the concourse, and additional parking is available nearby.

Westgate Plaza Hotel, at 2nd and C streets, is one of the world's leading caravansaries and one of the very few new hotels to be built in the heart of a city. A true luxury hotel, it's full of "wasted" space and such "wasteful" appurtenances as Aubusson tapestries, Baccarat crystal chandeliers, and famous paintings. It's worth a stop to look at the lobby, a re-creation of an anteroom at Versailles.

The San Diego Public Library, at the corner of 8th and E streets, is one of the most modern and well-stocked libraries in the country. It's open daily except Sunday. Its collection goes back 4,000 years to Sumerian cuneiform tablets (though you can't withdraw them on your library card).

Most of the stock brokerage houses are in the area of 3rd and B streets in new, ultramodern buildings. If you plan to peek in, remember that, because of the time difference between here and the East Coast, trading begins and ends early.

Elaborate facade *of Casa del Prado is stunning sight in Balboa Park.*

Shakespeare *is revived each summer at Balboa Park's Old Globe Theatre.*

For a bird's-eye view of San Diego, take the outside glass elevator at the El Cortez Hotel (7th and Ash) to the Starlite Roof. It's open daily for lunch, dinner, and dancing.

San Diego is beginning to restore some of her fine Victorian mansions. Villa Montezuma, considered one of the finest of this period, has been partially renovated, refurbished, and opened for public tours from 1 to 4:30 P.M., Tuesday through Friday, and on Sunday. It's located at 1925 K Street.

SAN DIEGO'S TWO GREAT PARKS

Two of the city's most outstanding attractions are examples of careful planning and foresight. Balboa Park, conceived in the 1880s, and Mission Bay Aquatic Park, developed a century later, are destinations for millions of tourists yearly.

The restored elegance of Balboa Park

The park came first. Then they built the city around it. Transformed from rattlesnake-infested, hilly chaparral to a public garden with sky-high eucalyptus trees, lush tropical plants and Mexican Churriqueresque buildings—this is century-old Balboa Park, one of the nation's greatest. Avenues curving through verdant foliage and grassy fields take you to almost any recreational or cultural activity you might seek: art galleries, museums of science and natural history, an innovative space theater, the world's largest zoo, a merry-go-round, a picnic grove, a golf course.

Optimism and foresight helped shape Balboa Park. In 1868, the city fathers set aside 1,400 acres (nine large lots at a time when the city had only 915 houses) "to be forever a public park." For 20 years the unimproved land supported a dog pound, trash dump, and gravel pit until horticulturist Kate Sessions set up a nursery on a few acres in exchange for doing a considerable planting in other areas of the park. By 1910, community planning and action had formed a park.

Two world's fairs added the massive and ornate structures for which the park is known. The 1915 Panama-California International Exposition, commemorating the completion of the Panama Canal, attracted 3 million visitors and is survived by the attractive Cabrillo Bridge (through which most out-of-town visitors enter the park) and much of the cultural center along the Prado area, still the park's center of activity. The Spreckels Pavilion contains the world's largest outdoor organ. Donated in 1915, it has provided Sunday recitals ever since. Built as the only permanent structure of this fair, the unique California Building (home of the Museum of Man), with its familiar Spanish-Renaissance tower rising above the treetops and its facade decorated with statues depicting California history, has become the symbol of the city of San Diego.

In 1935, the California-Pacific International Exposition contributed a series of structures representative of Southwest history. Added then was the building complex south of the Prado known as the Palisades area, as well as the Old Globe Theatre and the Spanish Village.

Four million visitors a year sample the attractions at Balboa Park, and countless more stroll the beautiful paths and picnic in special groves or on the lawns. You can spend an active or a leisurely day here. Walking is the best way to enjoy the lovely park, since the latest phase of development has now closed half of the Prado (east of the central plaza in front of the Fine Arts Gallery) to cars during the day, creating a new pedestrian promenade. At the Prado's east end is a spacious new plaza with an enormous fountain; at its west end is the Museum of Man.

Scattered throughout the broad mesa tops and canyons are plenty of recreation spots: golf and tennis, field and target archery, baseball, roque, lawn bowls, shuffleboard, horseshoes, badminton.

You enter Balboa Park from either 6th Avenue and Laurel Street or Park Boulevard and El Prado. There's parking in big lots in the Palisades area, at the zoo, and along Park Boulevard.

On the Plaza along El Prado, the House of Hospitality has free maps and information on the park. These are some of the major attractions:

The Museum of Man is known for its research on Indian culture of the Americas. Comprehensive exhibits of Mexican history are notable. It is open daily from 10 A.M. to 4:45 P.M.; admission is 50 cents.

The Old Globe Theatre, in a grove behind the California Building, was built for Shakespearean productions. Pre-performance entertainment on the green lends an Old English fair atmosphere to the three-month summer festival. Part of the complex is the Cassius Carter Centre Stage, an intimate, arena-style hall. Both theaters operate year-round.

The House of Charm, located on the west side of Plaza de Panama, has a model railroad (operating Sundays), exhibits of the Art Institute, and the Hall of Champions, a sports museum.

The Fine Arts Gallery, center for the arts in San Diego, maintains a fine collection of old masters, in addition to traveling exhibits. A small sculpture court has been enlarged by an adjoining garden, a large display area for some distinguished sculpted pieces. Located on the north side of the plaza, the gallery is open Tuesday through Saturday from 10 A.M. to 5 P.M. and on Sunday afternoons.

If you like art, you'll want to see the superb Old Master collection at the Timken Gallery.

Aerospace Museum exhibits represent pioneer flight days through the space age. The collection of gliders, planes, and space hardware is impressive but crowded. A move into larger quarters is being considered. It's open daily except Monday from 10 A.M. to 4:30 P.M.

Casa del Prado (next to the Botanical Building), a complex of buildings, arcades, and courtyards, is a replacement completed in 1971 for the decrepit Food and Beverage Building from the 1915 exposition. Casts of existing plaster ornamentation were made for reproduction in permanent materials.

The Natural History Museum has something for all kinds of explorers. Extensive exhibits and a large research library fascinate visitors, and bi-monthly nature walks attract adventurers. Ask at the museum for a self-guided horticultural walk around the Prado. This museum on Southern California environment opens from 10 A.M. to 4:30 P.M. daily.

The Reuben H. Fleet Space Theater and Science Center is the park's newest addition. In the theater, the screen is a tilted hemisphere; image and sound surround you. Not confined to showing the sky as seen from earth, its computer-controlled system of more than 80 projectors takes you into space, past planets, in view of stars changing configuration as you move. In the adjoining science center, you operate ingenious gadgets demonstrating principles of sensory perception. Listen to your heartbeat; look at the inside of your eye; create pop art with a harmonograph; or match wits with a computerized teaching machine. It's open daily from 10 A.M. to 5 P.M. and from 7 to 9:30 P.M.

San Diego Zoo is extraordinary. Here the world's largest collection of wild animals lives in surroundings as natural as man can provide. Lions roam

Colorful, convenient Skyfari *at San Diego Zoo gives visitors overall view of animals and Balboa Park.*

freely on the other side of good-sized moats, and exotic birds fly free in a tropical rain forest. You may even see a guinea fowl strutting independently on the walk, helping hold down the insect population. This manmade jungle holds some of the rarest animals in the world.

High above the zoo canyons, an aerial tramway called Skyfari whisks you on an exciting 5-minute ride over the grottos and mesas that are home for the animals in this cageless zoo. The Skyfari leaves near the zoo entrance over a lagoon colored by Chilean flamingos and black swans, rises over the nearby seal show (free performances in the afternoon), and travels above the active and popular residents of the Great Ape Grottos in Monkey Mesa. When you're not looking closely at animal activity beneath you, you can enjoy a spectacular overview of Balboa Park.

The orange gondolas reach their highest point of 170 feet over Stork and Crane Canyon and terminate at Horn and Hoof Mesa, where inhabitants include antelope, bison, kangaroos, and wallabies. If you do not choose to make the return immediately, you can disembark here and tour the western end of the zoo before returning by tramway or walking back along the zoo's winding pathways. The skyride one-way costs 50 cents for adults and 25 cents for children under 12.

On the ground, you can see the 128-acre zoo on a guided tour bus that takes in 3½ miles, including areas not easily reached by walking. You can save steps and time this way, planning where you'd like to revisit and also catching a performance by stage-struck bears or other animals that are cued by your guide. The guide's lively commentary almost puts you on a first name basis with the animals. The 40-minute bus ride is $1 for adults, half price for those under 12.

The zoo remains open all year in San Diego's mild climate. Your visit takes you on pleasant meandering paths through rare tropical and sub-tropical plantings that have become a famous botanical garden. This stunning horticultural collection is worth as much as the prized animal exhibits. The deep canyons of the zoo are linked with upper levels by two of the world's longest moving sidewalks, saving you the climb.

Look for picnic groves north and south of the zoo entrance, a restaurant near the entrance, and refreshment stands throughout the park. The zoo is open daily from 9 A.M. to dusk, though the admission gates close at 6 P.M. in the summer and earlier the rest of the year.

The Children's Zoo, a wonderful zoo within a zoo, puts the 4-year-old nose to nose with the animal kingdom's younger members. Benches and drinking fountains are also appropriately scaled down. Garden paths wind through an aviary in which tiny, colorful finches fly overhead and perch in nearby branches and birdhouses, past swimming turtles to the baby elephants begging peanuts. A cuddly but lazy koala sleeps in the V of a tree, a tolerant Galapagos tortoise offers a ride on his great hulking shell, and friendly little deer and barnyard animals come to be petted and fed by their equally friendly little visitors. One of the most delightful attractions is the small hatchery where you can watch baby chicks peck out of their shells. If you wish, you may hold some of the fluffy yellow newborns in your hands. Another treat is the nursery for baby animals unable to be cared for by their mothers. You're apt to see diapered infant chimps and orangutans romping in playpens with their toys, anticipating the bottle of milk administered by nurse attendants. Signs identify the "babies" as to name (one such is "John Gorilla"), birthdate, weight, feeding and sleeping schedule.

The Children's Zoo, a short walk past the aerial tramway, opens at 9:30 A.M. There is a small admission charge.

Mission Bay Aquatic Park

Mission Bay, now a beautiful aquatic playground right on the edge of downtown San Diego, was once a vast and productive estuary, home for resident waterfowl, resting place for migratory birds, and nursery for fish and other sea creatures. Originally named "False Bay" when Cabrillo mistook it for San Diego Bay, it degenerated into a silt and trash collector, popular as a fishing hole for those who could brave the mosquitoes until later-day community action transformed it into one of the most beautiful resort areas on the coast.

Twenty years of dredging and development has created a maze of islands and lagoons, 27 miles of beaches, free public boat-launching ramps, picnic areas, campgrounds and trailer park, children's playgrounds, golf courses, a marine park, and miles of beautifully landscaped, grass-covered coves.

The hotels of Mission Bay are worth seeing for their unusual architectural qualities, as well as for their location. Many have now gone high-rise to take advantage of the view. Vacation Village makes extensive use of streams and lagoons for landscaping. The San Diego Visitor Information Center, just off Interstate 5 at Mission Bay Drive, provides information on hotels and maps of the park. Reservations are a "must" during peak summer months and three-day holiday weekends.

Vacationers who like to "rough it" can easily settle in at Campland, on the north shore by way of Olney Street. Here resort-equipped campsites renting for $4.50 to $6.50 a night (depending on the season) are near a parking area for boats, a swimming beach, and complete rental facilities (from campers and bedding to boats and skis). You can reserve a campsite for up to two weeks by writing to Mission Bay Campland, Inc., 2211 Pacific Beach Drive, San Diego 92109.

Water sports are Mission Bay's reason for being. At the many marinas, visitors can rent paddle boats or ocean-going sloops—any type of boat they desire. Traffic on the bay is organized so that one water activity is separated from another. Water skiers use a 1½-mile course with several beaches reserved as pick-up and landing areas; power boats roar over the same 3-mile course used by hydroplanes and competition speedboats during organized races; sailboats reign in the western cove of the bay. Small racing sloops, tiny dinghys, exotic outriggers, and swift catamarans dart across the cove all year long.

Fishing is enjoyed from a comfortable lawn chair on the beach, from a small skiff, or from the deck of a sportfishing boat. Within the bay, fishermen land halibut, flounder, bass, croaker, and perch.

Sea World makes a big splash. San Diego's fascinating aquatic park within a park is one of the world's largest oceanariums, featuring some popular added attractions as well. Besides outstanding aquarium exhibits and a variety of water shows, you'll find a Japanese Village, a sky tower, an aerial tram and hydrofoil boats.

Water show stars include Shamu, a remarkably agile black and white killer whale; Google, a trained elephant seal weighing 1½ tons; a water-skiing chimpanzee; and a penguin on skates. At the Water Fantasy Show, colorful lights and explosive dancing fountains perform like fireworks set to music. All shows are free. Presented on the hour and half-hour, they average 20 minutes in length; to see them all, consult your time schedule and the map distributed at the gate.

The Sky Tower ride, highest of its kind in the United States, makes slow turns up and down its 320 feet, giving you an unobstructed 360° view of Mission Bay and surrounding territory. The Skyride tram takes you up 70 feet over the waters of Mission Bay to the Atlantis Restaurant, where you can stop for lunch or sightseeing.

Hydrofoil boats zoom over the bay's famous speed course at up to 30 miles per hour. A ride costs

Hydrofoil *skims along at 30 knots out of Sea World into Mission Bay's water-ski area.*

Seventy-foot-high *aerial tram crosses Mission Bay from Sea World to Atlantis Restaurant.*

60 cents for adults, 35 cents for children under 12. If you plan to go on more than one ride, save money by purchasing combination tickets.

An exotic feature of Sea World is the Japanese Village, which flies the giant Koinobori fish kite. Here Japanese pearl divers will retrieve a pearl-bearing oyster for you from the bottom of the pool. You can have the pearl extracted on the spot and mounted into jewelry. Pause for tea and cookies in the pavilion.

Walking through mature gardens between the arenas and exhibits, visiting the manmade tidepool, and shooting pictures at pre-picked spots will be a pleasant part of your visit. Sea World's horticultural exhibitions, like the San Diego Zoo's, are outstanding. If you need to, rent a whale stroller for the small ones and check out the diaper changing facilities on your map before you begin your stroll. It takes about 5 hours to see all the park, open daily from 10 A.M. until dusk. One-time admission ranges from around $4 for adults to $2 for children over 3. Sea World is on Perez Cove at the southern edge of Mission Bay Park; follow Sea World Drive.

UP THE COAST

Many of the area's attractions are located north of San Diego—off Interstate 5 and along the coast on State 21, as well as inland on U.S. 395 and State 78. You could make a fast loop trip in one day, but you may want to take more time to visit quaint seaside communities, flower fields, a famous biological institution, an oceanographic museum, rare Torrey Pines, and the large San Diego Wild Animal Park.

Captivating La Jolla

Fronting the sparkling Pacific and its broad beaches and built over beautiful coves, caves, and cliffs, La Jolla is aptly named. It means "hole" or "caves," according to the Indians who once lived there, but the usual interpretation today is from the Spanish word meaning "jewel" or "gem." La Jolla is not a touristy place. It is the quiet edge of the big city of San Diego, a 5-mile section of Mediterranean California at its most beguiling.

If you come north from the main part of San Diego—as most visitors are likely to do—the quick way is by Interstate 5, taking Ardath Road exit. You can also drive the older, longer route up La Jolla Boulevard from Pacific Beach. Neither route reveals much of the La Jolla experience, which begins when you get out of your car.

Most visitors come during the foggy summer months, but La Jolla reserves its greatest charm for those who visit from fall through spring.

The sea beauty of La Jolla is the reason for everything else here. You'll find all the beach pleasures: swimming, diving, surfing, rock fishing, tidepool exploring, beach walking.

Offshore you see the fishing party boats that come here from Mission Bay to probe the kelp beds or the deep, cold waters of the submarine canyons.

The beaches are a magnet here, and every beach has a character of its own. Some vary considerably with the tides, as well as with the seasons. Below Prospect Street, which curves through the heart of the old village, the beaches nuzzle under sandstone bluffs in a series of small crescents and coves. If you stand on the sidewalk on Coast Boulevard and look over the railing above La Jolla Cove (the northernmost of the beaches below the city proper), you'll see why it has been a favorite for years of sunbathers, swimmers, and skin and scuba divers. Intimate and protected, it has a gentle surf. The clear water and undersea gardens hold such prizes as spiny lobster and abalone. On the bluff above the cove is Ellen Browning Scripps Park, where you can stroll green lawns or sit and enjoy the sea air, watching the beach below.

South of Boomer Beach (ideal for the expert body surfer) and connected to the park and the cove by a promenade is the Children's Pool. This small beach has a curving breakwater that keeps the surf gentle enough for small children.

At the foot of Bonair Street is Windansea Beach, celebrated as one of the best places on the coast for surfing. Swimming here can be dangerous.

To visit one of the La Jolla caves, go to the end of Coast Boulevard and enter through a curio shop, descending 133 wooden stairs (not recommended for the infirm). You pay a small admission charge. Just seaward of the cave entrance, a bluff-top trail (part of an ecological reserve) runs easterly through about a half mile of semiwild city park past a rocky gorge called Devil's Slide. The view of La Jolla Bay is spectacular from this sometimes dizzying overlook. Close by, on the sheer face of the cliffs, you'll see birds—cormorants, pelicans, sea-gulls—watching the waters for fish.

There's no beach at the foot of these cliffs. You have to get well north of the village before you see the second kind of La Jolla beach—wide, hard-packed sand with shallow water some distance out. Kellogg Park and the La Jolla Shores Beach are public and equipped with fire rings, play equipment, rest rooms, showers, and a lifeguard all year. The southern part of the beach is reserved for swimming, the northern for surfing. The private La Jolla Beach and Tennis Club, with its Spanish architecture of the 1930s and striped beach tents reminiscent of F. Scott Fitzgerald novels, marks the south end of this stretch of beach.

Exploring the village should please you. The charm of La Jolla today owes much to its isolated setting on a natural peninsula bounded by Mt. Soledad

La Jolla Cove *has been a favorite of swimmers and divers since town was settled as resort around 1886.*

Diver enters *La Jolla's intriguing undersea gardens. Caves in cliff walls are inviting.*

and the ocean and to the efforts of its tradition-minded citizens. Residential-scale buildings, mature trees, brilliant tropical flowers, and the old tower of La Valencia Hotel fit into the context of the classic old resort town.

La Jolla is for strolling. Parking places are almost impossible to find; the layout of the streets is confusing; pedestrian traffic is erratic. Although the main street (Girard Avenue) has as wide a selection of shopping as you'll find anywhere in San Diego, the best walking is along the mile or so of Prospect Street from the cottage shops and plazas on the north to the museum on the south. Shops range in character from one specializing in understated tweedery to one selling Scandinavian imports. The varied restaurants here often occupy old houses; several have a sea view. The popular old La Valencia Hotel offers meals indoors or out, along with a view from the tower. The La Jolla Museum of Contemporary Arts fits well into this community of many artists. Hours are from 11 A.M. to 5 P.M. Tuesday through Friday, 12:30 to 5 P.M. on weekends; Wednesday evenings. Tours are at 1:30 P.M. on Wednesday, Saturday, and Sunday.

Sherwood Hall, adjacent to the museum, is active year-round with productions by the La Jolla Civic Orchestra, lectures, films, stage plays, ballets, and other cultural events. Here, too, are found the University of California, San Diego, and the Salk Institute.

Scripps Institution

La Jolla is world-famed as the center for research on the secrets of the sea. Located on the pier north of La Jolla Shores Beach is Scripps Institution of Oceanography, well known for its ocean study and now part of the University of California at San Diego. The aquarium museum offers studies of tide motion, archeology, and beach lore. Hours are from 9 A.M. to 5 P.M. daily. Admission is free; there's a small fee for parking. The pier is not open to the public.

The beach around Scripps Pier is a favorite for swimming, and you'll probably see considerable surfing action north of it.

The San Diego-La Jolla Underwater Park was established near Scripps to preserve the shoreline and underwater life of La Jolla Canyon. Buoys and shore markers define the limits of the reserve.

Torrey Pines Mesa

The expanding edge of La Jolla is a former wilderness thick with groves of eucalyptus and unique stands of the rare Torrey Pines. Torrey Pines Road

Wild ducks *and geese socialize with domestic birds at Buena Vista Lagoon, just north of Carlsbad.*

Soaring gliders *are in action every weekend near 300-foot cliffs at Torrey Pines Park, near La Jolla.*

takes you from La Jolla up onto the mesa to join the old coast highway. Set in the thickest of the eucalyptus forests is the University of California at San Diego. Drive through the campus and visit the art museum at Revelle College.

At the top of North Torrey Pines Road, just past La Jolla Farms, the surrealistic city of concrete that rises above the trees is the Salk Institute for Biological Studies. Named for Dr. Jonas Salk, it was founded in the hope that scholars from different disciplines—including the arts—could move toward an understanding of life. The exterior has been called the most powerful architectural statement on the West Coast. Guaranteed to make you react, it creates a proper setting for the energetic study that takes place inside. Tours are offered on Monday through Friday from 10:30 A.M. to 3 P.M.

Next to the Institute is an active sail plane area where, on weekends, you can watch the pleasant sport of soaring—and often hang gliding—over the waves. A little farther north are two municipal golf courses. Even if you don't golf, you can have lunch at the restaurant (the only one on the mesa) with its grand view of the ocean. The complex also includes a comfortable motel.

Torrey Pines State Reserve protects some rare trees. The only natural grove of Torrey Pines in the world grows along the ocean in this area and on Santa Rosa Island 195 miles away. The rare pines in this beautiful, wind-shaped area are gnarled relics of the Ice Age. The slanting trees were clinging to the eroded yellow sandstone cliffs when Cabrillo's ships first sighted California in 1542.

Occupying the whole northern tip of the mesa, the park is reached by N. Torrey Pines Road. It is a good place for family hiking, having well-marked trails and picnic facilities. To hike along the ocean, use the north entrance to the park off U.S. 101. For beach hiking, consult a tide table to avoid being caught by rising waters.

Torrey Pines Reserve opens at 8 A.M. and closes at 10 P.M. from April to October; it closes at 5 P.M. during the winter. Admission to the reserve is free, but there is a parking charge. Most people find that merely driving through doesn't seem enough. The refreshing and fascinating change of scenery invites close-up exploration.

Coastal towns

Between Torrey Pines and Oceanside along the coast is strung a chain of small beach communities, interspersed with state and county beaches. These are some of the more interesting attractions:

Del Mar, a commercial flower-growing center, is best known for its horse-racing track (open from July to September).

Rancho Santa Fe (turn off Interstate 5 at Via de la Valle) was originally a Spanish land grant. Douglas Fairbanks, Sr. founded Rancho Zorro in the 1920s, and Bing Crosby later owned the original ranch house. In and near the town are more eucalyptus trees than anywhere else in California—the result of an unsuccessful try by the Santa Fe Railway to use the wood for railway ties. The Rancho village has a small shopping area reminiscent of old time La Jolla and a good tea room and restaurant.

Encinitas, with its acres of flower fields, is a colorful sight when the flowers are in bloom. The largest poinsettia fields in the state turn nearby hills red in December. "Safest beach in California" is the city's claim.

Carlsbad built its reputation around the similarity of its mineral water to that of the original Karlsbad, Germany, in what was then Bohemia. The Alt Karlsbad Hanse House (now a gift shop) is built over the spring. Nearby Twin Inns is a Victorian memento, having served country-fried chicken to happy diners since 1919 on the same blue willow pattern plates.

Oceanside

Gateway to Camp Pendleton, an important U.S. Marine base, Oceanside has been a beach resort since the 1800s. The original fishing pier was operating in 1910. Jutting into the ocean for 1,900 feet, it attracts throngs of fishermen. At one end of the 4-mile beach is a boat harbor and the replica of a Cape Cod Village. There's good surfing, swimming, and skin diving.

Visitors are welcome to drive through Camp Pendleton. On the grounds is the former ranch house of early Spanish Governor Pio Pico.

From Oceanside you can follow State 78 inland to Escondido, avocado capital of the world. The famous Hunza House Bakery (from U.S. 395 turn right on Grand Avenue, three blocks down and around the corner) turns out over 50 varieties of delicious health bread and its celebrated whole-wheat doughnuts. Approximately 9 miles east of Escondido is the site of one of the least-known battles in United States history and almost the only one fought in conquest of California. A marker commemorates the battle in 1846 between General Pico and his native Californians and General Kearny and the U.S. Army. The U.S. troops lost in what historians called the "bloodiest battle" of the Mexican War.

From Escondido, pick up the Highway to the Stars (State 6), another approach to Palomar Observatory. It also can take you fishing in pretty little Lake Wohlford, where boats and fishing tackle are for hire; to the Bates Brothers Nut Farm for tours; and to groves where, in season, tree-ripened tangerines and Valencia oranges are sold from roadstands at cut-rate prices as in days gone by.

San Diego Wild Animal Park

An innovation in American public zoos, the San Diego Wild Animal Park is also on State 78 near San Pasqual. The first zoo to give its breeding herd animals so much roaming room that resembles their native habitat, it's already had some births, rare for animals in captivity. Developed in 1972 in chaparral terrain evocative of the dry upland plains of Africa, the park is home to some 1,000 animals— many of them rare and endangered species—who live on 500 of the park's total 1,800 acres. This compares with 5,500 animals in the parent San Diego Zoo's 128 acres.

You watch mostly from a distance that doesn't interrupt the animals' lives. A monorail train takes visitors through the park on a 5-mile drive that lasts a little less than an hour. One tip: bring a pair of binoculars. The animals are most active and visible in late afternoon and early morning when the sun is mildest and the crowds thinnest. And you can walk for some distance past the animals (who are kept in their areas by moats).

Nairobi Village, just inside the park entry, presents animals in a more close-up setting. You walk through a giant, free-flight, free-form aviary. You will also see babies in the animal nursery, lemurs on an island, flamingos in a lagoon, newborn animals, green iguanas, lowland gorillas, and less exotic animals in a kraal (corral) for petting.

Open daily from 9 A.M., the park closes at 7:30 P.M. on weekends, 6 P.M. on weekdays. Admission is $1.25 for everyone 16 or older. There is an additional charge for the train ride.

To reach the park directly from San Diego, take Via Rancho Parkway exit from U.S. 395 east onto San Pasqual Road; then follow the signs.

Rancho Bernardo

Red tile roofs are all you see of the town of Rancho Bernardo from U.S. 395, south of Escondido, but it's worth turning onto the Rancho Bernardo exit just to visit the Mercado. Of all the enclaves of art and craft shops that have sprouted up in Southern California recently, this is one of the most handsome and lively. About 20 minutes north of San Diego, it's still within the city's far-flung boundary.

Bold graphics and bright banners stand out against the two story, tile-roofed buildings, faintly Mediterranean in inspiration. Grouped around courtyards at plaza level and on balconies are 40 shops, studios, and eating places. Variety is built in. Artesans concentrate on creating pottery, jewelry, candles, and many other wares.

You can visit on Monday through Saturday from 10 A.M. to 6 P.M. or on Sunday from noon to 6. Some craftsmen are always there; you'll see most on weekends. The big event of the year is the Indian show in May, largest in Southern California. Another big event is August's four-day display of the work of Mercado craftsmen.

The Back Country

Oceanside is a good jumping off spot for a loop trip of the back country of San Diego County. A land of rural charm and historical intrigue, it offers rambling hills, meadows, rocky mountain peaks, and desert. Two or three days will go fast in the back country—it is full of Indian lore, past and present; California mission and gold mine history; pleasant ranches and farms; spectacular views; good hiking, riding, and camping. Not the least of its charms is that it offers the rare treat of unhurried country driving. Camp overnight in a forested state park, stop at a dude ranch in Warner Springs, or stay in the old Julian Hotel. For a circle trip of the area, follow State 76, 79, and U.S. 80 between Oceanside and San Diego.

A historical tour

In addition to some lovely hill and valley scenery, a trip into San Diego's interior reveals some of the area's rich history. Cuyamaca Rancho State Park was formerly a Spanish rancho and, prior to that, a gathering place for Indians. Step back a century at Julian, one of the gold mining towns of the 1800s. And you'll see missions—from San Luis Rey, largest in the chain, to Pala, its small branch, and Santa Ysabel, the *asistencia* of the San Diego Mission. Through these hills ran the stagecoaches—and, on some of the back roads, you might not be too surprised to see one still appear.

Mission San Luis Rey

Off State 76 just 5 miles east of Oceanside is one of the most impressive restorations in the mission chain, Mission San Luis Rey. Crowning a hill that dominates a beautiful valley, the "King of the Missions," founded in 1789, was the largest and most populous Indian mission of both Americas. Known for its artful facade, the gracious and dignified mission building (which at one time covered 6 acres) was built by a padre and Indians who had never before worked with tools.

The first pepper tree in California, which provided the padres with peppercorns to be ground for seasoning, was brought from Peru in 1830 and still stands here. The trees were so widely planted that they are now called "California pepper."

On the always colorful grounds, you'll find picnic tables in a shady grove, an old cemetery, a small museum, and a gift shop. Now a seminary,

Mission San Luis Rey is open to the public from 9 A.M. to 4:30 P.M. on Monday through Saturday, from 9:30 A.M. to 4:30 P.M. on Sunday. Take one of the special tours conducted by the Franciscan fathers who know this charming mission so well; the cost is 50 cents for adults, 25 cents for juniors.

Pala Mission

Located in the tranquil river valley a little farther east on State 76, San Antonio de Pala Mission, actually an *asistencia* (or branch) of Mission San Luis Rey, is the only chapel in the mission chain still used by a predominantly Indian congregation. This is the original building, built in 1815, with Indian frescoes still on the walls and an attractive separate campanile.

Behind Pala, the Tourmaline Queen Mountain echoes days of lucrative gem mining that rivaled the activity in the gold rush town of Julian.

Palomar Observatory

Southeast of Pala, State 76 goes through Pauma Valley, site of the Palomar Observatory. The turn-off to Palomar is 5 miles beyond Rincon Springs, where the road rises abruptly through chaparral and rock-covered countryside and offers a winding but scenic ride.

High on Palomar Mountain is the great silver dome of the 12-story observatory, operated by the California Institute of Technology, and a museum-exhibit hall, where a tour will brief you on the workings of the large telescopes. The Hale, a 200-inch telescope weighing 500 tons, is viewed from a gallery. You may want to wear a sweater; the working interior of the dome must be kept at night-time temperatures, since even a few degrees of variation can cause distortions. The observatory is open daily from 9:30 A.M. to 4:30 P.M. in winter, from 8 A.M. to 6 P.M. in summer.

From the road up Palomar Mountain, you can turn west to Palomar Mountain State Park. This Sierra-like country has many camp and picnic sites, good views, and trails to explore. You'll probably see wild pigeons after which this area was named. As you drive in, ask the ranger for directions.

If you would like to explore this country, a road that offers seldom-seen, spectacular views of distant ranges and avocado groves is the Nate Harrison Grade. It connects Lone Fir Point in

Cattle drives are still part of life in border country near Cuyamaca Rancho.

Rope on pulleys *moves raft-ferry from shore to island in one of Santee lakes.*

Old mining town *of Julian, at 4,235-foot elevation, is now prime agricultural area.*

Palomar Park with the highway. Along the way is a little shrine at the spring that belonged to Nate Harrison, a former slave who died in 1920 at the age of 101. Though the unpaved grade is steep, winding, and dusty, it is worth following.

If your vehicle is heavily loaded, you should approach Palomar from Lake Henshaw, where the road is more gradual and less rough. The lake has boating and fishing. No matter what way you go up, you may want to descend this way to continue your loop trip.

You can spend some time at Warner Springs, a few miles off the loop on State 79. A ranch and golf resort, Warner Springs accommodates you in simple or luxurious adobes.

Santa Ysabel

The white-stuccoed chapel of Mission Santa Ysabel is on the site of the *asistencia* of the San Diego Mission, built in 1818. Rebuilt in the mission style about 1920, the church is still used. Surrounded by pleasant trees, a wishing well, a windmill, and picnic tables, it welcomes visitors.

In the little town of Santa Ysabel, the old general store claims to have been founded in 1870. A good

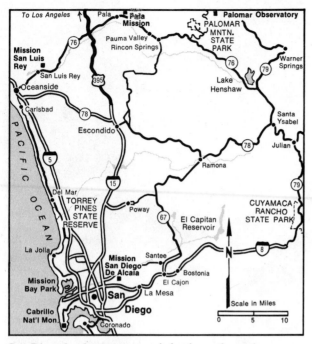

San Diego back country *roads lead you through many historic sights, peaceful mountains and farmland.*

reason for stopping here is the Dudly Pratt Bakery, where nearly 50 varieties of bread are made. A little beyond here, on State 78, you can take a trip into the Anza-Borrego Desert State Park, headquartered in Borrego Springs. (This desert country is discussed on pages 110-111.) A few miles farther along State 79 is the old gold rush town of Julian.

Julian

High in the pine and oak-covered hills, you'll find the mountain settlement of Julian, where a town started over a century ago and time stopped before the false front stores could go out of style.

A gold strike in 1869 started Julian thriving as the second largest town in the county. The end of the boom halted progress and settled the town into a comfortable little agricultural community letting supermarkets, super highways, and subdivisions pass it by. Even today, you reach Julian on meandering, tree-lined country roads nearly empty of traffic and uncluttered by commercial development. Appaloosa ranches; cattle-speckled hillsides; apple, pear, and peach orchards; and fruit and homemade jam stands comprise the scene.

Main Street in Julian has its original false front stores, wooden sidewalks, the Julian Hotel (built in 1887), homey restaurants and stores selling homemade pies from locally grown wares, and real sarsaparilla. You'll even find an adaptable parking lot offering space to "horseless carriages, stuttering bicycles, and mothers-in-law." Hardly changed, old homes still cling to the hillsides around town, and the old George Washington Mine, the first operated in the area, is still reached from the end of Washington Street on a footpath. The entrance has been shored up, and you'll see ore cars on tracks running into the mine. You can also look into an assay office and a blacksmith shop—both reconstructed.

Another mine in the area, the Eagle, is open for tours. To reach it, take C Street in the middle of town and follow the signs to the mine. It is open daily from 9 A.M. to 5 P.M. The short tour includes an explanation of gold mining by the guide. Admission is $1.25 for adults, 75 cents for children.

The friendly, proud residents of Julian, some 500, are always inviting visitors. Julian is famous for the Apple Festival in late October and also sponsors the Wildflower Festival in May and the surprisingly fine Weed Festival in August. Go early, for native weed exhibits are for sale, and the best ones disappear rapidly. No matter when you visit, you'll find the fruits of the season offered to you.

The Julian Museum, located where State 79 turns west for Santa Ysabel, is in an old masonry building once used as a brewery and a blacksmith shop. It is open from 11 A.M. to 5 P.M. on weekends. A more recent article of memorabilia is a mail pouch with parachute, dropped by the Coast Guard in 1938 to inaugurate Julian's first air mail delivery.

If you are visiting only Julian, the fastest route from San Diego is via U.S. 395 to the Poway exit and along the old stagecoach route (State 67 and 78) through Ramona. Otherwise, your circle trip continues south through some high country. Look for the desert view after about 3 miles, where you can see Anza-Borrego country and all the way to the Salton Sea. Driving, walking, horseback riding, and camping are good all through the country fanning south from Julian.

Cuyamaca Rancho State Park

An area of rugged mountain terrain and intermittent streams, Cuyamaca Rancho State Park lies about 40 miles from urban San Diego with the ocean to the west and the desert to the east. Its wilderness is graced by much bird and wildlife and wildflowers in all seasons.

Formerly a Spanish rancho which had been isolated Indian country, the state park now has Los Caballos Campground, accommodating horseback riders; a nature trail at Wooded Hill; and an Indian exhibit, containing relics of early Indian life. Some of the things depicted here, such as acorn gathering, are still practiced by Indians in this region.

The name "Cuyamaca" is a Spanish version of the old Indian word for "the place where it rains." Proud and fiercely independent, these Indians were never brought under the control of the missionaries and managed to maintain their way of life until about 1870, when gold was discovered in the Julian district of Cuyamaca. As the miners poured into the area, the Indians were forced to relocate onto a reservation.

For those who like to ride and hike, there are over 75 miles of trails to explore. From the Paso Picacho Campground, you can climb to three peaks. On a clear day on top of Mt. Cuyamaca, you can see from the Pacific Ocean to the Salton Sea and from Mexico to San Bernardino. Allow about 3 hours for the round trip. Stonewall Peak trail climbs about a thousand feet in 2 miles and also offers magnificent views. On the trail to Middle Peak, you follow an all-year stream and pass many large Indian mortars. Hiking trails also originate from Green Valley Campground, including a 3½-mile self-guided nature loop that takes you to Indian camps, hidden meadows, streams, and abandoned ricks of wood once intended to fuel the mill at Stonewall Mine, where most of the $2 million in gold from Rancho Cuyamaca was dug.

For wonderful desert views and spectacular color in the fall season, you can take another short loop, turning off State 79 just before Lake Cuyamaca onto Sunrise Highway and back on Interstate 8.

Santee

For a pleasant break on your way back to San Diego on Interstate 8, turn off to the small community of Santee, which you reach by going through Bostonia on State 67. Here an aquatic park with six small reservoirs has islands, reached on a pulley-operated raft-ferry, channels for small boats, and fish to catch. Near the lakes are picnic tables shaded by willows and sycamores, playground equipment, volleyball and horseshoe courts, snack bars, and a swimming pool.

Santee Recreation Lakes is on Lake Canyon Road in Santee and is open in the summer from 10 A.M. to sunset, daily except Monday. Winter hours are from 10 A.M. to sunset on weekends and holidays.

Bird-lovers might want to continue a few miles farther to the Silverwood Wildlife Sanctuary near Lakeside. The 167-acre reserve, set in chaparral-covered hills, has eight trails radiating between inner and outer loops, a trailside display, and picnic spot. Two special treats: a bubbler that attracts a wealth of migratory and resident birds and hand-held bottle feedings for hummingbirds.

There's a resident naturalist on duty when the park is open (Wednesdays and Sundays from 9 A.M. to 4 P.M.). He also leads nature walks on other days.

To reach the park from Lakeside, turn right on Maplewood and left on Ashwood, which becomes Wildcat Canyon Road. The sanctuary is 5 miles.

You can see *Palomar Observatory's famous Hale telescope through a glass wall inside this structure.*

Grist mill *remains in Wilderness Gardens, on San Luis Rey River, near Pala, include iron water wheel.*

Across the Border to Mexico

Mexico is right next door when you're in San Diego —and most visitors find it an irresistible lure. Though Tijuana receives most of the traffic, there are two other border crossings—Tecate nearby and Mexicali beyond the mountains. It's only 2 hours to Ensenada, south of Tijuana, on scenic Bahia Todos Santos; and San Felipe, on the Sea of Cortez, is only 127 miles south of Mexicali.

After passing through the sleepy village of San Ysidro on Interstate 5, you come to the dry Tijuana River bed and the gateway arch sweeping over 16 lanes of traffic that marks the end of California and the beginning of Baja California, Mexico. At the border (just 15 minutes from downtown San Diego), the bustling city of Tijuana brings you instantly to Mexico. The scenic Silver Strand is a beautiful coastal alternate to the freeway from San Diego to Mexico.

Border Field State Park is the beach with one foot in California and the other in Mexico. Once a Navy field, it's now a 372-acre park with beach front, lagoons, and salt marshes. Mexicans flock there on sunny weekends; there's usually lots of elbow room on the American side. To get there, turn off Interstate 5 at Palm Avenue, go west to 19th Street, south to Monument Road, and west to the park.

A TASTE OF MEXICO

Even though the towns along the border's edge are more tourist-oriented than most of the Mexican cities, they do give you the feeling of being in another country. The cheerful parade of streetside vendors adds to the atmosphere, and you can enjoy it all without speaking a word of Spanish.

Tijuana is the closest and largest of the cities mentioned. If time permits, try to visit some of the others; each is different and has the added advantage of being "foreign."

Tijuana

Tijuana (te-wah'-nah) lays claim to the title of most visited city in the world—with some 30 million border crossings each year. It's easy to see why the attraction is so strong. Many who come are weekenders attracted by horse and dog racing, the summer Sunday bullfights, or camping on the beach seaward of Tijuana. Many are active and curious shoppers seeking out the fine handicrafts and import stores and colorful arcades. And yet others come to experience a foreign culture, so accessible from the United States. Realize that, as a border town, Tijuana is not entirely a typical Mexican village.

To enjoy your visit more, it is best to know what to expect of this very diverse and busy city. The Tijuana Convention and Visitors Bureau has visitor information booths both at the border and on the main street (Avenida Revolucion).

You can park a car on the U. S. side of the border and walk across where a Mexican taxi takes you downtown for 50 cents. If you decide to drive across, stop at one of the Mexican insurance offices; American insurance is usually no good once you are over the border.

At San Diego's Santa Fe Station at the foot of Broadway, the Mexicoach buses have done away with the former necessity for changing buses at

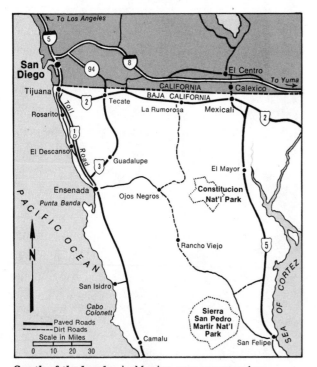

South of the border *in Mexico, you can travel on good roads to east, west coasts of Baja California.*

The ancient art *of the bullring unfolds each Sunday, spring through fall, in Tijuana.*

Wrought-iron *lamps exemplify Mexican folk art available in Ensenada shops.*

Fronton Palacio, *a Tijuana landmark, is home of colorful, centuries-old sport of jai alai.*

the border. They leave at 9 and 11 A.M. and at 2 and 6 P.M. Roundtrip, curiously, is cheaper on weekends: $2. Weekdays, it's $3.60. Because this is a common carrier crossing the international border, even California residents now can bring back one quart of liquor. Tequila and Kahlua are the best buy. You can also take Greyhound (120 W. Broadway) or the San Diego transit line buses (board them at downtown Horton Plaza or anywhere along the route) to the border.

Signs from the border direct you downtown to Avenida Revolucion. Revolucion is brassy, shabby, and insistently commercial; yet it bustles, sings, laughs, and invites you to walk and search for its cheerful surprises. You're sure to see the patient burros with painted zebra stripes waiting on corners to be photographed with you in colorful sombreros. At the tourist booth on Revolucion and

between 3rd and 4th streets, English-speaking attendants will help you locate shops and attractions. At 7th Street is the impressive jai alai Fronton Palacio, a city landmark.

Shopping finds in Tijuana range from the richest Mexican folk art to the gaudiest of tourist gadgets, from fine imported woolens to the most dubious of costume jewelry, all displayed in great profusion.

Most of the shopping is concentrated along Revolucion between 2nd and 9th streets. There is also a growing area on 2nd Street, east of Revolucion, that specializes in furniture and picture frames. On Constitucion, which parallels the main street, you'll find a little different flavor. This is where the Mexican people shop. Generally, English is the common language along Revolucion and in the arcades; it is much less common in the local trade stores on Constitucion. Most prices are marked in dollars for your convenience; if not, just remember each Mexican peso is worth 8 U. S. cents. It is not necessary to change dollars into pesos.

These solid-looking shops that have fixed fronts and regular doors also have fixed prices; elsewhere you may bargain. But bear in mind it is very difficult for you to get the better of the merchant in this kind of bargaining unless it is late on a cold or rainy night and you are talking to the proprietor, who has had a bad business day and is in the mood to close up and go home. Very often the best-looking stores offer a fairer price than you can get in a stall or arcade.

Services favor the visitor. You won't need appointments for men's haircuts and women's hair styling. Take shoes to be repaired as you start your shopping day; pick them up later. Craftsmanship is reliable and cheap.

Since an estimated 70 per cent of all Mexican handmade goods filter through this border, plenty of easy-to-pack items will catch your fancy. The most outstanding folk art selection anywhere is at Tolan, across from the Fronton Palacio.

What should you look for? Handmade pottery; handcarved wooden boxes, mirror and picture frames, figurines and chess sets (Mexican wood-carvers are numerous and do interesting work in many styles); tin ware; copper ware; papier mache work; silver jewelry; gold jewelry (generally about 30 per cent under the world market price); pure wool *rebozos* (stoles, also used as table runners); shirts for men and women, as well as other clothing in Mexico's wonderfully long-lasting cotton; bright wool area rugs (they can double as wall hangings or bedspreads); paper flowers; bark painting; yarn "painting"; handblown glass; colorful tiles.

Inco, the Tijuana glass factory across from the Fronton Palacio, invites you to watch glass blowers at work and has installed a visitors' gallery for your comfort. Most of its production is now given over to reasonably priced colorless glass for terrariums. Appealing to plant enthusiasts are the yards of clay pots, all east of Revolucion. At 2nd and Oporto Streets, turn north at the stoplight or drive east down 4th Street. Be prepared to bargain.

Tijuana enjoys free port status. You'll find good selections of such imports as Scottish cashmeres, Pucci silks, French crystal, Spanish leather coats and jackets, Italian gloves, Swiss watches, Belgian glass, and a few worthwhile things from China.

Although Tijuana has several major hotels (Palacio Azteca, Royal Inn, El Conquistador), the most satisfying dining is to be found at Reno's, near the southwest corner of Revolucion and 7th.

You'll find wonderful buys in fresh fruits and vegetables at small stands, as well as in the CaliMax supermarkets. At the glass teepee tourist booth, you can check an approved list of what produce may be brought back across the border. If you are traveling down the south coast by camper, plan to load up with this superior and cheap local produce. By driving almost to Caliente Racecourse, you also can pursue economy at several agencies selling both chilled beer and delicious apple-flavored Mexican soft drinks by the case. A *sub-agencia* exists on the old 2nd Street approach to the Ensenada toll road.

Remember the law permits anyone over 16 to bring back $100 in goods duty free (families may pool their $100 exemptions to make one big important purchase), but these purchases must be incidental to your trip.

Sports are varied and different south of the border. The biggest crowd-attractor to Tijuana is Caliente Racecourse, a couple of miles from downtown on Agua Caliente Boulevard. A fire in 1971 destroyed much of the track, but it has been expanded and rebuilt. Its beautiful modern facilities include good restaurants and shops. Thoroughbreds race Saturday and Sunday the year-round. Wednesday through Sunday nights, the course is converted for greyhound racing.

Jai alai (hi-li), a colorful and often dangerous sport that is billed as the world's fastest ball game, is four centuries old. Traditionally played by the Basques in a show of grace, skill, and strength, jai alai offers thrills and pari-mutuel betting from Thursday through Monday evenings most of the year in the imposing Fronton Palacio on Revolucion at 7th Street.

Tijuana has two bullrings, both named and patterned after the famous ones in Mexico City. The downtown ring, El Toreo de Tijuana, is easily reached via Agua Caliente Boulevard. Great ceremony and excitement accompany the classical art of bullfighting, celebrated here Sunday afternoons from late spring through early fall.

Plaza Monumental, 5 miles out of town near the ocean and the border, is the second largest bullring in the world (the largest is in Mexico City). Whether or not it is the day of a bullfight, it is a wonderful place to visit. You'll enjoy beautiful landscaping, Andalusian patios with Mexican tiles and murals, views of the Pacific Ocean, and the lovely chapel of the Plaza Monumental, where the *torero* stops to pray as soon as he arrives at the arena.

Occasionally on Sundays the *charros* (cowboys) stage rodeos (or *charreadas*). There are several arenas; ask at the information booths if a rodeo is scheduled and how to find it.

Other attractions in Tijuana include over 25 churches. Some are distinguished. The cathedral (Nuestra Senora de Guadalupe), downtown at 2nd and Ninos Heroes, has twin towers, a big blue and yellow-tiled dome, and deep-throated bells. At the

Bienvenidos!– Crossing to Mexico

Although it's easy to visit Mexico, your trip will be even more enjoyable if you familiarize yourself with some information before you cross the border.

Tourist cards. You don't need a passport to visit Mexico, but if you go more than 75 miles into the interior (Ensenada and Mexicali are within this limit) or stay longer than 72 hours, you will need a tourist card. They are free from the Mexican Consulate and the Mexican Government Tourist Office in San Diego, but you must supply proof of your U.S. citizenship.

Car insurance. It is better to obtain auto insurance from a Mexican insurance company before you cross the border. American agents are not licensed to do business in Mexico, where an automobile accident is a criminal offense for which you can be detained until claims are adjusted. The Convention and Visitors Bureau in San Diego will provide a list of reputable insurance firms. Some are located on your way to the border crossing, and short term Mexican insurance is not expensive.

Driving. Traffic regulations similar to those in the United States are enforced. Speed limits are posted in kilometers (1 km=.62 miles), so be sure to make the reckoning. Road signs are generally in Spanish, but shapes and symbols are universally understood. Baja California has some new highways (including the new road to its tip), but they are unfenced, so watch for livestock on the road. Major highways (1, 2, and 15) are well patrolled by Mexico's green emergency repair jeeps. Service is free, except for cost of parts. Gasoline is generally available; plan ahead as you do north of the border.

Currency. Most Mexican stores will accept either pesos or dollars. You can change your currency at banks, your hotel, or currency exchange booths. A peso is worth 8 cents in U.S. money (12.50 pesos = 1 U.S. dollar) and is indicated by a dollar sign with a single bar.

Customs. United States Customs permits each person to bring back $100 worth of goods without duty. Beyond that amount, you must itemize each purchase. Check the *Customs Hints* booklet, free from customs offices, for detailed information on declaring purchases over $100. California residents may not bring back alcoholic beverages unless returning by commercial carrier (boat, train, bus, or plane), in which case the limit is one quart.

Rooms and meals. Good accommodations at reasonable prices and restaurants where you can eat with confidence are found in the Mexican towns discussed in this chapter. Along with Mexican restaurants, there are many North American, European, and Oriental establishments.

Profusion of fruits at Tijuana fruteria *draws tourists to examine strange and familiar foods.*

fringe of downtown (11th and Ocampo), the graceful, single-towered church of the Sagrado Corazon is a natural color subject for photographers. The most striking church and the one most representative of modern Mexico, Espiritu Santo is in the Chapultepec subdivision in the hills above the golf course, reached along Avenida Sonora.

Tijuana does not follow the pattern of conventional Mexican towns which traditionally center around a plaza—the focal point of the town's public

Heading for Ensenada, *yachts jockey for position in Newport Harbor-to-Ensenada race.*

Ensenada Bay *is home for commercial fishing industry and major sportfishing fleet.*

life. But it does have a city park where you can relax on green lawn among tall eucalyptus. On Sundays it teems with a carnival atmosphere, including band concerts in the central pavilion, many colorful vendors, and an occasional itinerant entertainer. There's lots of local color here. Few north-of-the-border people visit Teniente Guerrero Park, six blocks west of Revolucion between 3rd and 4th.

Tijuana to Ensenada

Outside of Tijuana you find the ramshackle hillside huts of the Mexican poor. You'll also find industry, part of the new diversification of Tijuana, particularly eastward from Caliente Racecourse on the Tecate Road, also known as Mexican Highway 2.

By following the 2nd Street extension to the ocean (or taking the direct route from the border), you encounter a change of scenery at Playas de Tijuana. Here you can pick up the scenic freeway taking you 65 miles south from Tijuana to the seacoast town of Ensenada. This four-lane, divided toll road ($2.40 one way) in many places parallels the old Ensenada Libre (free) route, which takes you through rural Mexico but also slows you down. The 90-minute freeway drive routes you past spectacular cliffs and sea views.

Enroute to Ensenada, at La Mision, you'll come upon La Fonda motel, gift shop, and restaurant. The restaurant has an outdoor dining terrace with a dazzling water view. You can climb down cliffside stairs to an unspoiled beach.

Ensenada

Ensenada's pace is much more relaxed than Tijuana's, and the setting is much more inviting, curving gracefully around the bay of Todos Santos. And shoppers delight in the fact that in Ensenada is Mexico's northernmost state store, with great variety in folk art at reasonable prices.

Lack of irrigation water discouraged the settlements of Cabrillo (who discovered the area in 1542), Father Serra, and the Dominicans. In 1870 a gold rush brought a short era of progress here, but it was the sportsmen who finally lighted upon the real advantages of the delightful seaport town. Game in the hills is abundant, and fishing is so excellent that Ensenada is known as the "Yellowtail Capital of the World." Pleasure boats abound in the protected harbor; cruise ships head in for a short stay. The world-famous Ensenada-Newport International Yacht Race, held during Mexico's Cinco de Mayo (May 5) independence celebration, attracts more than 500 participants.

The mood of Ensenada is contagious. Life is informal and relaxed; yet there is no lack of activities. The city has become a summer playground for Mexicans, as well as for foreign visitors, because of mild air and water temperatures, excellent fishing, and Mexican festivals. New hotels, excellent and varied shopping, and scenic attractions nearby all make Ensenada a popular vacation spot. It's also full of good places to eat. If you prefer the independence of your own camper, you'll find plenty of open space and more than 20 trailer parks dotting the countryside around the city. Estero Beach, 6 miles south of the city, is a good spot for camping and also has a fine hotel, shops, and restaurants.

Punta Banda is a magnificent high bluff at the southern end of Ensenada Bay. Past here is the famous La Bufadora, a spectacular sea geyser created by the beating of the sea against the coastline. There is a campground and beach at Punta Banda and, nearby, a large colony of sea lions on the rocks. A popular surfing beach lies immediately south of the point. Magnificent views, ruins of missions, and old wineries are in the Ensenada area.

Water exercise *is step toward slimming at Tecate's Rancho la Puerta.*

"Happy Feet" *is Rancho la Puerta exercise class that revitalizes many.*

Guadalupe Russian Village (probably the world's largest olive plantation) and Santo Tomas Winery are short excursions from Ensenada. Check with the Tourism Office on Avenida Lopez Mateos for their locations and for other attractions.

Ensenada has often been thought of as a stepping-off place for the rest of Baja California to the south. This is even more true since the completion of the transpeninsular highway. Visitors going below Ensenada or those staying anywhere in Baja for more than three days must obtain a tourist card. Good for six months, the free cards are available at any Mexican consulate, tourism office, or office of Aero Mexico.

Tecate

As Mexican border towns go, Tecate is relatively quiet and uncommercial, but you will find it busy for a town its size, especially during festivals. It is about 30 miles east of Tijuana and 72 miles from Ensenada on good roads.

A famous beer that bears the town's name makes Tecate a popular refreshment stop. The brewery and Hidalgo Park are the town's main attractions. The city has a good restaurant (Los Candiles) and a small hotel (El Dorado). A few miles west of town along Highway 2 is Rancho la Puerta, a widely known health spa that attracts many Southern Californians.

Mexicali

Mexicali, the capital of Baja California, has about the same population as Tijuana (400,000). Located in the center of a vast cotton-producing valley, Mexicali has a lively agricultural and industrial life. It does not cater to tourism, nor is the U. S. dollar the chief currency. English is spoken at the main hotel (Lucerna), at the few tourist shops, and at some restaurants. Folkloric music, rodeos, nearby campgrounds and lakes, intriguing restaurants, and a concentrated area of curio shops invite travelers to linger.

The road to Mexicali from Tijuana offers one of the region's most spectacular views. From the great Cantu grade, you can look over the entire valley of Mexicali and the vast playa of Laguna Salada.

South of Mexicali, the scenery on Highway 15 changes to typical Sonoran Desert. The road drops over the edge of the sand mesa to the somewhat primitive town of San Felipe, 127 miles away. San Felipe is primitive but not undiscovered. Especially on three-day holidays, it swarms with North Americans who overwhelm the few motel/hotel accommodations and sleep—if at all—on the beach.

Palm Springs
& the Coachella Valley

Perhaps nowhere else do mountains and desert meet more abruptly than at Palm Springs, famed desert playground about a hundred miles east of Los Angeles. To the west, the San Jacinto Mountains—often snow-draped in winter—drop sharply to the valley floor thousands of feet below. To the east, the sun—most important resource of the Southern California desert country—rises and shines all year, and the air is warm and dry.

Palm Springs, center of an expanding community of resorts, stands in desert that is mostly tamed. But close by is land rugged and open enough to urge your investigation of its tenacious plants, its shy animals, its rocks and sands, its silent canyons. And the mountains, pine-covered and verdant in their upper reaches, offer spectacular views from the heights and some surprises in the easily accessible side canyons.

Two great desert parks—Joshua Tree National Monument and Anza-Borrego Desert State Park—reveal the differences between the high and low desert.

Nearby is Salton Sea, once a dry desert wasteland and now a recreation area popular for motor boating and water skiing. Undeveloped desert canyons and unusual rock formations around the sea invite exploring.

The Colorado River, boundary between California and Arizona, is a mecca for boating enthusiasts. Lake Havasu, formed by a dam on the once-wild river, is a water world playground. On the Arizona side in Lake Havasu City is the London Bridge, reassembled from its original site on England's Thames River.

One of the great virtues of this vast land is that it seems far removed from California's more populous regions. Here, understated resorts provide bases for exploring, and campgrounds abound on empty stretches of sand, along the water's edge, or among pine-forested mountains.

Rain-water basin *in Joshua Tree National Monument lies behind dam built during cattle-range era.*

Palm Springs Offers Privacy

Looking at Palm Springs from the air, it appears to be developed in a kind of checkerboard fashion —residences and commercial establishments in one giant square area, open desert on another. There's a good reason.

The city is divided into mile squares, every other one belonging to the Agua Caliente Indians, original settlers of the land. The land on which the Palm Springs Spa Hotel is located, as well as much other local real estate, belongs to the Agua Caliente Indian Reservation.

If you drive up into verdant Palm Canyon, south of town, you'll enter the Indian reservation and pay a toll to proceed to it and other tributary canyons along the east side of the mountains.

Palm Springs is a wealthy community—but, in a sense, its real wealth perhaps still belongs to its original owners.

SOMETHING FOR EVERYONE

No longer considered only an exclusive resort community for wealthy businessmen and glittering personalities, Palm Springs offers a variety of activities for a wide range of visitors. If you like to swim, golf, play tennis, hike, picnic, ride horses, bicycle, ride dune buggies through the sand, fly planes, watch polo or baseball, shop, or relax in the sun, Palm Springs can supply excellent facilities.

The sporting life

Known as the "Golf Capital of the World," Palm Springs has golf courses that stay green all year. The entire community boasts almost three dozen courses. The Palm Springs Golf Course, one of the few public courses, is located at 5500 E. Palm Canyon Drive. To play golf at the private clubs, you usually must be the guest of a member, although a number offer reciprocal privileges to members of other private clubs. Some hotels provide guests with temporary cards; two major hotels have their own courses.

If you are interested in tennis, 14 public courts are playable, and more are planned. Eight of the courts, at Ruth Hardy Park in the center of town, are lighted for night play. The other six, at Palm Springs High School, are open on weekends and holidays during the school year and every day in the summer. Several of the major hotels provide courts for guests; the well-known Palm Springs Tennis Club allows hotel and cottage guests to use its courts, but the Palm Springs Racquet Club is strictly private.

Other popular sports include horseback riding and cycling. You can rent bicycles on E. Palm Canyon Drive. A riding stable on Toledo Avenue offers guided horseback tours of the scenic canyons extending from the desert floor into the foothills.

The California Angels, an American League baseball team, maintain spring training headquarters here. Visitors may attend the spring practices and exhibition games, mostly in March, at the baseball stadium at E. Ramon Road and S. Sunrise Way, not too far from the airport.

Shopping and culture

Shopping Palm Springs is a popular diversion. Many of the top national and California retail stores have branches here. The colorful shops provide opportunities for both window gazing and serious shopping. New fashions are introduced in this pace-setting community in October before being put on the general spring market.

Palm Springs is also becoming known as an art center. Its galleries and exhibits attract many visitors each year. Most of the galleries are along the main downtown streets; the town also has an excellent desert museum.

Your season in the sun

Palm Springs' magnet is its climate, especially from mid-October to mid-May. The days are generally sunny, warm, and cloudless, with dry air. Winter temperatures are comfortably warm—70° to 90° during the day; desert winter nights can dip to 25°, though 40° is a more usual minimum. In the summer, daytime temperatures average in the 100°s, but the humidity is very low. Rainfall is scant. Most of the under-3-inch annual average falls in brief storms from November through April.

Nestling at the base of the steep San Jacinto range, Palm Springs has an unusual climatic factor: the receding afternoon sun abruptly disappears behind the mountains, leaving the town in cool shade while the valley to the east is still bright with sun. Winter or summer, the mountain wall creates a lengthened, but early, twilight. The mountains also give Palm Springs one more weather bonus:

Guests *at Palm Springs Spa Hotel and Mineral Baths soak in Indian hot springs.*

Golfing *at many fine courses gives city its title, "Golf Capital of the World."*

Tennis, *enjoyed year-round, is another sport that thrives under desert sun.*

"MUST SEES"

AERIAL TRAMWAY (Palm Springs)—climb from desert floor to top of Mt. San Jacinto in 15 minutes; snow fun in winter

BORREGO SPRINGS (Anza-Borrego Desert State Park)—resort oasis in untamed desert wilderness; base for exploring

DATE GARDENS (Indio)—have a date shake; wander through groves; watch movie on date growing; see rose gardens

DESERT MUSEUM (Palm Springs)—devoted entirely to desert and local history; fine art museum; Sunday concerts

LAKE HAVASU (Colorado)—beautiful blue lake offers water sports; Lake Havasu City (on east side) has London Bridge

TWENTYNINE PALMS (Joshua Tree National Monument)—from Visitor Center take nature trail to forest of palms

PINES TO PALMS HIGHWAY (State 74)—scenic route through San Jacintos to desert floor southeast of Palm Springs

SALTON SEA (State 86)—float in below sea level salt water lake, once inland sea; popular for boating, fishing, camping

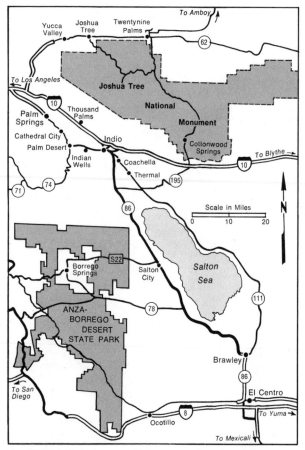

Southeast desert *area offers recreational activity, primitive desert; invites exploration.*

they act as a barrier to the ever-encroaching smog from the west.

The Palm Springs "winter season" is from mid-December through April. During these months, particularly in January, February, and March, advance reservations are advisable. You'll find equally good weather (and fewer people) during the fall and spring seasons.

What to wear in Palm Springs? It's almost always "shirt sleeve" weather, with an accent on casual sports clothes. Men and women wear shorts downtown, but bathing suits are restricted to pool lounging. Women's sun dresses and pants outfits are popular, as are men's sport shirts and jackets.

Accommodations are many and varied — but "motel" is a word you won't find used here. Hotel and motor inn rates in general are competitive with those in other popular resort communities. You'll find rooms for two ranging from $10 to $65 a day—and up. If you're traveling with children, look for hotels offering family rates. Room rates vary according to season. Summer is the most economical time.

A number of trailer parks (complete with desert landscaping, pools, and recreational facilities) are located in the city and surrounding vicinity.

Write to the Palm Springs Convention and Visitors Bureau, Palm Springs 92262, for specific information on accommodations and reservations.

EXPLORING THE CITY

As you approach Palm Springs from the northwest, the shadowy blue and dusty pink bulk of the layered San Jacinto Mountains provide an imposing backdrop of constantly changing colors and shadow patterns. Both contrasting and harmonizing with its surroundings, the city at its base has assimilated the colors and textures of the desert.

Your first introduction to Palm Springs is Palm Canyon Drive, lined with more than 1,800 palm trees along 5 miles of its length. Illuminated at night, the beautiful palms are the only street lamps of this major thoroughfare. Not artificial importations, the palms have been native for centuries.

From the moment you enter the city limits on State 111, you notice the absence of billboards. In addition, there are no above-ground power lines, no telephone poles, no large signs, no prices displayed, no neon or moving signs, and no high buildings. The uncluttered and unobtrusive character of the city is closely guarded by city ordinances, all strictly regulated in the same spirit of the law which forbids any building to shade another property or street from the desert's all important commodity—the sun.

The street grid makes it easy to find your way around Palm Springs. Palm Canyon Drive (a one-way route going south) is both the main arterial and the main shopping street. Indian Avenue, the secondary arterial one block away, runs one way to the north through the central part of the city. At Tahquitz-McCallum Way, the street numbering divides between north and south.

The older portions of Palm Springs are worth visiting for their lush garden plantings and handsome old trees. W. Arenas Road leads you to one interesting district near the Palm Springs Tennis Club. In the north part of the town, Via Las Palmas takes you west into a neighborhood of elegantly landscaped homes. Numerous movie stars and entertainers have homes in these areas of Palm Springs. To the south, one neighborhood off Camino Real (a main thoroughfare) has streetside plantings of desert trees and shrubs.

Palm Springs at night

Downtown Palm Springs is relatively tranquil in the evening. There are numerous good restaurants, though many of the most popular eating places are southeast of Palm Springs toward Rancho Mirage. Art galleries often extend their hours during the winter season; a wax museum (219 N. Palm Canyon Drive) offers a glimpse of famous people, including replicas of some of the desert residents (probably the closest look you'll get), for a fee.

With an emphasis on sports and sun activities, this is an early-to-bed community. Unless you know some of the residents, you're not likely to get a peek at the social life of the city's glamourites.

An historical corner

A good place to begin your exploration of Palm Springs is at the corner of Tahquitz-McCallum Way and Palm Canyon Drive. Here is the Palm Springs Spa Hotel and Mineral Baths, an elaborate structure that houses the bubbling hot springs sacred to the Agua Caliente Indians. If you are not a guest at the spa, you can enjoy these hot springs for a reasonable admission charge. You can take your pick of mineral baths, individual Roman "swirl-pools," rock steam and infrared inhalation, needle-point showers, massage, immersion in a 104° outdoor mineral pool, and an exercise gymnasium.

An 1853 government survey party noted that the Indians attributed special healing powers to the springs and considered them sacred. Today, the only reminder of this sacred shrine is a memorial plaque on the building—and, of course, the same "healing" waters.

Palm Springs Desert Museum mounts an excellent collection of natural history exhibits, Indian lore, and cultural artifacts. Presently located at 135 E. Tahquitz-McCallum Way, the museum is building a striking new home at the foot of the mountains on Museum Drive, between Tahquitz-McCallum Way and Andreas Road. Space for natural history and fine arts exhibits will be greatly enlarged, and a 450-seat auditorium will be added. In addition, a sculpture court financed by Frank Sinatra will enhance the 5½-acre grounds.

Now on view in the museum is the "Saga of the Desert" panorama, depicting wildlife, plants, and minerals of the surrounding desert. One room is devoted to the history and art of the local Cahuilla Indians, and an upper gallery has changing displays of the fine arts and primitive and folk art. A schedule of year-round evening programs and Sunday afternoon concerts is available. The museum is open from 10 A.M. to 5 P.M. Tuesday through Saturday (2 to 5 P.M. on Sunday) for a small fee.

Next door to the museum is one of Palm Springs' oldest houses, built with railroad ties in 1893. The home of Miss Cornelia White, it contains memorabilia of early Palm Springs, including the town's first telephone. Maintained by the Palm Springs Historical Society, it follows the museum's hours.

The Living Desert Reserve, also operated by the Desert Museum, is a 360-acre parcel of the Colorado Desert located in Palm Desert, about 15 miles southeast of Palm Springs. Featuring outdoor exhibits with a palm oasis and bird display, the reserve has 3½ miles of self-guided nature trails and is open daily (except Monday) from 9 A.M. to 5 P.M. Adults pay a nominal fee. Take State 111 southeast to Palm Desert; turn right on Portola Avenue and drive for about 3½ miles.

Everybody's Village, an unobtrusive complex at 538 N. Palm Canyon Drive, is the home of a privately supported arts and crafts school. Anyone can participate in the painting, sculpture, drama, and language classes and in the discussion groups and other activities offered. You can join a group even for only a day's stay.

Moorten's Desertland Botanical Gardens, started in 1938, contains plants from world deserts—North American, Baja Californian, Central American, African—grown in special sections that have been designed to simulate their original environments. You'll see interesting shapes, rare plants, and blooming cactus—some with obvious personalities and names like the "bearded grandfather." Courses are conducted and research carried out in a fascinating cactus conservatory called a "cactusarium."

By special arrangement the owners will take you on an interesting guided tour; otherwise you can stroll the 4-acre gardens on your own. Benches in some surprisingly verdant places provide spots for resting and observing birds and wildlife. Some interesting books on desert plantings are sold at the gardens' entrance; you can also buy rocks, minerals, and plants. Located at 1701 S. Palm Canyon Drive, the gardens are open daily from 9 A.M. to 5 P.M. Expect a moderate admission charge.

Aerial Tramway

When days get hot on the desert floor, Palm Springs residents and visitors have an instant escape route to the high country of Mt. San Jacinto, where the air is pine-scented and temperatures are 40° cooler. Beginning in the rugged Chino Canyon on the north edge of town, the tram trip up the mountain is refreshing, exciting, and beautiful any time of the year. You get an excellent view of the valley desert carpet, dotted with green palms and 5,000 blue swimming pools. Because of the awesome engineering challenges presented in its construction, the tramway has been called "the eighth engineering wonder of the world."

In a period of two years, 20,000 helicopter missions hauled men and materials to narrow ledges for construction of the towers. Today, the two 80-passenger trams move up and down one of the sheerest mountains in North America, over granite

Aerial tramway *hoists sightseers high above desert floor to top of Mt. San Jacinto, a 2½-mile climb.*

portation is also available from Palm Springs. The Valley Station has a gift shop, snack bar, and cocktail lounge. Be sure to save your tramway trip for a clear day; a desert haze will play havoc with the view.

SAN JACINTO MOUNTAINS

Although the tram is the most dramatic way to reach the upper level of the San Jacintos, you can reach this mountain recreation area by way of Banning (Interstate 10) or the Riverside-Hemet route (U.S. 395 and State 74). The latter is the Pines-to-Palms Highway, part of an enjoyable loop drive to Palm Desert or Palm Springs.

Small in area but high on the horizon, the craggy ramparts of the San Jacintos support a cool, green, much-sought-after summer retreat between the hot wheat and orchard country of the San Jacinto Valley on the west and the hotter desert of the Coachella Valley on the east. The forested backbone slants up gradually from south to north until it breaks away suddenly at the tremendous north face of San Jacinto Peak—one of the world's most abrupt escarpments, rising from near sea level to 10,831 feet, face to face with Mt. San Gorgonio (Southern California's highest mountain) across San Gorgonio Pass.

Jumping-off place for exploring the upper San Jacintos by road or trail is the forest community of Idyllwild—a logical headquarters until you become acquainted with the region and decide where most of your interests lie. Available are hotels and motels, restaurants, camping supplies, and pack and saddle stock.

Mt. San Jacinto Wilderness State Park has more than 50 miles of hiking trails. Only two campgrounds in the park are accessible by automobile— Idyllwild and Stone Creek—but many primitive areas stretch along the riding and hiking trails. Whether you enter the wilderness area on horseback or by foot, you'll need a permit. Apply in person or write the park headquarters (P.O. Box 308, Idyllwild 92349) or the Long Valley Ranger Station at the top of the tramway.

San Gorgonio Pass

If you take Interstate 10 east to Palm Springs, you pass Beaumont and Banning, lying in the divide between the San Bernardino and San Jacinto mountains. Side trips off the freeway in early spring reveal billowy colors of cherry and peach blossoms in nearby orchards and of apples up in Oak Glen. Later in the summer, you can pick your own fruit or get it from a roadside stand. Some apple stands around Oak Glen also offer homemade pies and cider.

recesses deeper than the Grand Canyon. The climb to the Mountain Station (8,516 feet) from the desert floor takes 18 minutes. This station is situated at the threshold of San Jacinto Wilderness State Park, where chattering jays and chipmunks attest that you are indeed in a different world. The top of Mt. San Jacinto is a 6-mile hike from the tram station. Below sprawls the great desert expanse of the Coachella desert valley, including the Salton Sea; on a very clear day, the mountain ranges of Las Vegas are visible. At Mountain Station you can eat in the restaurant (open for lunch and dinner), shop in the gift shop, and watch a free movie on the dramatic construction of the tram.

Behind Mountain Station a thermal sidewalk leads down to Long Valley, where you can picnic in the summer and rent sleds and sliding saucers in the winter. If you bring your own skis, cross-country skiing is good from this point.

To reach the tramway base, turn off State 111 north of town and follow the signs. Public trans-

Desert Hot Springs, north of Interstate 10 and just beyond the Palm Springs turnoff, has a Hopi Indian-style museum. Single-handedly constructed by Cabot Yerxa over a 20-year period, the 35-room structure has 150 windows and 65 doors—17 leading to the outside. A combination art gallery, trading post, and museum containing Indian artifacts and relics, the museum is open daily from 9 A.M. to 5 P.M.

Canyons east of the mountains

The scenic and historical canyons close to Palm Springs, for centuries the home of the Agua Caliente Indians, offer beauty and exploration for hikers, horsemen, bird watchers, botanists, and camera enthusiasts.

Tahquitz Canyon, containing a 60-foot waterfall, is the closest to town but is closed to the public.

Palm Canyon cuts south from Palm Springs up into the mountains for more than 14 miles, dividing the San Jacinto from the Santa Rosa mountains. This valley was the traditional summer retreat of the Agua Caliente Indians, who still own this land of shady palm groves and cool streams. There are traces of old Indian campsites in remote sections.

To reach the canyon, drive south on Palm Canyon Drive. Shortly after the road enters the Indian reservation, you'll come to a toll gate, open from 9 A.M. to 5 P.M. daily except during the period from May 15 to October 15, when the canyon is closed to the public because of extreme fire hazard. During a "wet" year, the canyon will be closed from June to September. Admission for adults is 50 cents; for children, 25 cents.

You pass a number of interesting tributary canyons along the way, all containing fine stands of palms, many more than a hundred years old. Proceeding south, the valley narrows, and you cut through the slot of Split Rock. Then the road climbs steeply to a level parking area called Hermit's Bench, where a souvenir shop, cold drinks, and rest rooms are located.

The steep but well-improved trail starts here, first dropping down into the canyon. Picnic tables are available, but there is no drinking water. The palms here reach an impressive height; for a short, pleasant outing, walk a mile or two along the trail winding beneath them. This is a popular trail for horsemen.

Andreas Canyon's parking area is just over half a mile off the main road in a grove of sycamores and cottonwoods. A clear stream runs year-round. You'll find picnic tables, rest rooms, and a wading pool (2 feet deep after a rain). The grounds are well cleared, shady and pleasant, often crowded on weekends. Look for mortar holes gouged in large rocks near the parking lot; the Indians once used them for grinding meal. A trail follows the stream for about 4 miles along a climbing, winding route up to the head of the canyon.

Near the parking area stands a particularly impressive grove of native California fan palms (*Washingtonia filifera*), their skirts trimmed well above the ground to reduce fire hazard. These are survivors of ancient groves once widespread throughout the valley.

Murray Canyon has a stream flowing most of the year. From the Andreas parking area, you walk south to the canyon on a well-marked trail. Another trail leads up to a stand of fine palms.

THE COACHELLA VALLEY

Southeast of Palm Springs and the nearby resort areas is Coachella Valley, part of the Colorado Desert which extends east to the Colorado River and south to the shores of the Gulf of California. The valley is endowed with a great variety of plant and animal life. There's a special fascination here in the transformation to rich farmland that has been wrought by 20th-century irrigation. Average rainfall is under 2 inches a year, but artesian wells discovered around 1855 played an important role in the area's agricultural development. Many of the valley's 60,000 cultivated acres are below sea level.

From Palm Springs through Indio ("Date Capital of the United States") and south to the Salton Sea, 200,000 date palms yield 40 million pounds of dates of numerous varieties annually. You pass thick gardens of date palms along the highways. Dates are sold at roadside stands on State 111 and 86; here is your chance to try a date milkshake. At Shields Date Gardens, 3½ miles west of Indio, watch a 25-minute film on how dates are grown. There is also a rose garden well worth viewing. The popular Indio National Date Festival (held in connection with the Riverside County Fair in mid-February) features an Arabian theme, with camel races.

The most productive general farming in the valley is in the southeastern section, where the two largest cities, Indio and Coachella, are processing and shipping centers for a wide variety of agriculture. Not until you approach the Salton Sea does the desert take over again. Even here, development is underway, increasing the recreational facilities at this lake that is saltier than the oceans (see page 109).

South of the Salton Sea lies the Imperial Valley, greater in area than the Coachella Valley and acre-for-acre the most productive agricultural region in the world.

The High & Low Desert Attractions

In this region of Southern California's desert country stretch many miles of natural desert—both high and low elevation—very little of it untouched by man (though parts of it look pristine). Not far from the highly civilized resort areas surrounding Palm Springs and the activity of the Salton Sea are preserves of desert lands whose "stars" are the spiny ocotillos, sculptured Joshua trees, time-carved canyons, and wind-blown sands, all in the earth and sun colors of the desert.

JOSHUA TREE NATIONAL MONUMENT

Although civilization is changing the character of the desert surrounding Joshua Tree, this area remains a rare desert sanctuary. The monument (lying at the edge of two great deserts: the low Colorado and the high Mojave) is a transition land of beautiful desert studded with dramatic trees and plants and covered with wildflowers in spring. It is less a playground than an area dedicated to the preservation of a characteristic desert scene and the wildlife it supports. In Joshua Tree you can drive, hike, climb, picnic, and camp.

The monument covers more than 850 square miles and is located east of Palm Springs, less than an hour's drive away. The Cottonwood Springs (or south) entrance is 25 miles east of Indio on Interstate 10; the north entrance on State 62 can be reached through the towns of Joshua Tree and Twentynine Palms (the park headquarters).

The living desert

The distinctive plants and animals of this region are notable for their adaption to the heat and aridity of the desert habitat.

The Joshua tree (Yucca brevifolia), the most famous of the native plants, is actually a giant member of the lily family and one of the most spectacular plants of the southwestern deserts. Clusters of white blossoms, sometimes 14 inches long, appear at the ends of its angular branches; the plants have been known to attain a height of 40 feet. Growing at 3,000 to 5,000-foot elevations in the central and western parts of the monument, the Joshua tree will bloom in March and April, except during unusually dry years. Legend has it the Mormons named the plant "Joshua tree" or "praying plant" because of its upstretched arms.

At first, the newcomer might confuse it with the Mojave yucca (Yucca schidigera), more common at lower elevations and distinguished by much longer leaves and a shorter stature.

In addition to extensive stands of Joshua trees, the monument has the distinctive ocotillo, the feathery nolina, and many colorful kinds of cactus with large, showy blossoms. Stately California fan palms are found in several of the shady oases. One grove in Lost Palm Canyon contains more than a hundred of these trees.

The spring wildflower show at Joshua Tree is dependent upon winter rains. Average annual rainfall here is 5 inches. In a normal year, the color show begins in lower elevations as early as March and progresses to higher elevations through June.

Wildlife in the monument resembles that of other desert regions, but it is more abundant here because of the higher altitudes and a cooler, more varied climate. As with plant life, adaptation is necessary to the animals' survival. The kangaroo rat with long tufted tail is often seen around campgrounds at night. This creature and other native rodents manufacture water in their own bodies and can survive a normal lifetime without a drink. The largest animal, the desert bighorn sheep, is impressive but rarely seen. You're most likely to spot a coyote or the lively, side-blotched lizard (little brown uta). Thirty-eight species of reptiles and amphibians and 249 kinds of birds have been reported in the monument.

History unfolds in the monument

Joshua Tree National Monument has experienced a long history of human habitation. Artifacts discovered along an ancient river terrace in the Pinto Basin indicate the presence of primitive man in days when there was enough water to support a culture. Much later, Indians who mastered the art of desert survival settled at springs and waterholes and left traces of their campsites. Old mine shafts and mills on the hillsides attest to settlement by gold prospectors—the first white men to arrive around 1865. The cattlemen who followed left small dams or "tanks" at natural rock-collecting basins to catch rainwater for their herds.

Planning your visit

Because much of Joshua Tree is high desert, the weather is pleasant most of the year, particularly

Tall pines *along Hidden Lake, 1½ miles above desert floor, invite hiking, cool respite.*

Desert vegetation *of cholla and ocotillo grows profusely at opening to Coyote Canyon.*

Huge rock formations *challenge young climbers in Joshua Tree National Monument.*

on winter days. The altitude ranges from 1,000 to 6,000 feet in the Little San Bernardino Mountains. Since most roads are at the 3,000 to 4,000-foot level and go as high as 5,185 feet at Salton View, the monument seldom gets too hot for comfort even in summer. Most visitors come in October through May. Remember that desert nights get cold.

Camping is pleasant at several good campsites, but you will have to furnish fuel and water; gathering firewood within the monument is prohibited. Cottonwood Campground near the south entrance does have running water; otherwise, there are

water pickup stations between Ryan and Sheep Pass campgrounds and at the Visitor Center in Twentynine Palms. It's good to bring a container.

You'll find no lodging or eating facilities within the monument, but accommodations are available in and around the entrance towns.

Exploring Joshua Tree

Your visit can include several interesting stops and adventures on your way to (and inside) this diversified monument. If you are traveling State 62 to the

Desert bighorn sheep, *camouflaged among the rocks, thrive in Santa Rosa Mountains.*

north entrance, look for interesting antique and junk shops. Big Morongo Canyon Wildlife Preserve, at Morongo Valley, has a stand of large cottonwoods and springs that create a natural oasis.

Yucca Valley, between the San Bernardino Mountains and Joshua Tree, is built among fantastic rock formations, thick stands of Joshua trees, and spring wildflowers. Shortly after entering town, you can turn off to Pioneertown, site of many Hollywood westerns. The Pioneer Pass Road continues on to Big Bear Lake but is only accessible by four-wheel-drive vehicles. On a mountain overlooking the town, Desert Christ Park features large biblical figures sculpted of white concrete.

Along Old Woman Springs Road in Landers (north of State 62) are trailer parks for recreational vehicles and horsemen. This road also takes you to Giant Rock Airport; here, in three rooms hewn from a mammoth desert boulder, UFO buffs gather to discuss "sightings." Still another Yucca Valley attraction is the Hi-Desert Nature Museum.

Twentynine Palms, the northeastern gateway and headquarters to the monument, was once a watering place for prospectors. Now it is an oasis for health seekers, retired persons, aspiring artists, and tourists.

An early visit to the Visitor Center and Museum here will acquaint you with the fascinating land that you are about to explore. This building contains displays, desert artifacts, and maps and brochures. Ask the rangers for additional information. A self-guided nature trail leads through the nearby palm oasis.

At the south entrance to the monument in the Cottonwood Springs area just north of Interstate 10, there is also a small visitor center. From Cottonwood Springs, a 4-mile trail to Lost Palms takes you to an oasis of more than a hundred native palms that is also known for its birdlife.

Hidden Valley is a few miles in from the Joshua Tree entrance to the monument. Legend has it that the massive boulders and haphazard rocks here were once hideouts for cattle rustlers. Today, they shelter a campground and provide an intriguing jumble for agile explorers. To reach the valley from the parking lot, you can either climb through a narrow passageway under jumbled granite or take a surface trail. A 1½-mile nature trail winds through the valley.

Salton View, at the end of the paved road that runs south from Hidden Valley, is 5,185 feet high, giving you a panoramic view of the area stretching from Mexico and the Salton Sea (235 feet below sea level) to the San Jacinto and San Gorgonio mountains (over 10,000 feet above sea level). Nearby, the Lost Horse Mine area is rewarding for its display of desert plants and its view to Pleasant Valley.

Salton Sea *attracts fishermen. Area offers water skiing, boating, camping, picnic sites.*

Squaw Tank, a self-guided motor nature trail, is marked by a sign from the main park road. You'll cover 18 miles of sweeping views, inactive mines, and a fine stand of barrel cactus. Remnants of early Indian habitation are found in this area. Nearby, the climb to the top of Ryan Mountain (5,401 feet) is a steep 1.5 miles but well worth the effort. At the summit are outstanding views of the Queen, Pleasant, Hidden, and Lost Horse valleys.

Old Dale and New Dale, in the eastern section of the monument, is basin and range country, often overlooked by visitors.

Nature trails are numerous. Other than those already mentioned, there are well-marked walking trails at Cholla Cactus Garden and Cap Rock, each keyed to explanatory booklets available at the beginning of each trail.

Arch Rock, about 300 yards east of White Tanks campground, is a remarkable span of granite you can walk under. Descriptive signs mark the way.

SALTON SEA

Sandwiched between the rich farmlands and resort centers of the Imperial and Coachella valleys is one of California's most interesting stretches of desert — the below-sea-level depression that contains Salton Sea.

Once a dry desert wasteland, the sea was formed in 1905 when the Colorado River overstepped its bounds; billions of gallons of its flood waters were impounded in the basin. The sea remained at a nearly constant level until about 15 years ago. Then the water began rising steadily, overtaking deserted resort buildings and leaving them half-submerged in ghostly silence.

Salton Sea is a hot place in the summer, but winter temperatures stay in the comfortable low 50s to high 80s. Water temperatures drop as low as 50° in midwinter and climb to as high as 90° in summer. The best months are November, December, and the period from February through April.

The sea is circled by good highways—State 86 on the west, State 111 on the east. The highway between Anza-Borrego Desert State Park and Palm Springs passes along its southwest shore. Dusty side roads and rocky trails lead to hot mineral springs, Indian relics and petroglyphs, rock-hunting grounds, ancient shell deposits, colorful canyons, and sand dunes.

You'll find privately owned resorts. The 16,000-acre Salton Sea State Recreation Area, about 26 miles northeast of Indio on State 111, provides improved and primitive camp and picnic sites. Camping permits are available for a small fee at campground headquarters. Reservations are advisable in winter and spring; write to Park Supervisor, Salton Sea State Recreation Area, North Shore 92254, including a $1 reservation fee.

Motor boating and water skiing are the major water attractions, and racers consider the sea one of the fastest bodies of water in the world because it is below sea level, which is advantageous for internal combustion engines. If you are interested in seeing one of the larger racing or skiing meets, watch the Los Angeles or San Diego newspapers for times and dates. Strong winds create waves up to 10 feet in height at times; the park has a storm alert system.

Varner Harbor is the hub of most boating and fishing activities at the recreation area. The well-equipped marina offers rentals, supplies, and boat-washing facilities. The breakwater is popular with croaker fishermen; corvina and pargo fishing is best from a boat. Fish planted in the 1950s by the Department of Fish and Game have survived, but the gradual leaching of minerals from the land, making the sea more salty, has led to a decline in good fishing.

The nearby desert

Because the desert around Salton Sea has not been developed, it is full of fascinating natural features.

Mecca Hills, a choice desert country just north of Salton Sea, has three canyons that are favorites of desert explorers—Painted Canyon, Box Canyon, and Hidden Spring Canyon. All are reached along State 195 a few miles east of Mecca. The smoke tree (*Dalea spinosa*) and desert ironwood plant (*Olneya tesota*) found throughout the hills are full of purple blossoms.

Rocks and formations abound in this desert region. About 7½ miles due west of Mecca, you'll find the Fish Traps, circular pits formed from piles of large travertine-covered boulders. Archeologists aren't certain why these pits were built, but their favorite theory seems to be that the stones were collected by Indians and piled in these circular forms to trap fish in ancient Lake Cahuilla, which covered the Salton Sink from about A.D. 900 to 1400.

Travertine Rock is a mound of enormous boulders located approximately 100 yards off State 86 about 6 miles south of its intersection with State 195. Once partially submerged by Lake Cahuilla, the mound is covered with a scaly, knobby limestone (actually not true travertine but a calcareous rock called tufa). A climb to the top (about 200 feet) reveals a full view of the Coachella Valley and its miles of farms plotted in geometric precision.

The country south of Travertine Rock along State 86 is happy hunting ground for amateur geologists and rock collectors. Each year desert rains sweep clean the broad shallow washes of the

Santa Rosa Mountains and carry down brightly colored and oddly formed quartzites, flints, granites, schists, and sandstone. Look for them in washes around the south end of the sea—the farther from the highway the better.

ANZA-BORREGO DESERT STATE PARK

Anza-Borrego is a large desert. The area preserved within state park boundaries extends almost the entire length of San Diego County's eastern edge from Riverside County to the Mexican border. It ranges from 100 feet below sea level near the Salton Sea to 6,000 feet above on San Ysidro Mountain. You can't see it all in one visit. The nearly half-million acres are more than two-thirds of all the land in California's system of preserves.

The southern part of the present state park was originally a separate desert park named for Captain Juan Bautista de Anza, the Spanish explorer who pioneered this route to Alta California in 1774. Borrego State Park, taking its name from the Spanish word for "sheep," adjoined it on the north. In 1957 the two parks were combined.

Anza-Borrego is often pictured as a wrinkled wasteland of harshly eroded, nearly barren clay and gravel, possibly because its gullied badlands are its most extraordinary phenomenon. There is more to it than that: cool piney heights, springs and oozing *cienagas*, spectacular though brief waves of wildflowers in spring, and native fragrances of pervasive sage, subtle cottonwood, and even more subtle earth. Today's visitor can traverse a terrain nearly as wild and untouched as that found by early Spanish visitors. Many travelers consider November through May the best time of year to explore this desert—then it has a clean-washed, fresh look.

This state park is one of California's last untamed desert areas except for the privately owned enclave of Borrego Valley in the northern part of the park. Development has been isolated to this region so that Anza-Borrego can remain one of California's last frontiers. Like Palm Springs and Salton Sea, the valley taps underground sources for water. Nearby, 6,000 acres of former wasteland are cultivated for grapes, gladioli, citrus, and grains. Along with its farms, subdivisions, shopping centers, golf courses, and airports, the area offers tourist accommodations.

Driving is not difficult. More than 600 miles of roads follow the scenic, weathered hills and flatland. Although a deftly handled automobile can do surprisingly well in the desert, there are many roads that require high clearance or even four-wheel-drive vehicles. Pickup campers can get to some remote places; jeeps are advisable for the really tough routes.

Rangers conduct family cars in caravans to many scenic destinations and can point out roadside geological features, sea fossils, wildlife, and some unusual plants.

Camping has a unique feature here. This is the only California state park in which you may camp anywhere you wish. The only regulations are that you drive on established roads (horses and hikers are not restricted), that you not light fires on the ground, and that you leave things just as you found them. The nearest ranger will come to your rescue if you've camped off the beaten path and have failed to check in at a prearranged time the next day. Camping areas vary from highly developed (Borrego Springs) to less than the basic (your own site in a remote spot).

Desert camping is most popular from November through May, though there may be a few very cold nights or high winds during these months.

For a short visit to the park, it is best to select a relatively small area and explore it thoughtfully. If you can spend several days, establish a preliminary headquarters near one of the ranger stations, where you can attend campfire programs, get latest information on back-country driving conditions, and check out and back in for your own safety. Based on locations of active ranger stations, the most logical divisions of the park and some of their features are listed here:

Borrego Springs, a small resort community at the foot of San Ysandro Mountain a few miles north of State 78, is the center of park activity. Park headquarters is Borrego Palm Canyon, 3 miles northwest of Borrego Springs. For a list of lodgings, write to the Chamber of Commerce, Borrego Springs 92004. State 78 and U.S. 80 are the major routes leading into the park. The Borrego-Salton Sea Road (County Road S-22) parallels State 78 as a shortcut from Borrego Springs to Palm Springs, Indio, and the Salton Sea.

Wildlife is worth watching for. Some desert big-horn sheep still live in remote areas of the north end of the park and in the Santa Rosa Mountains beyond. At points farthest away from human activity, the natural desert is often a noisy place, with the humming of winged insects, the buzz of the cicada, the croaking of frogs in the springs and marshes, and the sounds of many birds.

About 600 species of plants are native to the park. Depending on altitude and exposure, desert flowers bloom profusely in March and April. Wildflowers range from tiny, pin-sized blooms to clusters of red on the ocotillo, which punctuate the landscape after a rainstorm. The California fan palm groves and the stands of smoke trees are among the finest anywhere, but Anza-Borrego is most renowned for its low, fat-boled elephant trees *(Bursera microphylla)*, fairly common in parts of Baja California but north of the border practically confined to the Anza-Borrego region.

Borrego Palm Canyon is the site of park headquarters and the most improved campground in the park. Its many conveniences include gas stoves, ramadas, showers, and trailer sites with hookups. Nearby are several points of interest: a 1½-mile, self-guided nature trail leading up to a canyon of palms; the most famous view point in the park, overlooking barren, spectacularly eroded Borrego Badlands; date groves; and a jeep road to Pumpkin Patch, a flat area covered with large, round concretions of unexplained origin.

Culp Valley is in high country, up to 4,500 feet. Here you'll find primitive camping on semi-wooded land with many huge boulders. From here a dramatic view extends across Borrego Valley to the badlands. Culp Valley is a cool retreat from the summer heat of the lower desert.

Tamarisk Grove has an improved campground that faces the beautiful, flowery slopes of the North Pinyon Mountains and a remarkable natural concentration of cactus. Good auto exploring is possible on a primitive road along San Felipe Creek

and Grapevine Canyon. Borrego Valley is a few minutes away by way of Yaqui Pass; Yaqui Well, an historic watering spot above Tamarisk Grove, has magnificent desert ironwood trees and a busy wildlife population.

Blair Valley can be reached on the Overland Stage Route, hacked through historic Box Canyon by the Mormon Battalion and still in use as County Road S-2. A year-round "use" area, Blair Valley has improved campgrounds at Old Vallecito Stage Station and at Agua Caliente Springs.

Fish Creek comes into view along a dramatic motor route up Fish Creek Wash through Split Mountain to Sandstone Canyon, with a jeep trail continuing through Hapaha Flat to the Pinyon Mountains. The eerie mud hills and elephant trees are features of this area. Supplies and meals are available in Ocotillo Wells.

Bow Willow has many palm groves, especially in the Mountain Palm Springs area: about 300 *torotes* (a Spanish word for "elephant trees") in Torote Canyon; a smoke tree forest; the old Carrizo Stage Station site; many inviting roads, jeep trails, and foot trails; the Well of the Eight Echoes (some say only seven); and the Dos Cabezas area, with monumental rocks, lava flow, a mine, Mortero Palms, and the giddy, canyonside tracks of the San Diego and Arizona Eastern Railway.

Desert campers *seek shade, cool breezes from their Pinyon Mountain camp site.*

In Borrego Palm Canyon, *tall palms provide shade from warm desert sun to hikers, campers.*

The Colorado River

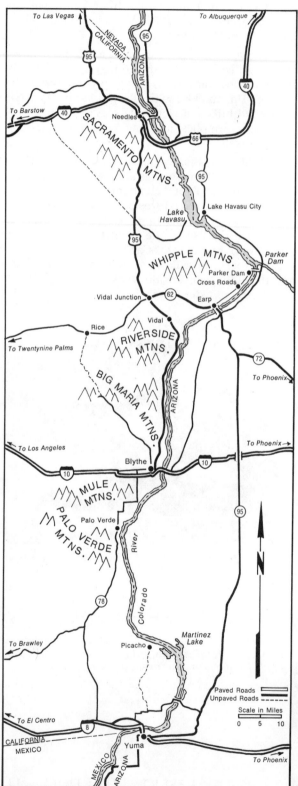

With its most renowned handiwork the Grand Canyon, the mighty Colorado carves through rugged terrain on the earth's surface, winding some 1,400 miles before reaching the sea. Once described as "too thick to drink and too thin to plow," the once-raging river (forming a natural boundary between California and Arizona) was used by early American Indians as a thoroughfare for canoe travel. Petroglyphs cut in rocks near Lake Havasu City are believed to be shoreline messages of these ancient river voyagers.

Important today as a major water supplier to the metropolitan areas on the Southern California coast, the Colorado River has been harnessed by dams and developed into a vacation and recreation area. Once traversed by paddle wheel steamers, the river is now dotted with campgrounds and marinas along its shoreline.

Most of the 265 miles of river from Hoover Dam in Nevada to the Mexican border are suitable for public recreation purposes. Along the lower Colorado River, Havasu Lake is the largest recreational development, increasingly popular each year.

This is "low desert" country where the summers are hot. Yet in July and August, boating, fishing, and water skiing at the lakes are outstanding.

THE NEEDLES AREA

At the Arizona border, the town of Needles is at the junction of two major highways—U.S. 66 (Interstate 40) and U.S. 95. Established in 1869 as a steamboat landing and supply station on the Old Emigrant Trail, Needles today has many boating facilities. Good beaches line the river and diversified fishing is possible in the Havasu National Wildlife Refuge. A marina and golf course add to the attractions. The nearby rock formations known as "The Needles" are visible from the highway crossing at Topock; they are a backdrop for the spectacular boat trip down through Topock Gorge to upper Lake Havasu.

Park Moabi is 11 miles southeast of Needles on U.S. 66. The park surrounds a lagoon opening into the

Colorado River *camp sites and marinas line the border between California and Arizona.*

Boating buffs *cruise placid Colorado River.*
Bear Canyon bluffs in Picacho park area tower above.

Famed London Bridge *rises above Lake Havasu City. An*
English village and London taxicab nestle beside bridge.

river, directly across from the wildlife refuge.
Launching facilities, boat docking, and boat rentals
are available (including houseboats). Secluded,
sun-bleached, sandy inlets invite camping, and
fishing is good.

LAKE HAVASU

Construction of Parker Dam in 1938 not only tamed
the lower Colorado River but also created a 45-
mile-long fresh water lake that, contrasting with
the raging red river, was quiet and very blue.
Named Havasu (an Indian name for "blue water"),
this lake is lined with deep bays and picturesque
coves. Set between the Chemehuevi, Mohave, and
Whipple mountains, the beautiful lake has become
a favorite destination for sportsmen and the setting
for an extensive recreational development—Lake
Havasu City.

Three national championship water sports con-
tests annually take place on Lake Havasu: the
Desert Regatta for sailing craft in May, the
National Invitational Ski Championships in midsummer, and the Outboard World Championships.

The London Bridge

The most conspicuous addition to the desert landscape around Lake Havasu is the London Bridge.
This historic span, moved block by block from its
site on the Thames River, was reassembled across
dry land. Then the mile-long channel now separating the airport island from the shore was exca-
vated beneath it. After the bridge was sold by the
city of London for almost 2½ million dollars, it
took an additional 5½ million dollars to dismantle

the 130,000 tons of granite, ship them 10,000 miles
to Lake Havasu City, and reassemble them. The
bridge looks at home in an English village setting,
with pub, restaurant, and shops built around it.
A London taxicab is parked on the waterfront.

Lake Havasu City, 19 miles south of U.S. 66, is
served daily from Phoenix and Las Vegas by
Apache Airlines. Hotels are located in the center
of the shopping center, overlooking the lake, and
near the golf course. Facilities for campers and
trailers are at Havasu Cove on the lakefront.

Lake Havasu State Park

A 13,000-acre preserve, this park has headquarters
at Pittsburgh Point on the airport island. Check
with rangers for information on camping around
the lake. There is no shoreline road, but roads do
penetrate to the shore at a few points for boat
launching. At some points are resorts, boating
facilities (including rental), trailer parks, and
camping spaces.

The park has wide, sandy beaches with picnic
tables, fountains, barbecue pits, showers, and rest
rooms. The blue-green bay offers good water skiing,
interrupted only by your endurance, and safe
swimming in exceptionally clear water.

Anglers usually catch their limit of bass, trout,
crappie, bluegill, and channel fish. The clear, cold
Colorado River waters connecting Lake Havasu
and Lake Mohave to the north are noted for good
bass and trout.

Hunters try for Canadian honkers, other geese,
and ducks. On the Arizona side, dove and quail
roam in season. Bighorn sheep can be hunted but
only by permit.

Mojave Desert
& East of the Sierra

 The desert casts its spell unevenly. Some people regard it as an obstacle to be avoided or crossed as quickly as possible, never responding to it at all.

But for many the desert holds a special magnetism. Drawing them back again and again, it lures them on to explore rugged hills and rocky canyons, thrills them with its sunsets and wildflowers, and shares the secrets of its shy creatures and hidden oases.

If you belong to the latter group, you will enjoy exploring the vast Mojave Desert. Stretching west and south to the San Gabriel and San Bernardino mountains, the Mojave reaches north and east into Death Valley and across to southeastern Nevada. Its altitude varies from 2,000 to 11,049 feet. Little of the water that falls on the Mojave reaches the ocean. Most moisture is evaporated by the dry, hot winds.

Contrary to popular belief, the desert is a region of many mountains. But in many areas, straight-line roads travel a seemingly unending line until gobbled up by the horizon at the edge of the sky.

It would be folly to claim that the Mojave of today is still the complete retreat from civilization that it once was. In places it is crisscrossed with roads, power lines, and pipelines. Modern desert cities are sprouting up in prime locations, and the once abundant wildlife is prey to people and their machines.

The best time to explore the Mojave is between February and May, after the winter rains but before the intense heat of the summer. In spring, the desert blushes with thousands of square miles of wildflowers. No seed was ever planted here by man; this is nature's garden, haphazard in arrangement, tended only by sun, rain, and wind.

Included in this section are Apple Valley, a high desert resort region; the country surrounding U.S. Highway 66 between Victorville and Barstow and beyond; Antelope Valley, the wildflower center; and Death Valley.

Reflecting the snowy tip of Telescope Peak is pool in Death Valley, 282 feet below sea level.

The Mojave Desert

Parts of the Mojave have never been fully explored. Much of it is rugged terrain, fit only for the seasoned desert traveler and his well-equipped car. Most of the trips mentioned in this chapter can be made in any well-maintained passenger car, but some include roads best negotiated by a four-wheel-drive vehicle.

Some parts of the desert are being closed to recreational vehicles under a Bureau of Land Management plan. These include sites of fragile Indian pictographs and places where endangered species are trying to maintain life. Before camping off the main roads, be sure you are not in a restricted area. When departing, leave everything as you found it.

Desert driving precautions

The rules for safe automobile exploration of the desert are few but mandatory. Don't turn off main roads without inquiring locally about conditions of side roads. Above all, don't hesitate to turn back if travel becomes difficult. Back roads are likely to become worse, not better.

Remember that you often gain necessary traction in sand by deflating your rear tires to about half normal pressure (take along an air pump so you can reinflate tires when you're back on hard surface). Be sure in advance that your engine's cooling system is in good working order. Always carry adequate supplies of water, gasoline, and oil. Don't count on desert springs as water sources; they are often dry. If stranded in the desert during the summer, don't leave the shade of your car.

Maps

Up-to-date, detailed maps are necessary to any back-road exploring. You can usually get good ones from counties, the U.S. Forest Service, state monuments and parks, and the U.S. Geological Survey. The Bureau of Land Management, the agency in charge of much of California's desert country, has section maps that indicate private or government-owned lands within the desert. For a free map, write to the BLM, Box 723, Riverside 92502.

APPLE VALLEY

Situated east of the Mojave River and north of the San Bernardino foothills, Apple Valley has the clean, dry air, beauty, warmth, and solitude of the desert. Once a sanctuary for early Indians, Apple Valley is now a resort community with golf courses, guest ranches, swimming pools, fishing lakes, an airport favored by sailplane pilots, riding stables, and a thoroughbred breeding farm where you can observe horses in training. Ranch clothes are in order here. Barbecues are reached by hay wagons, and Western entertainment centers around a crackling campfire.

The Apple Valley Inn—center of most visitor activity in town—offers both hospitality and private, detached cottages. Inside the inn you'll find game trophies, antique rugs, and old Western portraits. The Roy Rogers Museum, formerly on the grounds, is being moved to Victorville to form the nucleus of a new entertainment center—Western World—a 300-acre complex reached by taking the Palmdale offramp from Interstate 15.

Apple Valley is located southeast of Victorville on State Highway 18, which continues east through Lucerne Valley (also offering enjoyable guest ranches) on its way to Big Bear Lake. An unusual rock formation in Lucerne Valley is Hercules Fingers, a granite boulder 60 feet high. Drive out Camp Rock Road to the second power company road; turn east for approximately 3 miles; small bamboo sticks mark the road leading to the rock.

At the south end of Apple Valley Road is the Stoddard Jess Ranch, one of the southland's largest trout farms right in the middle of the desert. Huge reservoirs stocked with over a million trout a year offer weekend fishermen of all ages a chance to catch some "big ones." No license is required; there is a moderate charge. As a bonus you'll see some of the 400,000 turkeys the ranch raises.

Mojave Narrows Park is near here. This great oasis, halfway between San Bernardino and Barstow, is one of Southern California's least known parks.

Along a 2-mile stretch where the underground Mojave River rises to the surface, the park is an inviting expanse of green meadows, cottonwoods, willow thickets, and year-round water in river channels, creeks, bogs, ponds, and two small lakes. Birds and small animals come here from the desert, and beavers build dams.

Occupied by Indians at one time, the oasis was used by later travelers as a desert stop-off. Now you can camp, picnic, swim, and fish in a 50-acre lake, follow a nature trail through the river forest, enjoy

Restored house *in the old gold mining community of Tropico is among buildings open to view. Here you also see museums, mine, mill.*

Multicolored *Death Valley peaks and ridges are striped with reds, browns, yellows, and greens.*

Riders wind through *Calico Hills near ghost town of Calico.*

"MUST SEES"

CALICO (near Barstow)—authentic silver mining town now regional park; mine tours, train rides; see "boot hill"

EASTERN CALIFORNIA MUSEUM (Independence)—good starting point for local history; displays of Indian artifacts

BRISTLECONE PINES (White Mountains)—ancient forest of perhaps world's oldest living trees; good views of Sierra

PETROGLYPH LOOP TRIP (Bishop)—50-mile drive to petroglyph sites; includes reserve for rare desert pupfish

LAWS RAILROAD MUSEUM (Bishop)—1883 rail depot and narrow-gauge line now historic museum; tours of period buildings

LANCASTER (Antelope Valley)—starting point for wildflower wonderland; view valley from Saddleback Butte

MATURANGO MUSEUM (China Lake)—orientation for Mojave Desert; fossils and Indian artifacts; petroglyph tours

MITCHELL CAVERNS (Interstate 40)—underground limestone caves; Visitor Center view; walk Mary Beal Nature Trail

RANDSBURG (off U.S. 395)—more memories than houses remain in old gold town; Desert Mining Museum open

RHYOLITE (Death Valley)—turn-of-the-century boom town, now best known for house built of bottles

SCOTTY'S CASTLE (Death Valley)—architectural dream of Death Valley Scotty; tour interior and gardens

TROPICO (off State 14)—last operating gold mine in Southern California; tour mine, mill, and restored gold camp

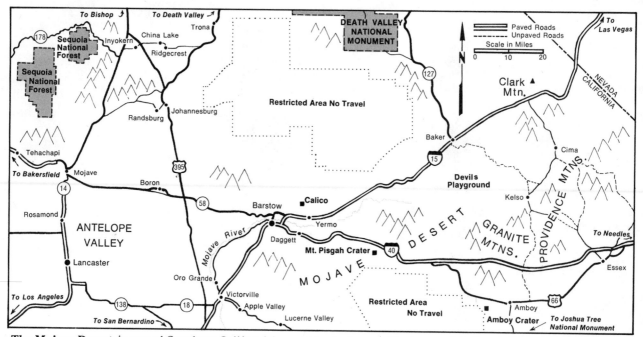

The Mojave Desert *is one of Southern California's most typical areas. To the north is Death Valley; east is the Colorado River; south is Joshua Tree; west is Antelope Valley.*

a farm atmosphere, or go boating (rowboats, kayaks, and paddle boats can be rented).

The park is open daily; there is a modest car entry fee. To get there, take Bear Valley cutoff from Interstate 15 east to Ridge Crest Road and then go north to the entrance.

FROM VICTORVILLE TO BARSTOW

As an alternate to the busy but stark Interstate 15 freeway from Victorville to Barstow, leave the highway at the downtown Victorville exit and follow the quiet country road (old U.S. 66) along the railroad tracks. Between Victorville and Oro Grande, you drive close to the Mojave River and have the opportunity to enjoy the several riverside picnic spots shaded by groves of tall cottonwoods.

Beyond Oro Grande the road continues through country planted in alfalfa and other forage crops, passing beautiful ranches, clusters of deserted buildings, and three sleepy hamlets before returning you to Interstate 15 at the outskirts of Barstow.

Barstow is a good base for exploring the surrounding countryside. You can venture into canyons, climb mountains, hunt gemstones, or follow trails leading to historic landmarks and old waterholes.

Nearby is Calico, a restored silver mining town. For a contrast, you can visit Goldstone, a space flight tracking station. The same areas that hide fossil beds and petroglyphs are rich in color when the wildflowers bloom.

The Mojave Valley Museum (open daily) has a variety of desert artifacts, mining exhibits, and a small Indian collection. For information on wildflowers, make this your first stop in Barstow; conducted tours (open to the public) are held during spring. The museum is located in Dana Park.

Southeast of Barstow, an area has been set aside for driving the ubiquitous dune buggies and motorcycles—so they won't overrun the entire desert.

Calico, founded in 1881 as the result of one of the west's richest silver strikes, is experiencing a new boom: an influx of tourists instead of prospectors. The town was named for the multi-colored mountains that lie behind it. The original residents were proud of the local saloon (Lil's), hotel, mercantile store, bank, railroad station, and schoolhouse— but especially of the high-producing Maggie Mine. Today you can explore its tunnels, ride the Calico-Odessa Railway, take a cable tram ride, and visit the buildings that are probably a bit more orderly and better scrubbed than before but still colorful. There's a slight admission charge per car, as well as a charge for specific attractions. You can also buy something to eat here. Hikers can explore a narrow gorge for a mile up Wall Street Canyon.

Calico was restored and opened to the public by Walter Knott of Knott's Berry Farm, whose uncle grubstaked the original Calico Hills prospectors. Later, the area was deeded to San Bernardino County, which now manages it as a regional park with emphasis on its mining history. Visitors enjoy Calico's Ghost Town spring festival in May.

A campground in the area allows you to spend the night in the "Old West." In addition, there are motels in nearby Yermo and Barstow. Calico is 9 miles east of Barstow (3½ miles west of Yermo) off Interstate 15.

The Calico Mountains are off the beaten track but not more than 20 minutes driving time from Barstow on primitive but safe roads. Doran Drive is a delightful, narrow loop that winds for 5 miles past high-walled gorges that are always good for camping. Mule Canyon is longer and wider and still offers views of the colorful mountain range. One-way Phillips Road makes a short side loop among many old mine shafts and tunnels.

Rainbow Basin, north of Barstow, is reached by taking Irwin Road to appropriately named Fossil Bed Road and turning west. By actual count, there are 25 individual fossil beds in this region. A 40-inch-high horse, rhino, dog-bear, and sabre tooth cat long ago roamed these now-sunken dry basins. Camping is available if you want to explore the region more thoroughly; remember to look but not dig. In and around this vividly colored canyon are some of nature's beautiful spring wildflower beds.

Goldstone, about 45 miles north of Barstow, is a complex of deep-space tracking stations designed for communication with spacecraft. To arrange for advance permission required to visit the Apollo and Mojave stations, telephone (714) 587-0641.

FROM BARSTOW TO THE BORDER

Leaving the old mining center of Barstow, two major highways take you through the Mojave Desert to the California border. Las Vegas is reached directly by Interstate 15 (U.S. 91); Interstate 40 (U.S. 66) goes southeast to Needles, the Colorado River, and the Arizona border.

Take the high road—Interstate 15 . . .

Instead of fighting the monotony of whizzing sagebrush and traffic along this fast interstate freeway, stop and take a look at the surrounding desert—it will seem more friendly.

Afton Canyon is 31 miles east of Barstow. The road comes to a dead end about 5 miles from Interstate 15 at the Union Pacific siding called Afton. Here the Mojave River emerges from underground and winds into beautiful Afton Canyon, where redwing blackbirds sing on swaying tamarisks and willows and fluted pink cliffs reach straight down to the nearly level sand. There is a campground here.

Rasor Ranch road leads to several inviting camping spots and finally to a deserted old ranch with buildings, corrals, and water tank still intact. Here

is the site of Rasor, a station on the long-defunct Tonopah and Tidewater Railroad. Some of the ties are still in place on the old roadbed.

Oro Fino ("fine gold") is one of several deserted but never-quite-abandoned mines southeast of Baker. It is located between Soda Lake and the lava beds that stretch 10 miles or more east of the Baker-Kelso road. Only four buildings remain.

The sand dunes (Devil's Playground) outside Kelso are perhaps the biggest and most spectacular in California. In spring, their undulating surfaces are carpeted with wildflowers.

. . . or the low road—Interstate 40

Heading southeast for the Colorado River and the California-Arizona border, the highway crosses the south side of low desert mountain ranges.

Daggett is a friendly, folksy pioneer town just 8 miles from where Interstate 40 leaves Barstow for its extension through the southern Mojave Desert. Here you can visit a blacksmith shop (now a museum), where 20-mule-team wagons were built.

Mt. Pisgah and Amboy craters are mountains of volcanic ash. Watch for Mt. Pisgah and Amboy craters along Interstate 40 and U.S. 66. Outstanding examples of cinder cones, they are particular favorites of photography buffs and of children, who love to climb through their weird formations. Because they are so much like the moon's surface, they were used by spacemen for practice walks.

An unpaved road comes within about a half-mile of the 200-foot-high Amboy Crater. From there it's a 10-minute climb up the steep side to the top; carry drinking water with you.

Mitchell Caverns State Reserve—underground caverns 23 miles northwest of Essex—is a fascinating place to visit. You enter the limestone caves at an altitude of 4,300 feet—about 1,000 feet above the desert floor. The higher view of the desert from the Visitor Center is magnificent.

An hour-long excursion (an easy hike of 1½ miles round trip) takes in Tecopa and El Pakiva caverns, a beautiful underworld of sculptured limestone. Rangers explain the complicated story of cave formation as they guide you through the caverns. Not too spacious, these chambers contain strangely beautiful cave coral, stalactites, and stalagmites.

To learn something about the flora and fauna of the region, walk the Mary Beal Nature Trail, a 1¼-mile self-guided loop. Descriptive folders explain some of the area's geography and geology.

Mitchell Caverns State Reserve is open all year; tours are scheduled at 1:30 P.M. weekdays and at 10 A.M. and 1:30 and 3 P.M. on weekends. The entrance fee to the reserve is $1 per car for both day-use and overnight camping.

Sand sailors *scoot across hard surface of El Mirage Dry Lake, pushed by a spanking hard breeze.*

Coast range foothills *meet desert at Western end of Antelope Valley, crossroads for many wildflower species.*

Some improved campsites with additional space are available for truck campers and trailers; water is limited and visitors are advised to bring their own supply. It gets cold on fall and spring nights (the favorite seasons for visitors).

ANTELOPE VALLEY

This corner of the Mojave Desert slopes gradually upward to the west as it narrows between the rolling foothills of the converging Tehachapi and San Gabriel mountains. The pastoral aspect of much of Antelope Valley sets it somewhat apart from the rest of the Mojave. Without its Joshua trees, it would not look like desert. Yet it is a part of the Great Basin, 2,000 to 3,000 feet above sea level, where cold winters, hot summers, and harsh winds discourage human settlement. Plants from the desert, from the Central Valley, and from coastal hills grow in Antelope Valley, making it a beautiful and popular destination in the spring. Even in other seasons there is much to observe. Antelope Valley's largest town, Lancaster, has fine motels and restaurants and is a convenient base for exploring open country a few miles to the west and east. Accommodations are also available in Palmdale, Mojave, Tehachapi, Lebec, and Gorman.

You get more than just a scenic view of the valley if you pull off State 14 (heading north) at the lookout point a few miles south of Palmdale. You can also see the valley's geologic features that have been formed by California's dominant rift zone, the San Andreas Fault. A plaque at the lookout shows the location of the fault line, extending west of Palmdale across the valley to its highest elevation at Big Pines Summit (6,862 feet).

Wildflower viewing is often at its best in Antelope Valley. Sometimes the show is shimmering and brilliant, but it is always unpredictable, so it's best to plan your outing with a double purpose in mind.

At the Lancaster wildflower center (open from late March until mid-May in the Antelope Valley Fairgrounds at 155 E. Ave. I), you can get a free map of the best viewing areas.

One suggested loop trip centers around State 14. Drive north from Lancaster to Rosamond and west to visit Burton's Tropico Gold Mine, Mill, and Museum. Continue 3 miles west to almost-deserted Willow Springs (just off the highway), a former stage and freight station and, in the early 1900s, a health resort. Head north to Backus Road; turn right past the headframe of the Cactus Mine.

Saddleback Butte State Park (formerly Joshua Trees State Park) is 17 miles east of Lancaster on Avenue J. At its northwest corner, a small headquarters building, a parking lot, and some picnic tables are all the civilized embellishments you will find. Beyond is a splendid, sunny, 2-mile sweep of yucca-studded desert, culminating in alluring Saddleback Butte. Ask the ranger where to find the large waxy desert candles.

Burton's Tropico Gold Mine, Mill, and Museum lies four miles west of Rosamond at the edge of a big forest of Joshua trees, not far from Mojave. Tropico is really two separate places. One contains the mine and mill—both real, and in operation until 1956—high on Tropico Hill; the other is the gold camp site below it. Both have museums.

In the cool gloom of the mine, you'll see gold ore and miners' gear; proceed through a stope (sloping cavity left after a vein is mined) to see the 900-foot shaft. Common mining methods and procedures are explained throughout the tour by guides as you follow the vein out to the "glory hole," an open pit created by steam shovel mining.

Walking 87 wooden steps down through the mill (and back up), you get a thorough idea of how gold is separated from ore. Still intact, the mill looks just as it did when the switches were pulled some 18 years ago.

The gold camp below—a village of old buildings richly furnished with antiques—includes an old one-room school, an assay office, and a combined bath-barbershop-dental office-post office. In the museum you'll see such relics as old period clothing and newspapers, displays of mining equipment, and a collection of rocks and gems. In the safe is a display of gold specimens and nuggets.

The mine is open all year from 9:30 A.M. to 4 P.M. daily except Tuesday and Wednesday. The gold camp, museum, and mill are open weekends only during the winter (October 1 to June 1) from 9:30 A.M. to 4 P.M. Admission, which includes the guided tour, is $2.25 for adults and $1.50 for children 5 to 11.

THE NORTHERN MOJAVE DESERT

The vast northwestern Mojave Desert is a land of great contrasts. To the west rise the high, imposing peaks of the Sierra Nevada; yet throughout this desert can be seen the low, crystalline sinks of ancient lakes. Human history is recorded in ancient Indian drawings on the rocks and in old mines and mining towns left by 19th century prospectors. Today, man is making his mark here with secluded military establishments and missile sites. At Brown, off U.S. 395 on State 58 north of Edwards Air Force Base, is the world's largest open-pit borax mine. Still active, the great pit yields snow-white hills of processed borax.

Randsburg, a gold town but not a ghost town, is hidden from U.S. 395, which passes through its neighbor, Johannesburg. From a distance it still resembles old photographs of early mining communities. Houses, some built with wood from dynamite boxes, stand weather-beaten and full of memories. The town has lived through three booms—gold (it had one of the richest mines in Southern California), tungsten, and silver. The Desert Mining Museum has miners' and Indian artifacts and objects from the famed Yellow Aster Mine. Nearby Koehn Dry Lake, resembling a snowstorm on the desert, is the site of still another kind of mining—mining for salt.

Natural history at China Lake

The most extraordinary concentration of prehistoric rock pictures in America is found in the Coso Mountains. The site in Renegade Canyon, within the China Lake Naval Weapons Center firing range, is now a National Historic Landmark. The Navy and the Maturango Museum, a geological treasure trove located on the Center, team up to conduct day-long caravans to the pictographs. There is no definite schedule for the tours; if you would like to join one, write to the museum at Box 5514, China Lake 93556.

To reach the museum, leave U.S. 395 or State 14 at the Ridgecrest-China Lake Exit and drive to the end of the road, where you'll come upon the Navy center's main gate. It's open only on weekends from 2 to 5 P.M.; admission to the museum is free. You will need a pass from the main gate.

Little Lake, just off U.S. 395 about 20 miles north of the road to China Lake, is worth a stop for a look at some notable Indian petroglyphs. You can see some of the rock drawings from the lakeshore, but others are best sighted from a rowboat (for rent at the boathouse at the north end of the lake). The greatest concentration of drawings are found on the basalt cliffs on the west shore and at the southeast end of the lake.

The fee for overnight camping includes bank fishing privileges. All campsites have tables, fireplaces, and water.

To reach Fossil Falls, turn east from U.S. 395 onto Cinder Road, almost 3 miles north of Little Lake. Turn southwest at the first intersection, left at the next intersection, and drive to the end of the road. It's a short hike to the falls on a marked trail. The falls were formed by ancient lava flows from the Coso Mountains and then eroded by the Owens River.

Trona Pinnacles

The Pinnacles make a logical side trip from the popular Wildrose Canyon route into Death Valley; you can see them at a distance.

Rising up from the desert floor south of the crystalline Searles Lake, the spires are believed to have been built up by algae from an ancient sea.

The northern approach to the Pinnacles is very primitive but gets you there in the least amount of time. If there have been very recent rains, a safer approach is on the rough but all-weather road from the south that runs more or less parallel to the Trona Railroad tracks.

A leisurely lunch stop among the formations will give you time for a brief exploration. You could easily spend a day investigating the area or camp overnight on the east side in the shadow of some of the tallest spires.

East of the Sierra

The full impact of the Sierra Nevada is rarely appreciated until you see its abrupt east side—the face it turns toward the desert. This eastern side of the mountains, to the west and north of Death Valley and east of Sequoia and Kings Canyon, offers a myriad of attractions for vacationers: high desert, spectacular mountains, uncrowded trails, good fishing, ghost mining towns, wildflowers, mineral deposits—most accessible by good roads. In winter, sections of these mountains offer excellent skiing.

One important highway, U.S. 395, leads north and south through the whole section, linking a chain of little towns. From this arterial highway you can go east into Death Valley or west a short distance into the towering mountains.

People may wonder why Inyo and Mono counties are considered part of Southern California when even the largest towns are 300 to 400 miles from Los Angeles. Mainly, it is because they are tied more closely with Los Angeles than with San Francisco, both economically and recreationally. Even residents of these counties themselves are most oriented to the southland.

OWENS VALLEY

The bending and cracking of the earth's surface that created the Sierra Nevada and the parallel ranges of the White, Panamint, and Inyo Mountains also sank a long deep trough between them—Owens Valley, a place of hot springs, craters, lava flows, and earthquake faults.

Owens Valley's first inhabitants were the ancestors of the Paiute Indians; then came ranchers and farmers. Today the most important industry has become the tourists who enter the valley.

Lone Pine is one of the points on U.S. 395 where you can turn off to the famed hiking trails of Sequoia and Kings Canyon. Going west on Whitney Portal Road, you pass through the picturesque Alabama Hills, named by Confederate sympathizers. Ringed by these knobby hills is Movie Flat, a favorite location for filming TV and movie westerns. One road to Movie Flat turns south from Whitney Portal Road, which also takes you to Tuttle Campground.

Independence, the turnoff for the Kearsarge Pass entrance to the Sierra high country, is also the home of the excellent Eastern California Museum. In its building at Center and Grant streets are natural and local history displays and Indian artifacts. The museum is open Monday through Saturday from 10 A.M. to 5 P.M. and Sunday from 1 to 5 P.M.

One block north of Center Street on U.S. 395 is the Commander's House, the only extant structure of Camp Independence, established in 1862 to protect early Owens Valley residents from Indian attacks. It is open Wednesday through Saturday from 10 A.M. to 5 P.M.

A little over a mile west of the highway north of town is the interesting Mt. Whitney Fish Hatchery, built in 1917 of native stone. You can picnic on its inviting, tree-shaded grounds.

Ancient bristlecone pines (some more than 4,000 years old) have been stunted and twisted by the harsh forces of nature so that they resemble upright pieces of driftwood decorated with green needles. The bristlecones grow above 10,000 feet in

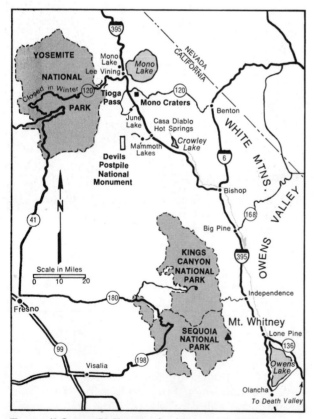

Tranquil Owens Valley *nestles between the Sierra to the west and the Nevada border to the east.*

Herd of 290 tule elk *run permanent reserve along U.S. Highway 395 in Owens Valley from upper end of Owens Lake to Tinemaha Reservoir.*

Fanciful, *often delicate tufa pinnacles line shores of Mono Lake to create sight that amazed Mark Twain.*

Most picturesque *in West is Mt. Whitney Fish Hatchery, near Independence, built of stone in 1917. Huge trout swim in this pool; tiny fish are kept inside building.*

the White Mountains; the drive up gives you a good view of the sheer eastern face of the Sierra. To reach this ancient forest, turn east on a secondary road to Westgard Pass, just north of Big Pine. Another well-marked road branches north, taking you to the first concentrated area of bristlecones at Schulman Grove. Here you will find a ranger station, information center, picnic area, and starting points to Pine Alpha and Methusela Groves.

The wildlife viewing point in the Poverty Hills is reached by an access road a few miles north of the

Goodale Creek road. Turn off the highway to the east on the Tinemaha Reservoir road. The viewing point looks down across an area known as a favorite of the rare tule elk. Take along binoculars; we can't promise a sighting of elk, but the site in itself is pretty enough to merit a stop.

Bishop, with a population of over 3,000, is the bustling metropolis of the Owens Valley. Known as the world's mule capital, the city stages a colorful Mule Days celebration on Memorial Day weekend. Its Chamber of Commerce, at 125 E. Line Street, has

"Big, Bad Bodie"– a True Ghost Town

Forgotten in Bodie *is elegant, 19th century horse-drawn hearse—a victim of progress.*

"Goodbye, God, I'm going to Bodie," was the conclusion to one little girl's prayer when her family moved to what was then one of the wildest mining camps in the West. Her dismay was not unfounded—there was allegedly at least one murder a day in "big, bad Bodie." Sixty-five saloons once operated there, and the girls along Maiden Lane and Virgin Alley were sometimes rewarded with gold nuggets from the big mines.

Now a State Historic Park maintained in a condition of "arrested decay," Bodie is a true ghost town. Weeds grow freely around the dozens of old weathered buildings, and no attempt has been made to restore them to original grandeur. A few rangers and their families are the town's only residents. Its edges curled by time, the old wooden boardwalk rises and falls along Main Street past the venerable Miners' Union Hall, the Odd Fellows Hall, and the brick post office. Other points of interest are the tiny Methodist church, the Cain home, the jail, and several "boot hills."

To reach Bodie, take U.S. 395 to a junction 7 miles south of Bridgeport; turn east on a dirt road that winds through barren hills for 13 miles. Bring your own lunch; there are no stores or overnight facilities.

useful travel literature for points of interest in this area. The 50-mile Petroglyph Loop Trip described in one of the chamber's folders is especially worthwhile and best for photography in the early morning or midafternoon. The loop takes you north on U.S. Highway 6 and then doubles back on a good dirt road through Fish Slough, with stops at four outstanding petroglyph sites. A short distance beyond the last site, you pass the 20-acre Owens Valley Native Fish Sanctuary, one of the state's first ecological reserves. Walk to the water's edge to get a good view of rare and endangered fish, including the tiny Owens pupfish.

At Laws, the rhythm of puffing steam engines, clanging bells, and freight platform bustle has long been stilled, but more people come to see this old Owens Valley railroad station now than ever came during its prime. The Laws Railroad Museum and Historical Exhibit has interesting daily tours of period houses and buildings (weather permitting). Located 5 miles out of Bishop and one-half mile off U.S. 6, it makes a good excuse to interrupt a long drive and give youngsters a run. The grounds are open all the time; the displays are open from 10 A.M. to 4 P.M. every day except a few holidays. There's no admission charge.

Crowley Lake, north of Bishop and above the monumental Stanley Grade on U.S. 395, is one of the most easily accessible fishing lakes in California. Popular with anglers for its giant trout, its waters hold fish weighing up to 10 pounds. A campground operated by the city of Los Angeles is situated a half-mile from the highway, just west of and in sight of the lake. It is cool at night at this 7,000-foot elevation.

MAMMOTH COUNTRY

Although Mammoth Mountain is only 30 air miles from Yosemite National Park and due east from San Francisco, it serves as a Southern California playground. There's a geographical reason for this. Part of the isolated eastern crest of the Sierra Nevada, Mammoth is reached easily from the south over U.S. 395 (though the drive takes at least 7 hours) but cut off from the west except in late summer when the high mountain passes are open.

This diverse area offers excellent winter skiing above 10,000 feet and all-year trout fishing and great inner tubing in the 28-mile stretch of the Owens River from Pleasant Valley Reservoir to Tinemaha Reservoir. (Bishop celebrates Huck Finn Day in August by decorating and launching anything that floats for river races.)

In the intermediate elevations from Mammoth Mountain to Owens Valley are abandoned mills and mines to explore, volcanic remains to discover, and picnic spots to enjoy.

Lake country

Visitors to Mammoth will find a variety of lakes and creeks. Most are fishermen's retreats; others are good for swimming, boating, and viewing. Turn east off U.S. 395 on the road to the fish hatchery to reach Hot Creek. The hot springs, a 25-foot-wide pool, are about 4 feet deep and have practically no current. High in mineral content, the water is unusually buoyant; you can vary the temperature by paddling away from the spring into the cool eddies of the creek.

For fishing, try Convict Lake, with access to trails leading to some 22 other lakes. Facilities include a resort, restaurant, and trailer park, as well as a pack station with horses, mules, packers, and guides. From U.S. 395, turn west about 4 miles south of Mammoth Lakes Road.

Mammoth Lakes, an area dotted with more than 30 lakes in a 9,000-foot basin, can be reached by a paved side road that cuts off U.S. 395 at Casa Diablo Hot Springs and meanders to the shore of Lake Mary, heart of the region. Five of the lakes, popular with fishermen for many years, may be reached by good roads. Mountain lodges offer woodsy comfort, log fires, and hearty meals. Forest Service campgrounds are usually crowded in midsummer but virtually deserted after the end of September. Summer aerial tram gondola rides on Mammoth Mountain are spectacular. Boats may be rented at Lake Mary and Twin Lakes, and packers offer pack and saddle animals and guides.

Mammoth Mountain ski area

While the steep eastern face of the Sierra Nevada contributes to Mammoth's isolation, it is one of the reasons skiing at Mammoth and nearby June Mountain is among the best in the state and certainly the best in spring, when at 10,000 feet there is still powder snow.

The lodge at Mammoth Mountain is 4 miles from the town of Mammoth Lakes. Lifts from here serve slopes to challenge any skier; for the sightseer there's a panoramic chair ride. Snow touring is popular—on skis, snowshoes, or dog sleds. Accommodations range from dormitories to chalets. For information on housing or package ski trips, write Mammoth Lakes Chamber of Commerce, Box 123 F, Mammoth Lakes 93546, or June Mountain and June Lake Reservation and Information Service, June Lake 93529.

Devils Postpile, in the midst of beautiful forest and lake country west of Mammoth Lakes and a few miles southeast of Yosemite, is a geological oddity on permanent display. Symmetrical basalt columns, some rising more than 60 feet and fitting together to resemble a great pipe organ, are remnants of a lava flow at least 915,000 years ago which cracked into these pentagonal and hexagonal forms as it cooled. Pumice so light that it floats on water and a soda spring with a nearby campground are points of interest in the northern part of the monument, as is the great crack in the earth—reminder of a past earthquake. The river offers good fishing.

Devils Postpile is open from mid-June to early October. From the northeast you enter along an 18-mile road off U.S. 395, crossing Minaret Summit at a 9,300-foot elevation.

Rainbow Falls, down the canyon from Devils Postpile, tumbles over a rocky ledge some 140 feet into a box canyon. When the light is right, you may see a colorful rainbow in the mist created where the water strikes the bottom. Park along the road and walk to the falls.

June Lake Loop offers a drive of great scenic beauty, as well as access to sports and recreation spots. Fishing is good in Rush Creek, running alongside the road. Nearby Grant Lake has a marina with boats you can rent for trolling. Boat rentals are also available on June, Gull, and Silver lakes. In summer, the June Mountain ski lift hoists visitors on sightseeing trips to a mountain top restaurant. Just south of June Lake Junction, you can follow a side road east about a mile to Devil's Punchbowl, the southernmost Mono Crater.

Mono Craters resemble gigantic ash heaps when you see them from U.S. 395. Actually, there are 20 craters forming a crescent-shaped range along the highway. These were thought to be extinct until 1940, when gas, steam, and hot water were discovered in the earth beneath them. You can explore the two northernmost craters from State 120 on the way to Mono Lake.

Mono Lake, at the northern end of the Mammoth area near Lee Vining, has been shrinking and taking on a more sulfurous smell since the Los Angeles Aqueduct extension began tapping its feeder streams. A shoreline walk reveals an amazing "moonscape" of delicate tufa formations rising out of the old lake bed. After seeing this, you'll know why Mark Twain called Mono Lake "one of the strangest freaks of nature."

Death Valley

Legendary Death Valley is distinguished from other desert valleys by its great size, low altitude, diverse desert, and colorful history.

It is unique among deserts for its great extremes, one of these being its summer heat. Its record high of 134° was set in 1913. Up the enclosing slopes, it may not be hot at all, but down on the flats it can stay about 100° all night long.

Another extreme is its low elevation. An area of about 14 square miles is lower than 280 feet below sea level. In the salt beds west and northwest of Badwater, two places 3 miles apart and 282 feet below sea level are the lowest points in the Western Hemisphere. Nearby Telescope Peak is 11,049 feet *above* sea level, another example of the dramatic extremes to be found in this valley.

MAN AND THE VALLEY

Throughout the valley you'll see evidence of human occupation, as well as geologic history. Indian petroglyphs appear in more than 200 sites. Many places carry names of pioneers and prospectors of the gold rush days. The valley, probably first referred to as Death Valley in January, 1850, did not really deserve its name. Although the pioneer parties crossing the area suffered extreme hardships, only one "'49er" died in Death Valley (but not from heat or thirst), and an obscure party of nine others also may have perished there. Death Valley's record of human lives lost, measured against that of the rest of the Western desert, is reassuringly low.

Natural features

All of the great divisions of geologic time and nearly all of the subdivisions are represented in the land formations of Death Valley. Fossils of prehistoric mammals discovered here show that the arid salt flats, gravel desert, and harsh peaks were at one time a fertile plain. As the climate became drier, ancient lakes evaporated into salt flat deposits and mud playas. Wind reduced granite into sand and blew it into dunes. Since the wind blows from all directions, the dunes remain in place.

Plants and animals

The popular belief that nothing lives or grows in Death Valley is discounted by the common animal and plant life that has tenaciously adapted to the burning heat and dryness. Almost all of the perennial plants have deep or far-spreading roots and special adaptations of leaves and stems to help tap and conserve vital water. Over 600 species of plants and trees flourish at all elevations in the monument, and 22 species—including the Panamint daisy, Death Valley sage, and rattleweed—exist only here. Bristlecone pines, thousands of years old, grow at 10,000-foot elevations on Telescope Peak.

On a favorable spring day, when the unexpected brilliance of myriad springtime wildflowers mantle the dark, alluvial slopes and narrow canyon washes, the name Death Valley seems inappropriate.

Visitors to Death Valley see few animals, for most emerge only at night in search of food. A great variety of natural life exists in a 2-mile area between Telescope Peak and Badwater, where the desert animals can find plants to feed on. Only the plantless central salt flats are barren of animal life. Even fish live in this desert. Descended from Ice Age ancestors, the rare pupfish or "desert sardine" thrives in Salt Creek, Saratoga Springs, and Devil's Hole and is an astonishing example of super-rapid evolutionary adaptation to changing environmental conditions.

Planning a visit

Although a visitor in summer may remember the blazing sun and intense heat, in other seasons Death Valley basks in a mild climate. Tourist facilities are in full operation from November to mid-April. In summer, a list of Hot Weather Hints, distributed in the monument, will help make your visit safe and pleasant.

State 190 from Lone Pine to Towne's Pass is the most spectacular and most improved route from the west into the valley. State 178 from the south to Wildrose Station is another popular approach.

State 127 from the southeast joins State 190 at Amargosa (Death Valley Junction). En route to the junction, the highway passes Tecopa Hot Springs, a unique watering hole where visitors partake of the baths free of charge. The curative springs once belonged to Indians whose ancestors brought their lame and sick to bathe. When they gave up the hot springs to the white settlers, it was with the stipulation that the good water be left free to all comers. And that is the way it has remained.

Clusters of trailers around the bathhouses make the little settlement visible for miles. For informa-

Pastime of guests *at Furnace Creek Ranch: muleback trip into canyons.*

Ubehebe Crater *is most prominent of several volcanic gashes at Death Valley National Monument.*

Crossing a rocky bajada, *jeep explorers traverse foot of Panamint Range.*

tion on camping, write to the Park Superintendent, P.O. Box 158, Tecopa 92389.

Amargosa Opera House, at Death Valley Junction, opens its weekend performances to the public. If no one attends, performances are still held, but the "audience" is a realistic, wall-sized mural.

Tours of Death Valley are popular; check with a travel agent for specific information. Las Vegas, Nevada, is the closest air terminal. There's a paved landing strip for light planes at Furnace Creek and a short dirt strip at Stove Pipe Wells.

Where to stay in Death Valley

Lodging is not really a problem except during Easter and Thanksgiving weekends and the weekend of the Death Valley '49ers Annual Encampment early in November.

Furnace Creek Inn is a luxurious resort hotel with resort prices that include meals. The inn has a swimming pool and tennis courts, stables, and an 18-hole golf course. Furnace Creek Ranch, a mile down the road, also has resort facilities on a more modest scale. Lodging is a choice between simple cabins or newer, motel-style accommodations. The inn is open from November 1 to April 31; the ranch stays open throughout the year. For information and reservations, write to Furnace Creek Ranch or Inn, Death Valley 92328, or Fred Harvey Reservations, 8601 Lincoln Blvd., Los Angeles 90045.

Stove Pipe Wells Hotel, actually about 6 miles from the site of old Stovepipe Wells, is a motel-style resort, open all year. The postal address is Death Valley 92328.

Wildrose Station, at 3,500 feet on the west side of the Panamint Range outside of Death Valley proper, has a coffee shop and cabins (with baths) to accommodate 10 guests. It is open all year. For reservations, write to Wildrose Station, Trona 93562.

Campgrounds provide scenic backdrops, ranging from whispering sand dunes to sweeping mountain views. Of nine monument campgrounds, the three most improved are in the valley: near the Visitor Center are Texas Spring and Furnace Creek (open all year but very hot in the summer); Mesquite Spring is south of Scotty's Castle. Other campgrounds are Sand Dunes (no water) and Midway Well, both in the Stove Pipe Wells vicinity; and year-round Emigrant Junction, with good mountain and valley views. The campgrounds at higher elevations are open in the summer. At all camps you furnish your own firewood; at some, the water must be boiled.

In the frequented parts of the valley, camping is strictly confined to established campgrounds. But back country campers are permitted to use outlying locations as long as they don't disturb or litter the ground or burn the plants.

Look for motels nearby in Trona, Beatty, Shoshone, and Death Valley Junction.

There's life in Death Valley

At first glance, Death Valley seems little different from the desert you have driven through to reach it. But as closeup follows closeup and you make your way to both labeled phenomena and some secret finds of your own, you perceive new dimensions. The unbreached mountain face seen from afar is really slotted with fascinating labyrinths that lead you on and on. The featureless salt flat is a vast maze of miniature crystalline Alps. The sand ridges in the distance are mountains in their own right—but mountains that yield underfoot and restore themselves to unmarked pristinity with every fresh breeze. The unnatural splotch on the far hillside is a waste pile marking an abandoned mine

Death Valley guests *soak up sun around pool in heart of valley at Furnace Creek Inn.*

Young visitors *to the Racetrack puzzle over mystery of the moving rocks.*

with tunnels, shafts, headframes, and railroad beds still more or less intact.

Death Valley can be explored on over 500 miles of improved roadways. Additional miles of primitive roads wind through the back country.

Furnace Creek, because of an excellent and dependable water supply from nearby springs, has always been a center of activity. Go to the all-year Visitor Center here to plan your stay. You can buy maps of varying scales and a wide variety of useful publications. The Visitor Center museum contains exhibits showing geology, plants, and wildlife.

The Borax Museum nearby exhibits an outdoor assembly of implements once used in the extraction and refining of borax and other minerals. Here are the great 20-mule-team wagons, nearly as sound as when they were maintaining their remarkable schedules 80 years ago.

Zabriskie Point, southeast of Furnace Creek on State 190, is an area of 5 to 10 million-year-old lake beds that are especially dramatic at sunrise.

Artist's Drive, off the main road south of Furnace Creek, takes you through a rainbow canyon colored by oxidation. The even more intense color of Artist's Palette is splashed on a hillside halfway through the canyon.

Badwater, a few miles farther south, is known as the lowest point in the Western Hemisphere (−282 feet below sea level). Often crusted over, the salt pools at close range reveal weird formations of rugged rock salt.

Dante's View, on the crest of the Black Mountains, is one of the most spectacular scenic overlooks in the United States, rising 5,775 feet directly above Badwater.

Charcoal kilns, resembling giant stone beehives, blend into the hillside of the Panamint Mountains. They appear as good as new after 90 years of existence. These kilns reduced pines and junipers to charcoal for the Modoc Mine smelter, 25 miles west. To reach the kilns from the Wildrose Ranger Station, follow the road to upper Wildrose Canyon.

Skidoo was the one boom town near Death Valley that really did pan out. At the end of its two-year existence, it was ahead by 3 million dollars.

Rhyolite, Nevada (a ghost town), is just outside the monument on State 58. Here a $130,000 railroad station without a railroad houses a museum and store. The Rhyolite Bottle House, with walls built of 51,000 beer bottles set in adobe, is still occupied by a Rhyolite citizen who sells desert glass and curios. Once a spirited boom town around the turn of the century, Rhyolite thrived for only five years.

Titus Canyon is reached by a one-way dirt road that must be entered from State 58 on the east. This

The Clock Tower *of Scotty's Castle is isolated from the rest of the desert castle buildings.*

25-mile trip through the wineglass-shaped canyon with changing colors and soaring walls is a memorable experience.

Scotty's Castle is the incredible desert mansion built by Death Valley Scotty (Walter Scott) and his millionaire friend Albert M. Johnson. Located in the extreme northern part of the monument, the Spanish-Moorish mansion, lavishly furnished, cost 2 million dollars and took about 10 years to build. Scotty's flamboyant escapades became part of the Death Valley folklore; the castle remains as a testimony to his natural showmanship and eccentric personality. Hourly tours are run daily from 9 A.M. to 6 P.M.; there is an admission charge. A gift shop and snack bar are provided for visitors.

Colorful Ubehebe Crater, one-half mile wide and 800 feet deep, was created 3,000 years ago by a volcanic explosion. It's not far from Scotty's Castle.

The Racetrack, 27 miles south of the crater, is a mud playa, occasionally subject to high velocity winds that are responsible for the "mystery of the moving rocks." When wet, the Racetrack is so slippery that the wind can move great boulders across it.

The Sierra
& the San Joaquin Valley

THE CLOISTER

Sequoia and Kings Canyon National Parks together encompass an exceptionally large portion of the Sierra Nevada. Each contains several thousand acres of the most massive trees on earth, the giant sequoias *(Sequoiadendron giganteum)*. Mt. Whitney's 14,495-foot peak rises from a region of magnificent granite mountains on the eastern edge of Sequoia National Park. The rugged back country of both parks offers unsurpassed mountain scenery and a hiker's domain of spectacular peaks and canyons, threaded with an intricate trail system that includes the southern end of the famed John Muir Trail.

The parks, joined end to end along the Sierra ridge and administered by the same headquarters at Ash Mountain, can be reached from the west on two main highways: State 180 from Fresno, which leads through the Grant Grove section of Kings Canyon National Park, penetrating the canyon of the South Fork of Kings River for a short distance; and State 198 from Visalia, which enters Sequoia National Park at Ash Mountain.

If you make advance reservations, park concessioner buses meet trains and buses at Tulare and Visalia to transport you to the parks. Air connections can be made at Visalia or Fresno.

For more information on the parks, including a detailed map of the back country, hiking trails, and campgrounds, write to Sequoia and Kings Canyon National Parks, Three Rivers, California 93271.

The Central Valley, lying to the west of the towering mountain range, is a broad agricultural belt, the scene of several of John Steinbeck's novels. It has a vivid historical background that has been too often overlooked. To the east of the Sierra Nevada is Owens Valley, offering some of the best access into the mountains. Visitors will find ghostly remains of mining towns, a 4,000-year-old forest, and, in the spring, an opulent display of wildflowers.

Towering sequoias *overwhelm a small boy. In Giant Forest soars this group called "The Cloister."*

Sequoia & Kings Canyon National Parks

Giant trees, awesome canyons, cascading streams, and sparkling lakes greet visitors to these spectacular mountain parks. Much of their natural beauty can be explored by mountain road or trail. Self-guided nature trails and naturalist-conducted walks allow everyone to sample some of the most unspoiled mountain country in the state.

The Generals Highway, connecting the two parks, takes you through groves of the "Big Trees" and leads to spur roads to Moro Rock (overlooking the Kaweah River Canyon), tree-encircled Crescent Meadow, and delicate Crystal Cave.

Access roads on both east and west sides of the Sierra offer an entrance into the high country reached only by hikers and backpackers. The shortest trip into the interior is from the west slope—11 miles by trail from Crescent Meadow. With advance reservations, you can stay overnight in the tent campground.

Where to stay? At Sequoia and Kings Canyon, rustic cabins in perfect keeping with the towering sequoias co-exist with more modern accommodations. Campgrounds are numerous, well equipped, and located in strategic and beautiful spots throughout both parks. Some allow trailers (but have no hookups); a few at lower elevations are open all year.

Giant Forest Lodge in Sequoia has one-room cabins scattered among the Big Trees and an excellent dining room. Rates are around $20 for two at this lodge, open from mid-May to early October. Camp Kaweah at Giant Forest Village is the only all-year lodging in Sequoia Park. Housekeeping cabins at reasonable rates are rented during summer.

Grant Grove Lodge in Kings Canyon is similar in price to Giant Forest. Meadow Camp offers housekeeping cabins. Farther north, Cedar Grove Camp has a limited number of canvas-top cabins.

You should make advance reservations for lodges and cabins, including a deposit. Write to Government Services Inc., Sequoia National Park 93262. During the summer season (May 1 to September 15), you can call the toll-free number (800) 742-2070 for information and reservations.

SEQUOIA NATIONAL PARK

The first national park in California and the second in the entire national park system, Sequoia was established to protect its groves of giant sequoias, found here in greater abundance than anywhere else in California—their only native habitat.

The southern entrance to the park through Ash Mountain is headquarters for both parks. But the center of activity is the Giant Forest region, 16 miles north along the Generals Highway.

Three miles from Three Rivers outside this park entrance, the road to Atwell Mill and Mineral King takes off steeply and winds for more than 20 miles into the high country. The remains of old Atwell Mill, where logging began in 1879, are visible today. You'll come upon a small, secluded campground and a ranger station at Atwell Mill.

Mineral King, at the end of the road 3 or 4 miles beyond Silver City, was an old mining community, now important as a jumping-off spot for trips to the high country. Pack stations with horses and burros are located here; nearby are several good fishing lakes. Closest lodging is in Three Rivers.

The Generals Highway

A visit to the park on the Generals Highway (State 198) is a journey not soon forgotten. This beautiful road connecting the two parks was completed in 1934. A hint of the care taken to preserve the natural scene around it is Tunnel Rock, a great boulder left in place to span the road. As you twist among the sequoias, look for other interesting spots along the 16 miles from Ash Mountain to Giant Forest.

At Hospital Rock, 6 miles inside the park, Indians lived in the shelter of another huge boulder. Legend has it that the sick were brought here for healing. Later, pioneers took refuge under it. Interesting reminders of the Indian camp are rock paintings and mortar holes in the flat rocks. Exhibits in a nearby shelter tell the story.

The best fishing reached by road in Sequoia is along the Middle Fork of the Kaweah River. An easy footpath takes you down from Hospital Rock. Fine scenic turnouts occur along this route. Amphitheater Point, 10 miles into the park, has one of the best overall views of Moro Rock and the Middle Fork's canyon.

Moro Rock is a giant monolith that juts out of Giant Forest to dominate the wide canyon of Kaweah River. Its commanding crest (6,725 feet) looks distant and unattainable from the Generals

From crest *of Moro Rock, you get unparalleled view of wide canyon of the Kaweah River.*

Bearpaw Meadow campers *sample joys of early wilderness, rising to fill backpacks with fishing gear.*

Kings River's *Middle Fork cascades down deep gorges cut through Kings Canyon National Park's jagged peaks.*

Highway but not nearly so forbidding when you get up on the plateau and drive the 2-mile spur road to its northern base. From the parking area, you climb only 300 feet to the summit.

Crescent Meadow was referred to as the "gem of the Sierra" by John Muir. A tiny stream runs through this lovely, crescent-shaped meadow surrounded by a wall of dark, stately trees. The road to Crescent Meadow branches left from Moro Rock Road and passes under a fallen sequoia called Tunnel Log, cut so that cars can pass through it.

A half-mile hike from the Crescent Meadow parking area brings you to Tharp's Log, in which pioneer Hale Tharp (first white man to see the big trees) spent his summers.

Among the giants at Giant Forest

In the Giant Forest region are clustered all of the park's lodging, stores, most of the campgrounds, and a Visitor Center. Yet the area still appears relatively natural and unspoiled. Giant Forest Village,

"MUST SEES"

SEQUOIA-KINGS CANYON NATIONAL PARKS — home of giant sequoia; view mighty Mt. Whitney; sample back country of High Sierra

FORT TEJON (Lebec)—old military post once housed First Dragoons and Camel Corps; restored as State Historic Park

TULE ELK RESERVE (Tupman)—remnant of once-large herds that roamed the valley; best view is afternoon feeding time

PIONEER VILLAGE (Bakersfield)—Kern County indoor-outdoor museum; collection of furnished historic buildings

CHINA ALLEY (Hanford) — joss houses, herb stores, and other remains of Chinese culture now being restored

even when summer's crowd overflows the parking space, seems old-fashioned and unhurried.

The General Sherman Tree, the world's largest tree (although not the tallest), is 102 feet in base circumference and 17 feet through at a height of 120 feet. One hundred forty feet above ground level extends a limb 6.8 feet in diameter, thicker than the bases of most forest trees.

Near the General Sherman Tree is the start of Congress Trail, a 2-mile loop that will take you to some of the more famous and spectacular of the trees: the Senate, House, and Founder's groves, as well as the President, McKinley, and Chief Sequoyah trees. At the beginning of the trail is a guide booklet explaining the numbered stakes along the way.

Crystal Cave is 9 miles from Giant Forest—but the drive takes 45 minutes. Here are beautiful natural pools covering veins of marble and crystalline limestone formations. The temperature is a constant 50°. Thousands of years of nature's handiwork are explained by a naturalist on daily tours in the summer from 9 A.M. to 3 P.M. Visitors over 16 pay a small fee.

High country

For nine months of the year, the park's high country is quiet, inhabited only by wildlife; during the other three months, this road-free domain is a playground for hikers and backpackers. The main traffic arterial is on the John Muir Trail, beginning in Yosemite Valley and running south for 225 miles to Whitney Portal. Much of its route lies within the boundaries of Kings Canyon and Sequoia parks.

To control the number of people in the wild area of the parks, backpackers are on a permit system. Although some permits are issued on a first-come, first-served basis, it is wise to write in advance, giving the dates of your trip, route, number of people in your party, and whether you plan to hike or use horses. Send your request to Sequoia and Kings Canyon National Parks, Three Rivers 93271.

Bearpaw Meadow provides a good sampling of the Sequoia back country in a short period of time; no camping permit is required. The trip is 11 miles one way by trail from Crescent Meadow. Perched on the edge of a tremendous overlook at the base of the Great Western Divide, the camp offers comforts and good food, in addition to a spectacular view. Side trails through bold mountains lead to good stream and lake fishing. The camp is generally open from late June to early September. Tent accommodations cost about $5 per person. Make reservations at Giant Forest Lodge well in advance of your trip. Trips to Alta Peak and to Heather, Emerald, and Pear lakes originate here.

KINGS CANYON NATIONAL PARK

Kings Canyon is both one of the oldest and one of the newer national parks. When established in 1940, it absorbed tiny General Grant National Park, a sanctuary set up after Sequoia was created in 1890, now known as the General Grant Grove.

The park is actually two entirely separate areas with the west side containing the only two developed sections—the General Grant Grove and Kings Canyon regions. Densely forested, it is usually comfortably cool (elevation varies from 4,600 to 6,600 feet). The largest area of the park is a rugged mass of spectacular peaks and canyons.

General Grant Grove region

Principal claim to fame in this area is in the three notable sequoia groves: General Grant, Redwood Mountain, and the remains of one other grove in the Big Stump area.

General Grant Grove is the destination of most visitors to the area since, along with all the park facilities, it has the famed General Grant Tree. Second largest tree in the world, the Grant Tree has a base circumference of 108 feet (actually 6 feet larger than the General Sherman) but a smaller total volume. Both of these trees were standing in the Bronze Age more than 3,000 years ago. Because General Grant is the nation's Christmas Tree, each Yule Season an impressive ceremony is held here. Roads to the grove take you near the base of the General Grant and also to its towering companions. One of its fallen friends, Fallen Monarch, once stabled horses in its strong shell. Nearby Centennial Stump, in striking contrast to the living giants, is all that remains of a great tree cut for the 1875 Philadelphia World's Fair and reassembled there to amaze fair visitors.

Informative campfire programs take place every summer night at the amphitheater. In the village you'll find posted schedules of daily ranger-conducted trips, full of facts and park lore.

If you just want to contemplate the wonders of nature, you can go to the landmark trees and groves without a guide. A labyrinth of trails radiates from Grant Grove Village. Within an area of 5 square miles radiate over 20 miles of trails, most of them comparatively level, where you can wander leisurely under the giants away from the sounds of civilization.

Big Stump Grove, a short and easy walk from the entrance station, contains Sawed Tree, Mark Twain Stump, and Old Adam (also called Burnt Monarch). Some sequoia stumps exhibit more than 3,000 annual growth rings.

Redwood Mountain Grove usually refers to the 10,000 acres in Redwood Mountain and Redwood

Sample the Sequoias in Winter

It can be delightful to drive slowly through a snowy forest, hearing no sound except the crunching of spotless snow under your tires. A route made to order for contemplation of a Western winter is the Generals Highway, the beautiful road linking Sequoia and Kings Canyon national parks, between Giant Forest and General Grant Grove. Except for brief closings during and after storms, it is kept open all winter. You can call (209) 565-3351 for a recorded message on current weather and road conditions. It's safe to take walks close to the road in Giant Forest; north of Giant Forest Village you can walk out into Round Meadow encircled by Big Trees.

A mile beyond the General Sherman Tree in Giant Forest is a side road to the Wolverton ski area. Crowds are small and skiing inexpensive (a family of four can ski for the day for about $12). Ski schools, geared to children and beginners, also offer cross-country instruction. All types of equipment can be rented; slopes agreeable to different degrees of skill are reached by four rope tows. Sleds, toboggans, and inner tubes glide down nearby hills. Wolverton is open according to snow conditions (normally December to April).

If you find the land of Big Trees beautiful in summer, you will find it so in a different way in winter. The air is crisp, the stars in the winter sky seem especially large, and a stillness settles over Giant Forest—a stillness in strange contrast to the bustle of summer. Again, you don't have to be a sportsman to enjoy this winterland. Put on your warm clothes and walk along the road some evening after dinner to find a new beauty and appreciation in the silence of the sequoias in winter.

Snow *along Generals Highway through Sequoia National Park prompts snowball fight.*

Canyon—the largest remaining concentration of giant sequoias in the world. Because it's off the beaten track, its solitude adds to its charm. Two guided walks from Grant Grove, Sugar Bowl, and Barton's Post Camp go into Redwood Mountain Grove. In cathedral-like Sugar Bowl itself, you can stand in one spot, free from the constant flow of people, and count 57 lofty sequoias.

Kings Canyon and Cedar Grove region

From Grant Grove you go to Kings Canyon and Cedar Grove on a 30-mile highway that drops 2,000 feet before reaching its destination. From parking overlooks on wide sweeping curves, you can gaze into the canyons of the Middle and South forks of the Kings River and beyond to the bewildering maze of jagged peaks that constitute the greater portion of Kings Canyon National Park. These breathtaking views are the best hints you will get of the country beyond. About 10 miles before Cedar Grove is Boyden Cave, 450 to 600 feet underground, which you can tour in an hour.

Cedar Grove has a store, coffee shop, ranger station, and a few cabins. A variety of conducted trips led by ranger naturalists are offered here, as are nightly illustrated campfire programs.

Summer days can be warm at this elevation of 4,600 feet; yet camping is delightful under the big pines on the bank of the boisterous Kings River.

The San Joaquin Valley

A flat basin dotted with small towns, the San Joaquin Valley is the southern half of California's so-called Central Valley—the only extensive expanse of flat land in the state (the northern half is the Sacramento Valley). It is a major agricultural producer of cotton, grapes, and other products that thrive in summer heat. Visitors will also see forests of oil rigs, most pumping furiously.

Hot, dry summer weather limits recreational opportunities in the valley itself and, with few exceptions, residents look to the nearby mountains or to the cool coast for their vacation and weekend activity. Still, significant vacation areas have developed around Fresno and Bakersfield, the area's two largest cities. Artificial reservoirs, part of large-scale irrigation systems, are sources for boating, fishing, and swimming.

Valley cities are also "gateways" to national parks and the high country of the Sierra Nevada. Because of this, they're centers of hurried activity throughout the summer.

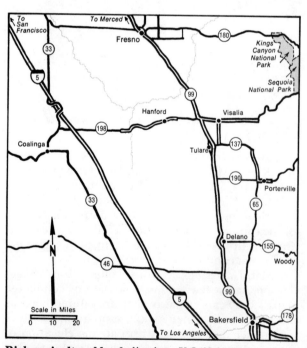

Rich agricultural lands *lie along U.S. 99 from Bakersfield to Fresno, north-south Interstate 5.*

OVER THE TEHACHAPIS

Years ago, to enter the southern half of California's Central Valley from Los Angeles you followed the "Grapevine," a twisting road with all the thrills of an amusement park ride on the Ridge Route over the Tehachapis and down into the outer limits of Bakersfield. No longer an obstacle course, today's road is a smooth freeway (Interstate 5), that gives no indication of the troubles once experienced in building a wagon route over this same pass.

Fort Tejon, an old military post established by the U.S. Army in 1854, is handily situated for today's travelers, just off the freeway near Lebec (30 miles south of Bakersfield). Fort Tejon once quartered the Army's most unusual unit—the First Dragoons and Camel Corps. Never the scene of any major military battles, the fort had as its main duties keeping peace between the miners, ranchers, and Indians and chasing down bandits.

Abandoned in 1864, the post was restored as a State Historical Park. It's open daily from 8 A.M. to 5 P.M.; admission is 25 cents for those over 18. You can picnic on the grounds in the shade of some lovely old trees.

Just south of Bakersfield, Interstate 5 and U.S. 99 divide. Interstate 5 heads through an almost isolated section of the San Joaquin Valley, marked only by turnoffs and a few gasoline stations and restaurants at posted intervals. Though it's the fastest route north, it's fairly monotonous.

Tule Elk State Reserve at Tupman, is the only real tourist attraction along the route. Saved from extinction, this small remnant of the great herds of tule elk that once roamed the vast San Joaquin Valley is kept in a 350-acre fenced range. Visitors are not permitted to roam the range; even though these are the smallest of elks, a bull can reach a weight of nearly 600 pounds. At the Visitor Center are picnic tables and a natural history display.

The best time to see the elk is at 3 P.M., when they gather for their supplemental feeding of barley and alfalfa pellets near the visitors' viewing center. At other times they move out of range and are less likely to be visible by eye or camera lens. Signs mark the exit from the freeway.

From vantage point *along Woodford-Tehachapi Road, look out over great Tehachapi railroad loop.*

Beale Tower *was rebuilt at Kern County Museum following 1952 earthquake.*

Bull wheel, *relic of long-abandoned oil derrick, decays in McKittrick Valley.*

BAKERSFIELD

Situated on the south bank of the Kern River in the southern end of the San Joaquin Valley is Bakersfield—county seat for Kern County and a junction of major highways through Southern California. Primarily a market city, Bakersfield is in the midst of an area rich in oil, minerals, and agriculture. Along the foothills to the east of the city lie the large oil fields; between these are spread ranches, pastures, vineyards, and orchards. This area was depicted in John Steinbeck's *The Grapes of Wrath* as the promised land for Oklahomans who drove

west to escape the Depression dust bowl.

Country music fans call the city "Nashville West," thanks to Merle Haggard, Buck Owens, and others of country western music fame. You can hear the sound on Chester Avenue.

Kern County Museum's Pioneer Village, a 12-acre indoor-outdoor museum, makes frontier history come alive. Outdoors, about 40 historic structures (originals and restorations) are laid out as a model town of the vintage 1870-1910 period. The Harry D. West Collection of vintage horse-drawn vehicles has everything from a pony cart to a logging wagon, from a Concord coach to a hearse. Other period

Basques in Bakersfield

Basque couples *join in traditional dance at annual celebration.*

Basques began arriving in the Central Valley almost a century ago. Originally from the French side of the Pyrenees mountains (separating France and Spain), they came as sheepherders, ranging up and down vast empty stretches of land with their flocks. This lonely occupation is today almost a disappearing way of life, although a few Basques (now mostly Spanish) come into the area on a work contract basis.

Bakersfield became home to many who gave up herding sheep to start other occupations, including cooking their distinctive food. You can enjoy a Basque meal at one of eight restaurants. Most are located in east Bakersfield around Sumner and East 21st streets (now called International Village): Noriega's, Pyrenees, Villa de Basque, Basque Cafe, and Woolgrowers Cafe.

Chateau Basque is on Oak Street, Chalet Basque on old Highway 99, and Airpark Restaurant at the Bakersfield Airpark, 3 miles south of town.

Noriega's serves boarding house style. Everyone eats together at 6:30 P.M., and there's no choice of menu. All restaurants feature some traditional side dishes (including stew and tongue), in addition to your entree. Lamb is a specialty; try "mountain oysters" in the spring. For a picnic, get your French bread at the Pyrenees Bakery, 717 E. 21st Street.

Late summer finds Basques and friends gathering for a special mass, picnic, and festival including dances from their original homeland. Though these activities are not generally open to the public, you can write to the Basque Club, c/o Highmoor St., Bakersfield 93308.

---

pieces include a steam locomotive, an 1898 oil derrick, a caboose, and a branding iron collection.

Indoors, the main museum houses fossils from the nearby McKittrick oil field area, a diorama of birds and mammals, Indian relics, and the most unusual curiosity—a dog-powered butter churn. The museum at 3801 Chester Avenue is open weekdays from 8 A.M. to 5 P.M., weekends and holidays from noon to 5 P.M. Museum admission is free; there's a small charge to visit Pioneer Village.

KERN RIVER CANYON

A popular recreation area beginning about 11 miles east of Bakersfield on State 178 is Kern River Canyon. Before reaching it, you will see the turnoff for Kern River State Park, a well-developed area known for its beautiful scenery, as well as for its swimming, boating, fishing, and hiking.

All along the twisting and churning Kern River, from its origin in the High Sierra to the thirsty valley floor, are scattered resort areas and mineral springs. Camping facilities are being prepared at Lake Ming.

Lake Isabella, some 45 miles from Bakersfield, is the largest manmade reservoir in Southern California. At Kernville, near the northern tip of the lake, you'll find a variety of accommodations and restaurants; the lake itself offers fine swimming.

In 1885 gold was discovered in considerable quantities on the Kern River, leading to a frantic boom in the southern Sierra region. Keyesville, first settlement to spring up in this new field, is now a ghost town. Gambling resorts and gunmen are long gone, but you can still see the remains of a rude fort erected for protection against Indian attacks that never materialized. The townsite is 4 miles west of Lake Isabella.

Lovely Rogers, a miner from Keyesville out looking for a lost mule, discovered the first piece of quartz that marked the beginning of Quartzburg and its rival, Whiskey Flat, later known as Kernville. Today, nothing remains of Quartzburg, and Whiskey Flat sleeps beneath the waters of the lake; the new Kernville was rebuilt several miles north of the original site. But bordering the highway, the old cemetery still remains. Modern Kernville proudly hails its predecessor's "lack of respectability" as an important part of its local history. Each February the citizens turn back the clock with Whiskey Flat Days, a rip-roaring, four-day celebration that recalls the exciting and often gaudy history of the old mining camp.

If you continue east on State 178, you will view some of the majestic scenery for which this section of the Sierra is well known. The road winds through the mountains, crossing Walker Pass (elevation 5,248 feet) to meet U.S. 395 southwest of Inyokern. You'll pass by the old flour mill at Weldon, and you can buy some homemade sausage at Onyx Store, a building that has remained virtually unchanged for almost 120 years.

A VALLEY SAMPLING

Three smaller valley cities have cultural or recreational attractions in or near them. Porterville (northeast of Bakersfield) is one of the entrances to the Sequoia National Park and to the national parks to the north. Seven miles east on State 190, Success Dam on the Tule River has formed a large mountain lake that offers fishing, boating, and water sports; camping and picnicking facilities are below the dam.

Tulare County Museum, near Visalia, contains historical collections that trace the heritage of this predominantly rural area. There's a surprising variety of old-time vehicles and an interesting cluster of historic buildings set amidst huge oaks in Mooney Grove County Park. The park also contains a small lagoon with boats, some zoo animals, shaded picnic tables, a playground, peacocks, and the original statue *The End of the Trail* from the 1915 Pan Pacific Exposition in San Francisco.

To reach the grove and museum (both open daily), follow Mooney Boulevard (State 63) for 5 miles south of Visalia until you see the Sequoia National Park turnoff.

Hanford (west of U.S. 99 on State 198) owes its name and its Chinatown to the Southern Pacific railroad. Although it's doubtful if anyone remembers who Hanford was, the large Chinese population employed in the construction of the railroad left some tangible evidence of their stay. Picturesque "China Alley," north of Seventh between Green and White streets, is a short street with photogenic brick buildings and sturdy old iron doors. Once these buildings were herb stores, laundries, fortune teller shops, and opium dens. Practically deserted in the early 1950s, it is slowly coming back to life. Notice the Taoist temple. The Imperial Dynasty restaurant serves gourmet dinners among Oriental art objects.

FRESNO

The largest Central Valley city south of Sacramento, Fresno is the rallying point of the fruit growers and ranchers who have turned the valley floor into a vast, productive agricultural area—an outstanding example of what can be accomplished through irrigation. Today, Fresno is the center of a large dessert wine industry. Roads through the city lead to recreation spots in the Sierra.

Though it is a progressive city, Fresno still retains some of its country flavor. On Tuesdays and Saturdays, visit the Cherry Auction, a rural version of a flea market, at which fruits, vegetables, livestock, and poultry are displayed side by side with the usual abundance of secondhand goods. Take U.S. 99 to the Jensen Avenue exit; follow Jensen west to Cherry Avenue; then go south 3 miles.

Roeding Park is a verdant, 157-acre oasis, well situated to break the long drive through the valley. Just east of the freeway at the Belmont Avenue exit, the large expanse of green grass under tall shade trees is a great place to picnic; food stores are close. Children can enjoy the zoo, amusement area rides, boat rides, and playgrounds.

Kearney Park, 7 miles west of Fresno, is the old estate of a wealthy, eccentric land developer named M. Theo Kearney. The old mansion is open to afternoon tours from Thursday through Sunday. The estate and both sides of Kearney Boulevard (leading to it from town) were planted with eucalyptus, palms, and oleanders in 1888.

The Underground Gardens, about 6 miles north of Fresno at U.S. 99 and Shaw Avenue, are one of the valley's coolest stopping places. An underground home of some 65 rooms, gardens, and grottos, this is the work of Baldasare Forestiere, often called the "human mole." The attraction is open daily in the summer (only on weekends and holidays in the winter); there's an admission fee.

Santa Barbara
& Up the Coast

 Santa Barbara is a city of obvious beauty and all-year allure. Spreading north from a wide and gently curving beach, the city lies in a sunny sheltered plain. Offshore to the south, the Channel Islands seem to be a protective barrier against the ocean beyond. And behind the city, the mountains of the Santa Ynez range form a rugged east-to-west backdrop. Yet its stunning setting is not the foremost thing you notice about Santa Barbara. Most likely you will be impressed with the signs of its perpetuation of history: the Spanish and mission architectures; adobes, old and new; tile roofs; bell towers; and the Spanish love of color.

Visitors have a varied schedule of events to choose from, ranging from the popular Old Spanish Days in August to the Summer Sports Festival earlier in the summer and the Fishermen's Festival in spring.

Some of Santa Barbara's warmest, sunniest days are in the autumn. Fishing holds up well into fall, and ocean temperatures remain warm enough for swimming into December. In September you will find a significant change in accommodation prices, for then off-season rates are in effect until June.

Spaniards who settled here called it "La Tierra Adorada" (the beloved land); today's visitors find it hard not to share their enchantment.

This chapter also takes you into the inland hills, where you can drive country roads or camp beside a peaceful lake. Solvang, in the Santa Ynez Valley, is a paradise for those partial to Scandinavian culture and shopping possibilities. The Ojai Valley is lake and mountain country, home of the largest land birds in North America—the condors.

Stretch your trip up the coast to include Pismo Beach (clam capital), inland San Luis Obispo, Morro Bay with its prominent rock formation, and San Simeon, headquarters for touring "Hearst's Castle," now a State Historical Monument.

Mission Santa Barbara's *massive twin towers dominate beautiful grounds in Mission Canyon.*

Santa Barbara Has a Spanish Flavor

The big earthquake of 1925 destroyed many of Santa Barbara's post-Victorian structures, forced early demolition of others, and opened the way for the city to express its Mediterranean consciousness in the course of rebuilding. An Architectural Review Board has been approving or rejecting designs for business and public buildings ever since. Spanish names were given (or restored) to the streets in the heart of town, with the one significant exception of State Street, which did not revert to the Spanish tongue-twister "Calle del Estado."

Most of the reconstructed adobes are within a block or two of De la Guerra Plaza. The bright stucco-and-tile newcomers, built to outlast anything the Spaniards or Mexicans ever erected in the Californias, are generously proportioned, about as functional as buildings in any other style, and, those that were built before 1942, impressively decorated.

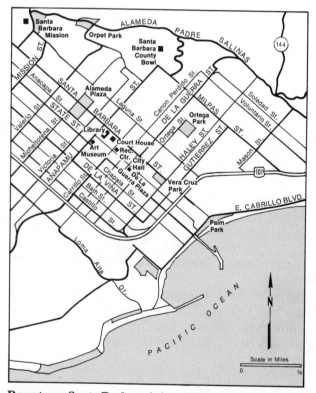

Downtown Santa Barbara *is laced with streets bearing names that testify to city's Spanish heritage.*

DOWNTOWN SANTA BARBARA

True to its traditional character, Santa Barbara not only has preserved and restored buildings from early periods but also has echoed them in new buildings. Contemporary stores, office buildings, theatres (preferred spelling in Santa Barbara), and gas stations bear the Moorish-Spanish-Mexican-California stamp in varying degrees.

The 12-block downtown area (bounded by Victoria, Chapala, Ortega, and Santa Barbara streets) includes Pueblo Viejo (Old Town), an historic preserve and original core of the city that was built around the Presidio. As you walk around, you'll find plaques and markers identifying early buildings. Only a few are open to visitors.

Walking through Santa Barbara

The easiest way to enjoy the flavor of the city is by walking along its streets. You can pick up a copy of the Red Tile Tour from the Santa Barbara Chamber of Commerce at 1301 Santa Barbara Street. Included in the brochure is a map and guide for a 24-mile scenic drive in and around the city.

To begin your walk, park in any of nine city lots shown on the downtown tour map; the first 90 minutes parking is free.

Santa Barbara County Court House is a good place to start. The building and grounds cover a square block bounded by Santa Barbara, Anacapa, Anapamu, and Figueroa streets. Built in 1929, the court house, with its great archway, wrought-iron balconies, gay mosaics, murals, red-tiled roof, romantic towers, and hand-carved doors, resembles a Spanish-Moorish castle. Above the entrance arch on Anacapa Street is an appropriate Roman motto in Spanish; the nearby English version reads, "God gave us the country. The skill of man hath built this town."

Built on the site of the first encampment in this area of peripatetic Portola and his men (1769), the court house and elaborate sunken gardens are the setting for pageants, concerts, and celebrations. Most notable is Old Spanish Days, held in the first part of August, when the participants wear costumes of the early period.

In the Assembly Room, huge, two-story murals colorfully depict Santa Barbara history, including

Graced *by the natural beauty surrounding it, the city of Santa Barbara lies between the Pacific Ocean and the Santa Ynez Mountains.*

De la Guerra Plaza *in downtown Santa Barbara is the site of the annual August Fiesta Marketplace.*

At County Court House, *Old Spanish Days are feted in August.*

"MUST SEES"

SANTA BARBARA COURT HOUSE (downtown)—Spanish-Moorish castle facade; historical murals; tower has good city view

EL PASEO (downtown)—Mediterranean shopping arcade built in and around historic adobes; indoor and outdoor cafes

MISSION SANTA BARBARA (Mission Canyon)—picturesque "Queen of Missions" still in continuous operation by Franciscans

MUSEUM OF NATURAL HISTORY (just north of the mission)—fascinating exhibits focusing on natural phenomena of the West

SANTA BARBARA BOTANIC GARDEN (1½ miles above the mission)—indigenous California plants displayed in their natural settings

CHANNEL ISLANDS (offshore)—take boat trip to islands now national monument (Anacapa and Santa Barbara); ranger on duty on Anacapa

SOLVANG (Santa Ynez Valley)—Danish village complete with windmills; don't miss bakeries; visit Mission Santa Ines

LA PURISIMA MISSION (west of Buellton)—restored mission now historical park; original crafts displays; large gardens

PISMO BEACH—California's largest expanse of sand dunes; camping available in nearby Oceano; clamming

SAN LUIS OBISPO—great place to look at an old California city; Path of History walk past mission, adobes, Ah Louis candy store

MORRO BAY—atmospheric seaside resort-fishing town dominated by Morro Rock; sportfishing and clamming popular here

THE HEARST CASTLE (San Simeon)—famous mountaintop mansion now historical monument; three guided tours of buildings

Old Mission Santa Barbara *is reflected in its fountain pool, part of early Indians' washing facilities.*

the arrival of Juan Rodriguez Cabrillo in 1542, the founding of Mission Santa Barbara in 1786, and the 1846 announcement by Colonel John Fremont about the new American sovereignty of California.

The tower, El Mirador, whose only access is the elevator operating on weekdays, provides an unequalled view of the city and court house grounds.

Today, many court house functions take place in the new county administration building located nearby, but the court rooms, law library, and some of the offices are still used. You can visit the court house on weekdays from 8 A.M. to 5 P.M. and weekends from 9 A.M. to 5 P.M. Free guide service is available if you want it.

The Santa Barbara Museum (corner of State and Anapamu streets next to the public library) is small, bright, and airy. An outstanding display of outdoor sculpture includes a kinetic Rickey piece on the front terrace and six Zúñiga bronzes in the garden behind. Soft natural light enters the gallery through skylights, falling on Greek, Roman, and Egyptian sculptures and priceless glassware; an encircling gallery and adjacent halls contain impressive collections of Oriental and American art from many periods. The museum is privately supported. It's open daily, except Monday, from 11 A.M. to 5 P.M. (Sunday from noon to 5 P.M.). A guided tour takes place Wednesday at 12:30 P.M.

The Santa Barbara Historical Society Museum, at the corner of De la Guerra and Santa Barbara streets, houses many of the city's historical treasures. A combination of the old and new, the building is made of adobe bricks formed from the soil at the site and enforced with modern steel.

One wing is devoted to the Mexican and Spanish periods of Santa Barbara's history and displays a carved statue of Saint Barbara from the Royal Presidio, fascinating old letters, costumes of the period, and items relating to Richard Henry Dana's famous visits to the city, including a model of the brig, *Pilgrim,* and a portrait of its captain.

The museum, home of the Santa Barbara Historical Society, offers free admission and is open afternoons except Monday.

Casa de Covarrubias, around the corner, was built in 1817 for Don Domingo Carrillo. Governor Pio Pico, his wife's brother, was a frequent guest. It was here, in 1846, that the last meeting of congress under the Mexican flag was held.

The Rochin Adobe, at 820 Santa Barbara Street, is sheathed in clapboard as protection from the weather. Built of adobe salvaged from the Presidio ruins, it is a double house with two street entrances. Privately owned, it is not open to the public.

Lobero Theatre, at the corner of Anacapa and Canon Perdido, stands on the site of the city's first theater.

El Presidio de Santa Barbara was the fourth and last Spanish army post in California. The two oldest buildings in Santa Barbara stand on the site.

El Cuartel, at 122 E. Canon Perdido Street, was built shortly after the Presidio was founded in 1782 as part of the original Presidio quadrangle and provided housing for Spanish soldiers. At that time, "The Barracks" had no windows and no fireplace. A scale model of the Presidio and other historical exhibits are on display Monday through Friday from 9 A.M. to 5 P.M.; admission is free.

La Caneda Adobe, across the street, was part of the original Presidio quadrangle. Lovingly restored as a private residence, it is closed to the public.

The Hill-Carrillo Adobe (11 E. Carrillo Street) was built by Massachusetts-born Daniel Hill in 1826 for his Spanish bride. The most modern house of its day, it had wooden floors instead of the usual hard-baked clay. Fully restored, it now houses the Santa Barbara Foundation.

El Paseo (15 E. De la Guerra Street) is a picturesque shopping arcade reminiscent of Old Spain, built in and around the adobe home of the De la Guerra family. It was begun in 1819 by Indians from the mission, and a brick in the wall of the passageway bears the date of completion—1826. Casa de la Guerra, noted for its hospitality, was made famous in Dana's *Two Years Before the Mast* as a setting for a colorful Spanish wedding fiesta.

Some of the shops spill over into the Oreña adobes next door. Here the antiques you see are really for sale. Elsewhere in El Paseo you can find stores specializing in leather goods, candles, books, Santa Barbara-made pottery, and Mexican, Scandinavian, and Oriental imports. Art stores and galleries are particularly at home here. The El Paseo Restaurant is a popular spot for full-scale lunch or dinner. For simpler daytime fare, the El Paseo Cafe offers an outdoor dining area.

Across the street is the plaza where the first City Council met in 1850 and where the first City Hall was located. During Fiesta Week, it becomes a colorful *mercado* (marketplace).

Mission Canyon

You can take many drives up into the hills behind Santa Barbara, but one of the prettiest is Mission Canyon Road. It begins at the old mission and takes you north into the hills to the Museum of Natural History and Santa Barbara Botanic Garden. This "back country," a beautiful, semi-rural area on the slopes of the Santa Ynez Mountains, is separated from the city by 500-foot-high foothills known as "The Riviera."

The scenic drive along the Riviera on Alameda Padre Serra goes through a pleasant residential area, giving you a beautiful view of the city and the ocean. You can turn into some of the little canyons, but they are somewhat difficult to navigate. To return to town easily, take Gutierrez Street.

Mission Santa Barbara, overlooking the city, sits on a knoll at the end of Laguna Street. The tenth in a long line of missions, it was founded in 1786 by Father Fermin Lasuen.

Having a unique stone facade—the only California mission to display two similar towers —"the Queen of the Missions" is a popular subject for photographers. Design for the facade was copied from a Roman book on architecture written by Vitruvius in 27 B.C. (The book is still in the mission archives.) The strange mixture of classical and mission style was retained later when the face was rebuilt because of earthquake damage and wear.

The water system developed by the mission padres was so complete that part of it is still used by Santa Barbara's water company. You can see an Indian-built dam in the Botanic Garden.

Off the arcade corridor (the floor tiles were made in 1811) are three of the original rooms, one a primitive kitchen. The rooms and artifacts in them suggest some of the quality of mission life when the Franciscans were teaching a primitive people not only religion and language but also agriculture and some 50 crafts.

Under huge pepper trees, the Moorish fountain flows into a stone laundry basin, at which Indian women once washed their clothes.

The old cemetery is entered through a Roman archway with two real skull and crossbones hanging above it, a common sight in Mexican churches.

The altar light in this, the only mission continuously in the hands of the Franciscan padres, has burned constantly since the mission was built. Still used daily as a parish church, it is open to the public from 9 A.M. to 5 P.M. weekdays and from 1 to 5 P.M. on Sunday. The chapel, curio room, and library contain relics of the mission days. Self-guided tours cost 50 cents for adults and are free to children under 16.

The Museum of Natural History, just north of Mission Santa Barbara, is located on two acres of wooded ground on Puesta del Sol Road. Its interest is centered upon, but not limited to, natural phenomena of the West. Well-conceived exhibits, comprehensible even to young children, feature some that perform mechanically at the push of a button. Hours of the museum are from 9 A.M. to 5 P.M. weekdays and from 1 to 5 P.M. on Sundays and holidays. Admission is free.

Gladwin Planetarium, also on the grounds, has closed circuit television enabling several people at one time to view the heavens through the large telescope. It is open to public viewing after the 8 P.M. planetarium show on the second and fourth Thursdays of the month.

Santa Barbara Botanic Garden shows indigenous California plants from wildflowers to giant redwoods in their natural settings on 75 acres in Mission Canyon, just 1½ miles above the mission.

Over 5 miles of trails wind through canyon, desert, channel island, arroyo, and redwood sections along historic Mission Creek and past the old dam and aqueduct built in 1806 to supply water for the mission. The History Trail takes you back to the days when the Indians of this area had to support themselves from the land, using plants for food, drink, soap, medicine, and household needs. Self-guided, the trail begins and ends near the Information Office. Plan about an hour for a leisurely walk.

Spring and summer offer the most colorful tours of the garden. Flowering shrubs, poolside plants, and brilliant wildflowers blaze in the meadow section; the ceanothus (mountain lilac) flowers white and blue; and the desert section comes alive with blooming cacti, yuccas, and wildflowers.

The Botanic Garden is open all year from 8 A.M. to sunset. On Thursdays at 10:30 A.M., you can take a guided tour. Admission is free.

Another Santa Barbara park of interest to gardeners is Franceschi Park on Mission Ridge Road, high on the crest of the Riviera.

THE WATERFRONT IS SPECIAL

It is a surprise to many people that Santa Barbara has a southern exposure to the sea. In fact, the California coastline runs almost due west from Ventura to Pt. Conception, the magic dividing point for California's coast. South of Conception, the climate is Mediterranean; north of it, waters grow progressively cooler. Santa Barbara is as Mediterranean in her waters as in her architecture.

In spite of navy missiles to port (Point Mugu) and air force missiles to starboard (Vandenberg AFB on Pt. Conception), Santa Barbara has one of the most alluring stretches of developed coastline that you will find. Miles of wide, gently curving beaches are lined with palms. Swimmers, surfers, picnickers, scuba divers, fishermen, and grunion hunters enjoy it all, except in a few places where oil rigs take over.

The main pier, Stearns Wharf, could be called an extension of State Street, the city's main thoroughfare. You can walk or drive out on the wharf for a view of the ocean and the Santa Barbara coastline; you'll find curio shops and a coffee shop.

Cabrillo Boulevard, a palm-lined drive along the ocean, is especially popular with strollers and cyclists. To the west of the wharf, W. Cabrillo Boulevard is lined with attractive motels, nearly all with swimming pools and many with balconies facing the yacht harbor. Nearby are a municipal swimming pool, a lovely shaded park, and—west of the yacht harbor and breakwater—another stretch of beach. The municipal pool, Los Banos del Mar, is open all year; there's also a wading pool.

The picturesque 92-acre yacht harbor, protected by a long breakwater, shelters the local fishing fleet, as well as hundreds of pleasure craft.

East of the wharf, the curving beach extends to the Andree Clark Bird Refuge at the end of E. Cabrillo Boulevard.

On weekends, the art activity on the Santa Barbara waterfront is so lively that rows of canvases and sculpture stretch as far as a mile along E. Cabrillo Boulevard. At this "Arts and Crafts Show," you'll find pottery, leather craft, metal work, handmade clothing, and jewelry, in addition to paintings. Open only to local artists, the non-restrictive, unjuried show is extremely popular.

Andree Clark Bird Refuge is a landscaped preserve for the protection of geese, swans, and other fowl. There are trails for biking and benches where one can sit and feed tame birds, photograph them, or just observe.

Just east of the refuge, turn right on Channel Drive to see the lovely gardens of the Santa Barbara Biltmore Hotel and the exclusive Montecito district, known in the 1920s as one of the greatest concentrations of wealth in America.

The Child's Estate

Situated on a hilltop on E. Cabrillo Boulevard is a child's garden of play and adventure. Overlooking the ocean and the refuge, this children's park has a charming garden zoo, playground, and picnic area. It is being developed by the community of Santa Barbara, which also sponsors and approves the displays.

Most animals at the zoo meet youngsters at eye level. From lacy white peacocks strutting frequently to ruffled little ducklings swimming with their mothers in pathside ponds, the animals seem at once natural and friendly. Their names are often presented in a child-like scrawl on signposts. From the zoo entrance, a 24-gauge miniature train takes you on a tour past the adjoining Andree Clark Bird Refuge and fresh water lagoon.

Athletic and popular seals show off in a sealarium with viewing portholes for visitors of any height. At the Rancher's Pet Park, children delight in mingling with tame animals—small deer, domestic and African pygmy goats, cows, and pigs.

Besides Susi the Chimp, Herman the Llama, the alligator, owls, bobcats, and the rest of the community, the park also contains a wild west playground of rocky hideouts, a covered wagon and tepee, and a rest area for parents. The fountain, pergola, and picnic area are peaceful stops.

The Child's Estate is open daily except Monday from 10 A.M. to 5 P.M. Adult admission is $1; students 13 to 18, 75 cents; children 2 to 12, 25 cents.

Aquatic flavor of Santa Barbara comes to the fore at the breakfront in Santa Barbara Harbor.

The beaches

Along the 70-mile stretch of coastline running due east between Pt. Conception and Ventura, there are a number of state and county parks centered around beaches characterized by their lack of strong winds and predominantly warm waters.

Jalma Beach, just north of Pt. Conception, is the most isolated and uninhabited of the area's beaches. No supplies are available, but it is the only point of public access to the Pt. Conception fishing grounds. Rough surf prevents swimming or boating; however, it is reached by a very scenic road. The beach is good for rock hunting, and it is probably the southernmost driftwood beach along the Pacific Coast.

Between Pt. Conception and Santa Barbara are five beach parks: Gaviota State Park (public fishing pier, boat rentals, swimming, campgrounds, trailer sites, picnic and camp fee); Refugio Beach (swimming, surf fishing, camping, picnic tables, picnic and camp fee); El Capitan Beach (campgrounds, trailer sites, boat rentals, boat launching, ramp, picnic and camp fee); popular Goleta Beach (sheltered cove for boats, electric boat hoist, fishing pier, swimming, picnicking); and Arroyo Burro Beach (surf fishing, swimming, picnicking) at the outskirts of Santa Barbara.

The long beach area in Santa Barbara is open to the public, except for a few spots that are reserved for occupants of some ocean-front hotels.

Carpinteria State Beach, just off U.S. 101 at Carpinteria (campgrounds, fishing pier, boat launchings, ramp, food concession, picnic and camp fee), calls itself "the world's safest beach." A long, sandy slope extends into deep water with no riptides. Emma Wood State Beach is about 3 miles north of Ventura (campgrounds, surf fishing, swimming). The last beach in this area is San Buenaventura State Beach, facing the city of Ventura.

Water sports

For many visitors, the activities centered around the ocean are the main attraction of Santa Barbara:

Surfing and snorkeling are good a few miles either way along the shore from Santa Barbara. You will find clear water for snorkeling and reefs that push the mild, incoming swells up into respectable, long-lasting, diagonal waves good for surfing. Some of the best water is at Arroyo Burro or Leadbetter beach, both west of the breakwater; they're rough but inviting.

Boating centers around the yacht harbor. There is a concrete launching ramp (fee required, 75 cents in quarters) and a large parking area for boat trailers at the foot of Bath Street. You can rent motor boats or sailboats in any of several classes. Check with the Chamber of Commerce for a list of boat rentals.

Water skiing takeoff area is the beach immediately to the east (lee side) of Stearns Wharf. After launching your boat at the yacht harbor ramp, you usually do your skiing between the wharf and East Beach. You can stay inside the natural breakwater formed by offshore kelp beds if the water is too choppy outside.

Offshore fishing is about as productive here as anywhere else along the California coast. Party boats usually head for Santa Cruz, largest of the Channel Islands, and anchor in a relatively sheltered zone. At a day's end, with ordinary luck, you should have more than enough rockfish.

Some charter boats are available at the yacht harbor for pursuit of albacore, big-game tuna, marlin, and sailfish. But for a day or a half day of less ambitious deep-sea angling at minimum cost, you can go to SEA Landing on the breakwater. They also have a harbor and offshore excursion boat. All equipment you will need and a temporary California fishing license are available here.

No license is necessary for pier fishing. Still-fishing with shrimps for bait may produce a nice haul of tasty perch.

The Channel Islands

Lying south of Santa Barbara across the Santa Barbara Channel are the Channel Islands. A clear day will reward you with a sight of them from the mainland; otherwise, only their mountainous outlines are hazily prominent in the mist.

Actually the islands are small mountain tops (the continuation of the Santa Monica Mountains), cut off from the mainland by water. These islands have retained rare primitive remnants of early California plant and animal life. To preserve some of the unique land and wildlife for study, the government designated the two smallest islands (Santa Barbara and Anacapa) as the Channel Islands National Monument. Anacapa has as its trade-mark the giant coreopsis, a curious perennial that dominates the wildflower display with brilliant splashes of yellow seen from the mainland and from far out to sea in late winter. The two largest islands, Santa Cruz and Santa Rosa, are privately owned and used for cattle and sheep raising. The farthest west island, rocky San Miguel, where explorer Juan Cabrillo is reportedly buried, is a Navy target range.

Wonderful for exploring, both Santa Barbara and Anacapa islands offer only limited primitive camping; day trips are most popular. For public transportation and tour information, write The Island Packers, P.O. Box 993, Ventura 93003, or check the Santa Barbara Chamber of Commerce.

Trips from Santa Barbara

The leisurely atmosphere and relatively slow pace you find in Santa Barbara also extends into much of the country around the city. U.S. 101 and the ocean beaches are normally crowded with vacationers, but just a few minutes away you can enjoy peaceful traveling or camping near a lake.

In this inland area, rolling hills and soft meadows dominate the landscape, and quiet little communities fit the slow tempo.

GOLETA VALLEY

One quick and easy trip is to the beautiful modern campus of the University of California at Santa Barbara, located 10 miles west of town near Goleta.

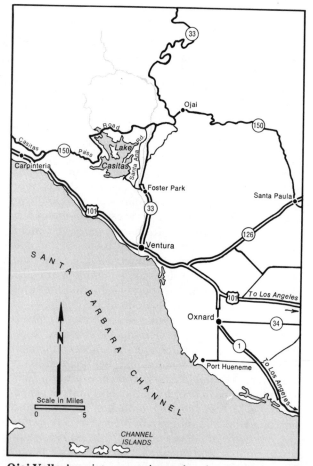

Ojai Valley's *quiet mountain roads take you past lovely views, recreation areas, town of Ojai.*

Follow U.S. 101; signs direct you to the seaside campus. Biking is a popular activity in Goleta, and you can easily find a bicycle to rent. Bike trails are marked; an easy ride will take you past many historic landmarks, the Santa Barbara airport, the marshland of Goleta Slough, along the beach, and through the college.

Stow House, heart of a once vast ranch, was built in 1872. This gracious country home, outbuildings, and gardens are now maintained by the Goleta Valley Historical Society. Wide verandas and gingerbread detailing adorn the outside; inside, the rooms are furnished with period antiques, including a square grand piano, a portable piano that folds up to the size of a trunk, and (in a child's room) an old-fashioned doll house. You can wander through the parklike gardens, a carriage house, and a bunkhouse containing a collection of Chumash Indian artifacts. To get there from U.S. 101, drive north toward the mountains on Los Carneros Road. The house is open Sundays from 2 to 4 P.M.

Stow Grove Park, on La Patera Road, was formerly a part of the Stow Ranch. Now the 13-acre park has picnic tables and a barbecue area in a grove of redwood trees, unusual for Southern California.

Dos Pueblos Orchid Company is one of the world's largest growers of cymbidium orchids. It is located off U.S. 101 at Ranchos Dos Pueblos (15 miles north of the airport). Visitors are welcome from 8:30 A.M. to 4 P.M. Sunday through Thursday.

Hope Ranch Park, just northwest of Santa Barbara (take La Cumbre exit from U.S. 101), is another pleasant drive through a luxury residential development that was formerly a great ranch.

OJAI VALLEY

For a pleasant lake and mountain loop trip from Santa Barbara or as a byway enroute to Los Angeles, the Ojai Valley has much to offer. The moon-shaped valley is well insulated by its altitude and by the Topa and Sulphur mountains against the fog, wind, and smog that sometimes bothers the nearby coast. Some say that Ojai (pronounced Oh'hi) is the Indian word for "The Nest," a name given the valley because of its protected location. Coming from Santa Barbara, leave U.S. 101 at Casitas Pass Road, which joins State 150 to the valley, for a drive through land that is dotted with

Nojoqui Falls *cascades in multiple ribbons, continually adding travertine deposits to rock wall.*

Solvang windmill *and steep, thatched roofs help give Danish village an Old World look.*

What better place *for a friendly game of touch football than sandy Ventura State Beach?*

orchards, streams, and ranches. Among California valleys, Ojai ranks high as a year-round resort.

Lake Casitas Recreation Area

West of Ojai, Lake Casitas is a favorite spot for camping, boating, and fishing (swimming and water skiing are prohibited). These activities are located at the upper end of the reservoir where boat rentals are available at the landing. You can fish or explore the many inlets and coves while you enjoy the shelter and scenery of the surrounding mountains. Campsites are numerous and spacious, though few are tree shaded; trailers are permitted. Day-use and overnight camping fees are small.

An observation point at Lake Casitas Dam on the southeast end of the lake is reached from State 33 or Santa Ana Road on Casitas Vista Road.

Ojai

The town of Ojai has changed very little over the years. It manages to preserve a pleasant atmosphere of the early Spanish days in some of its buildings and maintains a certain easy manner in its way of life. A shopping arcade with a facade of arches and the Post Office bell tower distinguish the main street. Civic Center Park in the heart of town is the hub of the community's active life. Cultural activities, arts and crafts, and special events are nurtured in Ojai. The Ojai Musical Festival held in May is the highlight of the year. A colorful Folk Dance Festival is staged every other year. Ojai Artists' Art Sunday is an extremely popular outdoor event. The inns, motels, and fine restaurants of this quiet town are inviting. The Ojai Valley Inn has resort facilities, including an 18-hole golf course.

Ojai is also a leading tennis center. In spring, it sponsors some of the best amateur tennis in the United States during the Western playoffs.

Many miles of wild and rugged mountain terrain stretch beyond this serene little valley, noted for its air of contagious leisureliness. For automobile explorers, there are creeks, campsites, and places to picnic. North on State 33, Wheeler Gorge at 1,000 feet is the largest and most popular of public camping parks. You'll go by scenic Matilija Dam. Farther north is a back road to Piedra Blanca, a spectacular outcrop of large, white sandstone rocks. On State 150 going east, several pretty little canyons—Bear, Sisar, Wilsie, and Horn—nip into the mountains, and side roads follow their streams for only a few miles. At Dennison Park, barbecue pits and tables are in the shade of tall oaks. Here is perhaps as nice a place as you can find for a picnic with a view of the Ojai Valley floor.

SANTA CLARA VALLEY

Santa Paula, at the junction of State Highways 150 and 126, is the shipping center for the valley. Here, lemons and oil compete for space. The valley had one of California's earliest oil booms, a fact memorialized in the California Oil Museum (Tenth and Main streets).

Condor country

Fillmore, east on State 126, is the entrance point into the Sespe Wildlife area of Los Padres National Forest, home for North America's largest land bird, the condor. Called "Thunderbird" by the Indians, this endangered species sometimes can be seen soaring effortlessly over the valley in search of food. Since these birds lay only one egg every two years and may abandon their young at the approach of man, much of the back country is closed to traffic. Because so many people come to see the famous birds, the Forest Service has set up an Observation Site about 15 miles north of Fillmore.

Follow A Street (later becoming Goodenough Road) about 3 miles north and then turn right onto an oiled road occasionally marked Squaw Flat (side roads lead to oil rig sites). When you reach a sign reading Dough Flat, park and scan the cliffs to the east. Condors can be seen above these cliffs before they leave the sanctuary to forage. There is also an observation point atop Mt. Pinos, accessible by dirt road off the highway in from Gorman. Plan to make a day of it to catch any of the big birds coming home to roost. Best time to visit is winter and early spring.

Ventura

Bypassed by the freeway, Ventura is well worth a stop. It has miles of beaches, a great pier for fishing, and is the cast-off spot for sightseeing trips to the Channel Islands. From October to March, the Monarch butterflies winter in Ventura, coloring the sky orange.

The Visitors and Convention Bureau (785 S. Seaward Ave.) publishes "mini-tours" of the areas with good maps and points of information; don't miss the Mission San Buenaventura (see page 152), the Olivas and Ortega adobes, and the Pioneer Museum.

Oxnard, south of Ventura on State 1, began life around the turn of the century as a sugar beet processing center. Little trace of the farming community remains; today, Oxnard has a strong U.S. Naval stamp because of the installations that take up so much of the shore south of Ventura at Port Hueneme and Pt. Mugu. Although Oxnard is set inland from the sea, it has easy access to beaches. The closest is McGrath State Beach, 7 miles south on Channel Islands Boulevard.

SANTA YNEZ VALLEY

Snuggled between the Santa Ynez and San Rafael mountains in back of Santa Barbara is the Santa Ynez Valley, a land of rich green hills and multi-colored flower fields, of cattle and horse ranges, and of stagecoach towns and missions.

Since its discovery by the Portola expedition in 1769, this valley has been known as cattle country. Modern ranchers were preceded by Indians, padres, and Mexican rancheros. Today, large ranchos from Spanish land grants retain their names, if not their original size, and the *Rancheros Visitadores* (by invitation) symbolically perpetuate the old Spanish custom of helping neighboring ranches at roundup time. Each May this dedicated group of horsemen start off on a 4-day ride.

This unspoiled pastoral valley, so steeped in history, is in sight of the rising missiles at Vandenberg Air Force Base at its western end, where its river meets the sea. Plan a loop trip through the Santa Ynez Valley from Santa Barbara along State 154 and State 246 to U.S. 101 for a pleasant day.

Time really hasn't stood still along State 154, but the back roads wander among the hills in gentle contrast to the rush and noise of U.S. 101. Climbing through historic San Marcos Pass, once the stagecoach route north, you'll have a panoramic view out over the foothills to the ocean.

Lake Cachuma

About 11 miles beyond the San Marcos Summit, you'll come to the entrance of Lake Cachuma Recreation Area. This 9,000-acre county park centers around Lake Cachuma, a reservoir created by a dam built across the Santa Ynez River in 1953.

California live oaks and native white oaks shade the grassy camping and trailer spaces. There are fire pits, tables, and shower and laundry facilities. A store, filling station, snack bar, and post office are inside the entry gate.

In winter when the water cools, the lake is stocked with fingerling rainbow trout and Kamloops trout from British Columbia. As on most Southern California lakes, angling slows down during the heat of summer. Cool spring and fall months provide the best fishing. Tackle and boat rentals are available. To reserve a boat during fishing season, send a $10 check or money order to Cachuma Boat Rentals, P.O. Box 287, Solvang 94363.

No swimming or water skiing is allowed because the lake supplies drinking water for Santa Barbara. But three swimming pools are open from April through October.

Lake Cachuma Recreation Area is open all year, 24 hours a day, and a ranger is on duty most of the time. Daily admission and parking fee is $1 per car. If you plan to stay overnight, the camping fee is $2. Crowded in the summer, the park takes no camping reservations, so plan to arrive early and make a day of it.

The little valley towns

On a short loop trip from Santa Ynez to Los Olivos and Solvang, you'll see a picturesque area affected only slightly by California's growth.

Santa Ynez, formerly the valley's busiest community, has retained its high front buildings and atmosphere of the old west, even having added a new Western Town complex. The white-steepled church, built in 1897 at the corner of Tivola and Lincoln streets, is one of the oldest church edifices in the valley. On Sagunto Street is a historical museum (open weekend afternoons) and a park.

Los Olivos was known as a stage stop for the famous Butterfield Stage Lines. Today, the old stagecoach inn, Mattei's Tavern (built in 1886), is a State Historical Landmark.

Ballard, established in 1880, was the first settlement in the valley. You'll still see some of the old homes and the Little Red Schoolhouse founded in 1883. A beautiful drive in the foothills from here is out Alamo Pintado Road.

Solvang

"Sunny valley" is the Danish translation of the name Solvang, a town that reflects its Scandinavian heritage. Windmills are prominent features. An old world appearance of homes and businesses comes from thatched, aged copper, or steep tile roofs with traditional storks on top, stained glass windows, and high dormers. More recent additions of gas lights and cobblestone walks set the scene for residents walking in *traeskos* (wooden shoes).

At first glance the town suggests a quaint environment manufactured for tourists. Then you discover it possesses the chief element of a true Danish community—real Danes and their descendants. The village was established in 1911 next to Mission Santa Ines as a place to educate immigrants from Denmark. It acquired its Danish facade (over its Spanish architecture) only after visitors began to discover it as a cultural enclave and source of European foods and goods.

Solvang Park, along Mission Drive in the heart

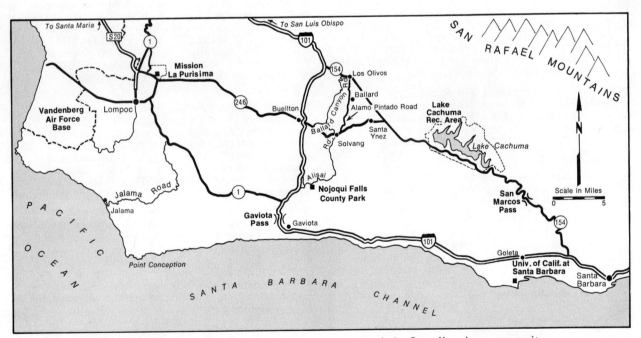

Santa Ynez Valley *trip loops through historic stagecoach towns and the Scandinavian community of Solvang, to beautiful mission grounds and bright fields of flowers.*

Five Missions
Off the Beaten Path

Mission la Purisima *lies in a quiet, rural setting west of Buellton. Original building methods, tools were used in the mission's extensive 1930s restoration.*

Missions are an important part of Southern California history. Most are well known; many are in the heart of a city that grew up around them. Along the central coast off U.S. 101 are five missions, less visited than those in larger metropolitan areas. This isolation is part of their charm. From south to north, rewarding detours will take you to these sites.

San Buenaventura (Ventura), last mission founded by Father Serra. The effects of an 1812 earthquake and the history of some unusual handcarved wooden bells are among the tidbits of information included on a tape for a guide-yourself tour of the church, museum, and grounds. You'll see some of the old books written and signed by Father Serra, the mission's original stained glass windows, and handwork of the Chumash Indians.

Santa Ines (Solvang), 19th in a chain of 21 missions. The first restoration of a deteriorating mission was launched in 1904 by Father Alexander Buckler. Continuing programs today have restored this "Hidden Gem of the Missions." With its simple straightforward exterior, Santa Ines fits one's impression of how a ripe old mission should look.

La Purisima (15 miles west of Buellton), now a State Historical Park. If you can just visit one mission now, especially with children, this should be it. Sixty years ago only bare ruins remained. But the C.C.C. of the 1930s restored La Purisima, using plans carefully worked out by National Park Service researchers and designers. Then the state took it over. Rangers—not padres—administer it.

San Luis Obispo (downtown), an example of a city growing around a church. The first mission to use tiles as roofing, this restored mission is both a parish church and a museum of the past. The attractively landscaped plaza between it and the creek was designed by students at California Polytechnic State University. Footbridges cross to shops and restaurants.

San Miguel (8 miles north of Paso Robles), founded in 1797 at a location halfway between Los Angeles and San Francisco. This is one of the most attractive and least spoiled missions, especially if you are interested in church art. Wall paintings by Spanish artist Estevan Munras and Indian assistants still look incredibly fresh. Franciscan friars maintain the mission as a parish church and monastery; visitors are welcome.

of town, has picnic tables and a Danish style bandstand. On weekends you can tour Solvang on *Honen* (The Hen), a motorized replica of a Danish streetcar of the last century. For two days in mid-September, colorful Danish Days bring out costumes in Solvang; you'll see the Danish flag flying everywhere.

Mission Santa Ines, another of the old missions still in use, is in Solvang (see page 152).

Shopping in Solvang leans heavily toward imports from Denmark and other northern European countries, with an emphasis on gourmet and delicatessen foods, traditional and contemporary housewares, toys, apparel (especially shoes), and things that can be classified only as gifts. These days you will also find imports from other parts of the world.

But the shops that really made Solvang famous are the bakeries, many of which serve pastries and coffee. If you visit some of the bakeries in the morning when activity is light, you may ask to watch the preparation and baking processes. Shops open by mid-morning but close up tight at 5 P.M.

Atterdag Road is worth seeking out. On it is Bethania Church, patterned after a typical rural church in Denmark. Inside you'll see an interesting, hand-carved wooden pulpit and a scale model of a fully rigged ship hanging from the ceiling facing the altar, a common tradition in Scandinavian churches. Farther along on Atterdag Road near the Solvang Lutheran Home is a famous chiming wind harp.

Buellton

Three miles west of Solvang is Buellton, a hospitable town which has the curious distinction of being the "home of Split Pea Soup" (a specialty of Andersen's Restaurant). At the crossroads of U.S. 101 and State 246, it is the gateway to the valley for freeway drivers, being only minutes from points of interest in all directions.

Look for La Purisima Concepcion Mission nestled in a valley 15 miles west of Buellton (see page 152).

Lompoc

Long, rainless summers in the Lompoc Valley help to produce over half of the flower seeds grown in the world. One of spring and summer's most beautiful spectacles occurs here beginning in May when several thousand acres of flowers bloom, turning the landscape into a rainbow of color. Hues of row after row of sweet peas, poppies, calendulas, nasturtiums, and larkspurs compete for your attention into September.

Fields are not open for public browsing because the flowers are grown commercially for seed, but you can see most of them from the road. Maps showing field locations are available from the Chamber of Commerce, 119 E. Cypress, Lompoc. The annual Flower Festival in late June includes a parade and guided tour of fields. You will also see fields as you enter the town of Lompoc from the north or south on State 1 and along the Santa Rosa Road from Buellton.

An extensive exhibit of Chumash Indian artifacts is available in the museum at Cypress and H streets. The museum is open weekend afternoons. Admission is free.

Nojoqui Falls

One of the most graceful waterfalls in all California is the highlight of the scenic drive along U.S. 101 between the coast and Solvang. You leave the freeway about 5 miles north of Gaviota Pass on a road marked "To Nojoqui Falls County Park." The 2-mile drive traverses choice countryside of green fields and native oaks. From the north, go to Solvang and then turn south on Alisal Road. It's 6.5 miles.

From the parking lot, a short walk on a woodsy path along a clear creek brings you to the waterfall, which is usually at its best in late winter and early spring—it usually dries up in summer.

Lompoc flower fields *spangle the valley with color each summer beginning in May. These are petunias.*

Up the Coast

Following El Camino Real (U.S. 101) northward adds even more memorable dimensions to your travel in Southern California. It's easy to see the Spanish and Indian influence on this portion of California, lying midway between Los Angeles and San Francisco, when the map spells out such musical names as Guadalupe, Santa Maria, Oceano, Nipomo, Arroyo Grande, San Luis Obispo, Morro Bay, Cayucos, and Cambria. You'll drive through valleys, pastures, and (on side trips) along the oceanfront.

Sleepy Nipomo (off U.S. 101) in its heyday was considerably larger than now-bustling Santa Maria. Today few of the original buildings remain, having fallen victim to fire or removal to the larger town. One exception is the Dana house, once home for the famous Dana family, original settlers in the area.

The freeway bypasses most of the historical and recreational spots. To see these, it's better to take to the back roads. Following State 166 west from Santa Maria to Guadalupe (on State 1), you pass through more large flower seed farms. Countryside tours take place from May to September.

PISMO BEACH AND NEARBY COAST

State 1 is the back entrance to the home of the Pismo clam. The broad, surf-swept arc of the bay provides an ideal environment from the clam's viewpoint. Their only trouble is that the shore is so accessible to clam-loving humans. One result is that the greater part of the beds is now a preserve. Only the north end of the state park, north of Oceano, is open to digging. But that is still the main reason visitors come to these pleasant towns and their wide and level beaches.

Adventure-seeking dune buggy riders also congregate in the area, particularly on the July 4th and Labor Day weekends. Most people bring their own vehicles; you can rent a ride at one of several spots along the beach.

Pismo State Beach, which has some 6 miles of shoreline, runs south from the town of Pismo Beach through Oceano and on into the north end of one of California's best and largest expanses of sand dunes. Shifting sands often overrun the camping area, but the dunes make the park special. Picnic, hike, climb, or slither up and down slopes.

Public automobile entrances give access to the beach. One is from Oceano, a once-aspiring seaside resort of the Victorian era. A couple of gingerbread houses still remain—one set incongruously amidst a mobile home park.

At the north end of the park, in the town of Pismo Beach, is a pier. Fish can be caught from it, and so can party boats for deep sea fishing. You will also find the necessary equipment and information for digging clams; there's good activity in the winter.

Avila Beach nestles within the north arc of San Luis Obispo Bay. Along the beach front is a small park, organized for active recreation. Water along the shore in this cove is warm, always above 60° and frequently into the low 70° range, ideal for ocean swimming. Facilities include a fishing pier, picnic tables, fire rings, charter boats, launching ramp, and rental concession for salty gear.

Set among hills of undoubted scenic worth, Avila Beach is the target for a lovely drive from U.S. 101. A freeway exit leads to the county road.

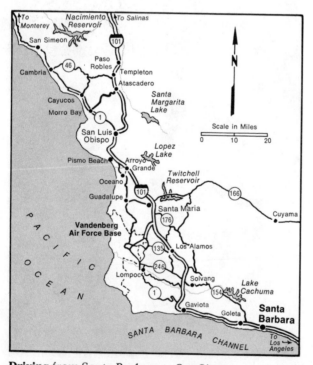

Driving *from Santa Barbara to San Simeon, you'll pass San Luis Obispo, an old California city.*

Huge Morro Rock *looms up behind fishing boats moored off Morro Bay.*

Hikers, swimmers *must dodge both waves and automobile traffic along shore just south of Pismo Beach.*

Castlelike Hearst estate, *backed by Santa Lucia Mountains, towers regally.*

SAN LUIS OBISPO AREA

Cradled in a small valley with the Santa Lucia Mountains forming a gentle backdrop, San Luis Obispo is the county seat and the center of a vast grain, livestock, poultry, and dairy region. The city grew up around Mission San Luis Obispo de Tolosa, established in 1772.

California State Polytechnic University, which has the largest undergraduate agricultural division in the West, is situated on rolling hills overlooking the city. Its Spanish-style and contemporary buildings spread over a 2,850-acre campus, attractively landscaped with tropical and semitropical plants and trees, some of them rare.

State 1 and U.S. 101 separate in San Luis Obispo, and from this point you can explore the Santa Lucia Mountains or follow the coastline north to Morro Bay and fabulous San Simeon.

Exploring the town

From the visitor's point of view, perhaps the best thing that happened to San Luis Obispo was to have a freeway relieve its streets of north-south highway congestion. If you detour into the city, though, you'll discover one of the most surprising showcases of California history on the coast. Starting with the Spanish era, nearly every period and contributing culture is represented, including the Chinese. Since many of the nostalgic remnants are lived in or nicely adapted to present-day use, San Luis is livelier than you might expect a museum town to be.

Exploring is made more meaningful by a *Path of History.* You walk (or drive) a route marked by a red line painted in the street. With no shortcuts, the walk is a little more than 2 miles and takes about 1½ hours. A free brochure, available at the County Museum (corner of Broad and Monterey streets) or from the Chamber of Commerce (1039 Chorro Street), describes about 20 stops on the way.

Among the high points are Mission San Luis Obispo (see page 152) and the Ah Louis store (800 Palm Street), first established in 1874. In addition to being stocked with herbs and general merchandise, the store served as bank and post office for numerous Chinese railroad workers. Across the street is Chong's, a delightful Chinese candy store.

In contrast to the old Dallidet Adobe and gardens, setting for an annual antique show, on Pacific Street is the still-modern building (now a medical clinic) designed by Frank Lloyd Wright. It is located on the creek at Santa Rosa Street. Keep an eye out for other discoveries along the route; the newer Sinsheimer Trust building plaza is set off with 200-year-old olive trees from the mission garden.

MORRO BAY

The attractive seaside resort-fishing town of Morro Bay spreads along the eastern shore of the estuary that gives it its name. Some travelers think of Morro Bay only as a stopover point, but this is a recreation area well worth the consideration of vacation planners or weekend sightseers. It is 12 miles west of San Luis Obispo on State 1.

The one prominent landmark that attracts your attention as Morro Bay comes into sight is high, rounded Morro Rock, looming 576 feet above the ocean just offshore from town. Unfortunately, distracting sea stack towers share the scene just inshore from the great rock. Named by Juan Cabrillo in 1542, Morro Rock means "crown-shaped hill." You can drive over a causeway from the beach area north of town to the rock. Although you can walk part way around it, going too far out on the jetties that reach into the bay is dangerous.

Fishing and clamming are good. Shore fishing from piers, the causeway, and the rock coast brings in perch and flounder. (You don't need a license for bay fishing from piers, breakwaters, or jetties.)

Sportfishing boats are numerous, taking parties out to deeper waters where prospects are better.

Clamming is very popular, and diggers have no trouble bringing in good catches of Pismo clams (limit is 10) at low tide. The ocean shore north of Morro Rock or south to Oceano is promising clamming ground. You'll need a license.

One all-year feature of Morro Bay is the Clam Taxi, which operates between the Morro Bay Marina at Fourth Street and the peninsula section of Morro Bay State Park. The water taxi takes clammers, fishermen, and assorted beachcombers across the bay to a landing area on the peninsula. From the landing area, it's about a quarter-mile hike across the dunes to the ocean beach, where you'll find the best clamming, surf fishing, and shell, rock, and driftwood collecting. Enjoy a picnic at tables near the landing area.

If oysters are your cup of stew, take in the annual March Festival. Wander through the beds and pick your own to take home. Free stew, boat parade, square dancing, and other activities fill a weekend.

Morro Bay State Park

A mile south of town, Morro Bay State Park spreads over some 1,500 acres that slope down to the bay. Spacious and verdant, it is an inviting place for camping and picnicking. You can play golf on an 18-hole course or rent a boat at the boat harbor.

Stop at the attractive Natural History Museum for a wonderful panoramic view of the bay and Morro Rock. The Museum and Visitor Center has fascinating displays of the area, including a history of the Chumash Indians. Movies feature wildlife and area history. You can peer through a telescope at a great blue heron rookery high in the eucalyptus trees beside the bay.

Montana de Oro State Park

Largely undeveloped, this 5,600-acre hiker's park faces the ocean south of Morro Bay. Made up largely of rugged cliffs and headlands, it also contains little coves with relatively secluded sandy beaches. Hikers can explore Valencia Peak and other 1,500-foot-high hills that overlook nearly 100 miles of coastline from Point Sal in the south to Piedras Blancas in the north. Spring wildflowers abound; the predominantly yellow color inspired the park's name—Montana de Oro means "mountain of gold."

About 50 campsites are located near the old Rancho Montana de Oro headquarters beside Islay Creek. Swimming and skin diving are popular, as are fishing and abalone picking (with a license). Access from Morro Bay State Park is on Los Osos Valley Road.

North of Morro Bay for some 30 miles, the coast continues to be hospitable to visitors in one fashion or another. Atascadero, Morro Strand, and Cayucos beaches offer miles of gentle, sandy ocean front. Although Atascadero has the only campsites, all are popular swimming spots.

AT SAN SIMEON:
A KINGDOM BY THE SEA

For William Randolph Hearst to have called his estate of San Simeon "the ranch" is an understatement if ever there was one. What you'll find here is a strangely eclectic but glamorous collection of mansions, terraced gardens, pools, fine art objects, exotic trees, bunkhouses, garages, and shacks crowning a spur of the Santa Lucia Mountains about 45 miles northwest of San Luis Obispo. The large central structure, *La Casa Grande*, looks more like a Spanish cathedral than a castle, but its imposing ridgetop position on "Enchanted Hill" has given it the aspect of a castle when viewed from afar. Parts of the estate were reconstructed from venerable European buildings that were dismantled and shipped to California.

The Hearst Castle today is a State Historical Monument to the memory of Hearst, the head of a vast publishing empire until his death in 1951, and his mother. Only the central cluster of impressive buildings and the immediately surrounding landscaped grounds have been deeded to California. The rest of the vast ranch—the cattle range, of which the castle served as a kind of baronial headquarters, the houses and barns, the airport, and most of the village of San Simeon—remains a single private holding. Hearst properties in the area once totaled 275,000 acres. During World War II, the corporation sold 140,000 acres as a site for a military reservation.

You must approach the estate by bus from the public entrance just off State 1. The road climbs and winds through rolling green hills to spectacular views of the rugged Coast Range and the ocean. The Hearst flair for the exotic extended beyond the house and furnishings to animal life. Perhaps the world's first "natural zoo" was at San Simeon. Hearst imported many wild animals and turned them loose to roam the estate; some have wandered off and established themselves as part of the "wildlife" of the Santa Lucia Mountains. Notables are the zebra, Barbary sheep, and white deer from Central Asia. At one time the estate had a zoo containing monkeys, cheetahs, lions, a leopard, a panther, and a polar bear.

Inside *La Casa Grande*, marvelous tapestries vie for your attention with outsize Oriental rugs and Pompeian floor mosaics. These and collections of furniture and art were shipped to San Simeon from all over the world. The huge indoor Roman pool under the tennis courts is tiled richly with lapis lazuli and gold leaf, watched over by white marble nudes and lighted by globes of pure alabaster. This million-dollar tank was turned over to hired help because house guests liked to swim outdoors.

Tours of the estate will reveal many delights: a classic Neptune pool, a walk-in fireplace, Cardinal Richelieu's bed. Unlike most parks and museums, the castle is not open for families to wander through at will. Visitors take only the conducted tours, which often require reservations.

There are three different tours of The Castle and grounds. Tour 1 takes in the grounds, one of the guest houses, and the lower level of the mansion.

Main dining hall *at Hearst Castle, seen by throngs of visitors each year, is resplendently European.*

You'll see the grand assembly room, movie theater, and the Neptune and Roman pools. Tour 2 takes in the upper level of the mansion, including bedrooms, Hearst's personal libraries, and the kitchen. On Tour 3, you get an intimate view of many bedrooms, sitting rooms, bathrooms, and works of art. Each tour lasts about 2 hours and requires considerable walking and climbing. They can be taken consecutively or on different days.

During the busy season, it's wise to make reservations in advance at Ticketron offices in large cities or by writing or telephoning the Hearst Reservation Office, Department of Parks and Recreation, P.O. Box 2390, Sacramento 95811. At the door, tickets are sold on a first come, first served basis. Prices below include a 35 cent reservation charge.

Tickets for Tours 1 and 3 cost $4.35 for adults, $2.35 for children 6 through 17. Tickets for Tour 2 are $5.35 for adults and $2.85 for children. The castle is closed on Thanksgiving and Christmas.

The well-marked entrance to the monument is just off State 1 at San Simeon, a little town 30 miles north of Morro Bay. Good motels and camps are available here. To be assured of accommodations, make reservations through the Chamber of Commerce in one of the nearby towns.

INDEX

Boldface indicates major
emphasis in text.

Photographers

Barry Anderson: 77; 137 bottom right. **William Aplin:** 63 left; 86 right; 89 top right, bottom right; 111; 114; 127 top left, bottom; 128 right; 129. **Gerhard Bakker:** 123 top left. **Robert Bander:** 155 top right. **Bishop and Associates:** 7 right; 35 top right. **Thomas D. Boyd:** 113 right. **John Boykin:** 120 right. **Ernest Braun:** 16 right; 19 bottom; 29; 149 top left. **California Historical Society:** 124. **Clyde Childress:** 155 bottom. **Glenn Christiansen:** 6; 7 top; 11 left; 83 right; 93 left; 95; 96 right; 101 top left, bottom left; 123 top right, bottom; 149 top right. **Dave Clark:** 73 top right. **Richard Dawson:** 50 left. **Disneyland:** 54; 57 top. **Richard Fish:** 20; 23 left; 25; 27 left; 73 bottom right. **Lee Foster:** 11 bottom right; 12 bottom; 14; 16 left; 22; 23 right; 28 left; 38; 46; 59 top; 67; 69. **Gerald R. Fredrick:** 27 right. **Cecil Helms:** 58 bottom. **Bud Hoffman:** 137 bottom left. **Walter Houk:** 7 left; 8; 30; 35 left; 40; 41; 42; 45; 49; 50 right; 57 bottom left, right; 59; 64; 73 left; 80 left; 89 left; 91 bottom; 107; 108; 117 top right; 149 bottom. **Milton W. Jones:** 104. **James Koski:** 37; 85. **Martin Litton:** 130; 133 top right, bottom; 140; 143 bottom; 157. **Ells Marugg:** 135. **J. N. Mathey:** 35 bottom right. **Alma McGoldrick:** 97. **Proctor Mellquist:** 127 top right. **Movieland Wax Museum:** 58 top. **David Muench:** 120 left. **National Park Service:** 117 bottom right; 133 left. **Ken Niles, Jr.:** 117 left. **Palm Springs Convention and Visitors Bureau:** 101 right. **Norman A. Plate:** 63 right; 128 left. **Annabel Post:** 138. **San Diego Convention and Visitors Bureau:** 70; 79; 86 left; 93 top right, bottom right; 96 left. **Santa Barbara Chamber of Commerce:** 143 top left, top right; 144; 146; 152. **Larry Smith:** 108 bottom. **Randy K. Taylor:** 81. **Frank J. Thomas:** 91 top; 155 left. **John Waggaman:** 83 left. **Darrow M. Watt:** 11 top right; 28 right; 32; 113 left; 153. **Robert Wenkam:** 98. **Peter Whiteley:** 43. **George Woo:** 137 top.